P9-AOA-130

DISCARDED

Brooks - Cork Library
Shelton State
Community College

A Collection of Biographies of
Women Who Made a Difference in Alabama

Compiled By
The League Of Women Voters Of Alabama

Edited By And Under The Direction Of
Miriam Abigail Toffel

COVER: The painting on the cover represents the diversity of Alabama women. It was painted in 1994 by the editor, M. Abigail Toffel.

Copyright © 1995 by the League of Women Voters of Alabama. Printed and bound in the United States of America. All Rights reserved. No part of this book may be reproduced in any form or by any electronic or mechanical means including information storage and retrieval systems without permission in writing from the publisher, except by a reviewer, who may quote brief passages in a review. Published by the League of Women Voters of Alabama, 3357 Cherokee Road, Birmingham, AL 35223. First edition.

ISBN   0-9649012-0-X

FOREWORD

The purpose of this book is twofold, to preserve the history of these women and to raise money for the League of Women Voters of Alabama. The money earned will be used by the State and local Leagues for workshops, debates, speakers, forums, publications, and other projects. There are so many notable women in and from Alabama that they could fill many books. The Alabama women in this collection were chosen for many different reasons. They are from a wide variety of backgrounds and the majority have not been written about in other books. Most are living, however, several said their age was private information. We hope you will enjoy reading about them. Our writers, while not writing scholarly biographies, give the most accurate picture possible with facts, interviews and research. We began each story with the woman's words of inspiration or words of wisdom.

These women are all heros in their own way. Heroes show us what can be done. They show us who we can become and how to go about it. We must take ownership of our past — it is what made us what we are. This collection recognizes the personal contribution and achievement of the women included in it. We encourage everyone to understand that all work is important for the dignity of the effort and the contribution to the whole of our society.

Many thanks to the writers for all their good work. Thanks to the proof readers, Joyce Mahan, Willita Zoellner, Joan King, Charlotte Gattrozzi and Suzanne Nasir. Thanks to Sybille Barron, State League Treasurer, and to President Sarah McDonald. Thanks to the local Leagues and to the State Board. Also special thanks to my local League, the League of Women Voters of Greater Tuscaloosa, and to its President Dena Strong.

Abigail Toffel, *editor*

Brooks - Cork Library

Shelton State

Community College

CONTENTS

THE WOMEN WHO MADE A DIFFERENCE

Photo courtesy of Sarah Cabot Pierce.

The speaker's table at the second State Convention of the League of Women Voters of Alabama held in Montgomery, Alabama, in 1952. Left to right - Mrs. Forrest Barker, 1st. VP LWV; Agnes Baggett, Secretary of State of Alabama; Mrs. T.L. Bear, Jr., Chairman, State Milk Control Board; Mrs. Ethel S. Gale, Chairman, State Pardon & Parole Board; Mrs. Lois Rainer Green, State Library Director; Sarah Cabot Pierce, State LWV President; Katherine Gurnett, National LWV Representative; Mrs. Marie Bankhead Owens, Director, State Dept. Of Archives and History; Sybil Poole, State Treasurer of Alabama.

ALABAMA LEAGUE OF WOMEN VOTERS CELEBRATES 75 YEARS!

On February 14, 1920, the League of Women Voters (LWV) was established at the National American Woman Suffrage Association's Chicago meeting. They were celebrating the 19th Amendment that had just passed to give women the vote. The League was a direct outgrowth of the Woman Suffrage Association and a century of struggle for women's rights. The 19th Amendment became law on August 26, 1920, after thirty-six states ratified it.

Two months after the LWV National Convention, the Alabama League of Women Voters (ALWV) was organized. Birmingham suffragist Lillian Roden Bowron was elected the president and Dixie Bibb Graves the vice president. Most of the activities of the first state ALWV meeting, held April 7-8, 1920, in Montgomery, centered around the organizational structure of the League, its purpose, and its constitution and by-laws.

The Alabama League's purpose was to foster education in citizenship, to support improved legislation, and to urge Alabama women to become enrolled voters. It had a nonpartisan plank to endorse neither a party nor an individual in an election contest.

One of the most important enterprises of the early League was the establishment of citizenship schools in the three major cities: Birmingham, Montgomery, and Mobile. The first school opened in September 1920, in Birmingham. The schools lasted four or five days and the lessons were divided between practical voting procedures and advanced lessons in political science. Following a vigorous League canvassing and education program, within a month of receiving the right to vote, 123,000 Alabama women registered to vote. Encouraged by these successes, in 1921, the Alabama League urged Alabama's public school system to institute citizenship courses to oppose ignorance about government and politics.

The ten standing committees of the ALWV represented the types of reform that concerned many Progressives, especially women: American citizenship, protection of women in industry, child welfare, improvement of election laws and methods, social hygiene, unification of laws, supply and demand, research, legislative, and membership. The ALWV voted to adopt the resolutions passed by the ALWV at the National Convention in February, 1920. The League of Nations received the total support of the ALWV, as did the following: universal compulsory physical training in the public schools in the state; raising the age of consent to marry from 14 to 18; an increase in teacher's salaries; abolition of the death sentence; an eight-hour day and a 48 hour week for women in all work; and full opportunities for the education of women along industrial lines.

As the Progressive era began to wane, so did the ALWV. The State League was disbanded in 1928 because of the active political participation of several local Leagues which was against the by-laws. A few of the local Leagues were still active. In the early 1930s, the Birmingham League members operated an employment service during the Depression years. The League declined again in the late 1930s, but there was a revival of interest in forming a local LWV group during the post-war period.

In 1947 a group of Montgomery women, led by Mrs. Fred Couey, began work on establishing a local League. In 1950, a State Organizational Committee was set up with representatives from each local League and the national League. The first state convention of the League of Women Voters of Alabama was held in the spring of 1951 in Tuscaloosa at Doster Hall on the University of Alabama campus. While local Leagues have come and gone, the state organization has remained strong.

The League of Women Voters is a "grass-roots" organization. Any citizen, male or female, who is eighteen years old or older can join. Members belong to the National League and to either a local League or are members-at-large. A nonpartisan organization, the League's work is divided into two parts. Voter Service informs the public on elections, voter registration, and amendments. It conducts candidate questionnaires and debates.

The second part is the Program. Every two years, League members at the three levels (Local, State, and National) choose one or more political or social issues to study and possibly take a stand on. The State League has studied taxes, education, election laws, Constitutional Revision, apportionment, and consumer affairs. And today encouraging citizens to play an informed and active role in government is still the cornerstone of League purposes.

Current state president Sarah McDonald, of Birmingham, points out that the League is still nonpartisan. "We do take positions on political issues. Nonpartisan doesn't mean nonpolitical. After studying and debating issues, the League develops consensus positions which we then actively work to support through grassroots lobbying. For example the Alabama League supports a new constitution for Alabama to replace the outdated 1902 constitution. Through consensus in our state-wide meetings we have developed many strong recommendations that we would like to have included in a new constitution."

The State League formally celebrated its 75th anniversary at its convention in Mobile on April 29, 1995. Local Leagues will mark the occasion throughout the year. For more information on the League or on our many publications, including this book, please contact our state office at 3357 Cherokee Road, Birmingham, AL 35223; phone 205/970-2389.

LEGISLATION IMPACTING UPON WOMEN'S RIGHTS

Legislation has been enacted over the years that has had an impact upon the rights of women. The following synopsis is a sample but not all inclusive list of some of the legislation, its purpose and the impact upon women.

1. **14th Amendment.** The 14th Amendment, commonly known as the "equal protection clause," prohibits states from denying to any person the equal protection of the laws of the United States. Case law has interpreted this amendment as prohibiting certain forms of discrimination on the basis of sex.

2. **19th Amendment.** The 19th Amendment reads as follows: "The right of citizens of the United States to vote shall not be denied or abridged by the United States on account of sex. Congress shall have the power to enforce this article by appropriate legislation." Ratification was completed on August 18, 1920.

3. **Title VII of the Civil Rights Act of 1964.** Title VII prohibits employment discrimination on the basis of race, color, religion, sex, or national origin. Title VII applies to failures or refusals to hire, discharge, compensate, or any terms, conditions, or privileges of employment. Title VII as originally enacted did not apply to state or local governments. An amendment in 1972 specifically included in the definition of "person" governments, governmental agencies, and political subdivisions. A 1976 Supreme Court case extended Title VII to state employees as a valid exercise of Congress' right to enforce the 14th Amendment. (42 U.S.C. 2000, et seq.) Title VII also established the Equal Employment Opportunity Commission, commonly known as the EEOC, which was charged with receiving and investigating complaints from persons alleging discrimination.

4. **Equal Pay Act of 1963** (29 U.S.C. 206(d)). The EPA prohibits discrimination between employees on the basis of sex by paying wages to employees at a rate less than it pays employees of the opposite sex for equal work in jobs requiring equal skill, effort, and responsibility and which are performed under similar working conditions. The EPA is part of the Fair Labor Standards Act of 1938 and does not require a complainant to file an EEOC charge before using this relief.

5. **Title IX of the Education Amendment of 1972** (20 U.S.C. 1681-1686). Title IX prohibits discrimination based on sex in education programs or activities receiving federal financial assistance. It reads "No person in the United States shall, on the basis of sex, be excluded from participation in, be denied the benefits of, or be subjected to discrimination under any education program or activity receiving federal financial assistance." It also prohibits, among other things, employment discrimination by an educational institution. Although Title IX contains no specific reference to employment, the Department of Education regulations prohibit sex discrimination in employment. (36 C.F.R. 106.51 (a)(1). Womens' Educational Equity Act of 1978 (20 U.S.C. 3041) This act was passed for the purpose of providing educational equity for women in the United States and to provide financial assistance to enable educational agencies and institutions to meet the requirements of Title IX of the Educational Amendments of 1972.

6. **Equal Credit Opportunity Act of 1974** (15 U.S.C. 1691). This Act was passed in 1974 with subsequent amendments at later dates. The purpose of this Act was to make it unlawful for any creditor to discriminate against any applicant with respect to any aspect of a credit transaction on the basis of race, color, religion, national origin, sex, or marital status.

7. **Title X of the Public Health Services Act** (passed somewhere around 1970). Title X provided funding for family planning clinics to provide services for low-income patients. The Act specified that Title X funds could not be used for performance of abortions but placed no restrictions on the ability of clinics to provide abortion counseling. In 1988 Congress adopted what has become known as the "gag rule." This rule prohibited Title X recipients from providing patients with information, counseling, or referrals concerning abortion. On January 22, 1993, (58 FR 7455) President Clinton signed a rule suspending the "gag rule" regarding abortion counseling. This rule stated in part that the "gag rule" endangers women's lives and health by preventing them from receiving complete and accurate medical information and interferes with the doctor-patient relationship by prohibiting information medical professionals are otherwise ethically and legally required to provide to their patients.

8. **Sexual Harassment**. Sexual harassment is a violation of Section 703 of Title VII, which prohibits discrimination on the basis of sex. The EEOC Guidelines, 29 C.F.R. 1604.11 provide that acts constituting sexual harassment include "unwelcome sexual advances, requests for sexual favors, and other verbal or physical conduct of a sexual nature" and those acts violate Title VII in three instances: (a) Submission to such conduct is made either explicitly or implicitly a term or condition of an individual's employment; (b) Submission to or rejection of such conduct by an individual is used as the basis for employment decisions affecting such individual; and Such conduct has the purpose or effect of unreasonable interfering with an individual's work performance or creating an intimidating, hostile, or offensive working environment.

9. **Equal Rights Amendment**. This amendment, which failed to pass, was worded as follows: "Equality of rights under the law shall not be denied or abridged by the United States or by any state on account of sex." This amendment was first introduced into Congress in 1943 and repeatedly thereafter in almost every Congress until around 1980. It failed to be ratified by the required number of states. This amendment was meant to be an all-encompassing amendment which would guarantee equal rights to women and avoid the need for piecemeal legislation.

10. **Family and Medical Leave Act** (29 U.S.C. 2601 (1993)). The purpose of this Act was to entitle employees to take reasonable leave for medical reasons for childbirth or for the adoption of a child, and for the care of child, spouse, or parent who has a serious health condition. Employees are entitled to 12 weeks of unpaid leave annually. This Act applies to all employers who employ 50 or more employees. Note: There has been recent talk about Congress repealing all or parts of this Act.

OTHER RECENT EXAMPLES OF LEGISLATION AFFECTING WOMEN

Women's Business Ownership Act of 1988 (13 U.S.C. 131)

Women's Business Development Act of 1991 (15 U.S.C. 631)

Displaced Homemakers Self-Sufficiency Act of 1990 (29 U.S.C. 2301)

Women in Apprenticeship and Nontraditional Occupations Act of 1992 (29 U.S.C. 2501)

CASE LAW

A recent Supreme Court case (1994) makes unlawful the use of preemptory challenges on the basis of sex. Attorneys cannot strike women from juries without giving a gender neutral reason for doing so.

Submitted by Linda K. Dukes

Why Bother to Vote?

The League of Women Voters of Alabama urges you to follow the example of the Suffragists - to take your rights seriously and get out and vote.

How important is one Vote?

Well . . .

- In 1645, one vote gave Oliver Cromwell control of England.

- In 1649, one vote caused Charles I of England to be executed.

- In 1776, one vote gave America the English language instead of German.

- In 1845, one vote brought Texas into the Union.

- In 1868, one vote saved President Andrew Johnson from impeachment.

- In 1876, one vote changed France from a monarchy to a republic.

- In 1876, one vote gave Rutherford B. Hayes the Presidency of the U.S.

- In 1923, one vote gave Adolph Hitler leadership of the Nazi Party.

- And in 1942, one vote saved the Selective Service – just weeks before Pearl Harbor.

How important is one vote? Your vote? A wise man once said, "Liberty means responsibility . . . this is why most men fear it." Do you dread to vote or do you consider liberty your responsibility . . . to be preserved where it counts most, in the ballot box? Is one vote all that important? You bet your free life it is.

Take Me Out to the Ball Game and Give Me the Right to Vote
by Elizabeth D. Schafer

Several decades before women would be invited to play professional baseball in "A League of Their Own" during World War II, Birmingham suffragists decided to use baseball as a platform to acquire the right to vote. Since the nineteenth century, women had played softball in female leagues and local matches, but were often jeered by male crowds or had their sporting interests considered improper and their morals and femininity questioned.

Birmingham suffragists arranged a baseball game on August 18, 1915, at Rickwood, to publicize their efforts to win the right to vote. Almost one thousand men and women were members of the Birmingham Equal Suffrage Association which had been established in 1911, with the male auxiliary forming in 1915. The members were prominent society women who sought progress and reform and sponsored suffrage schools, teas, and luncheons as well as hosted visiting suffragists such as Jane Adams who had established Chicago's Hull House.

To prove that women were equals of men, the women decided to show that they could be just as ardent baseball fans as their male counterparts. On "Suffrage Day" at the park approximately five thousand people watched the match between the Birmingham Barons versus the Chattanooga Lookouts. Among the suffragists arranging the ball games were Adele Taylor, Nell Freeman, Lillian Bowron, Mrs. Nixon Norris, Annie Shapiro, and Mrs. Sidney Ullman. Young Alfred Turner served as mascot, promising that "I'm going to bring all sorts of luck to the suffragists and help 'em make it the biggest day of the year in baseball circles!"

Sitting in grandstand boxes draped with yellow bunting, suffragists, their husbands and families, and members of the Men's Suffrage Association attended to root for the Barons. Many suffragists wore yellow clothes and "Votes for Women" buttons. Outside the park, suffragists sold tickets and inside the grounds they passed out yellow pamphlets and suffragist literature worded with baseball jargon to make their points.

The stadium was also adorned with yellow flags, ribbons, and pennants, and posters and signs, pinned to railings, declaring suffrage slogans such as "Votes For Women," "Justice," "Women's Equality," and "Equal Rights." Mr. W. D. Smith, president of the Birmingham Baseball Association, took the decorations in stride, comically commenting, "Wonder if the suffragists will have a sign out reading, 'Left handers are allowed to vote—why not us?'"

To show that women could play the same games as men, as well as understand and promote them, a one-inning game was staged between the Birmingham

Southern Bell Telephone girls and a group of Bessemer women. The girls had played for their municipal gymnasiums and wore traditional gymnasium bloomers and suffrage sashes. Lula Riggs pitched for Bessemer, and Annie Laurie Sparks coached the telephone company team.

The Birmingham Age-Herald reported that Sparks and the girls from the telephone company lost "but they put up a shapely game," noting that the men considered "it was very amusing." Most spectators considered the game merely a nuisance, delaying the professionals game. Edith Sparrow of the *Birmingham News* admitted that she did not understand much about baseball but that the girls who played "batted, stole bases, sacrificed, scored, and ran just as the men do, through not quite with the same air of practice."

After the women cleared the field, Annie Shapiro threw the first pitch to Lookout batter "Jud" Daly. She dramatically performed a windup then tossed a wide curve which was called a ball. Then pitcher Burleigh Grimes replaced her on the mound. The Barrons players were all bedecked in yellow suffrage sashes, like the ones worn by the "fans and fannets." The colors were also worn by W. D. Smith, their owner Rick Woodward, and mascot Taylor who were in the stands. The home team's sashes proclaimed their support for the suffragists, but they were quickly bedraggled by sweat, grime, and players exertions to catch balls and slide into bases.

For the first time women were allowed in the Rickwood press box. Pattie R. Jacobs, president of the Alabama Equal Suffrage Association, climbed the tall ladder to the high birds-eye-view roof seats with two other female journalists including Sparrow, a Chattanooga reporter, and Mrs. Ullman. Respecting their female colleagues, the male sports writers agreed that profanity would be taboo in the box during the suffrage game.

In the stands women joked that they wished they had a "vote" to influence the outcome of the game. Jacobs admitted that female fans were not capable of producing the same kind of noises as men "but their treble tones were just as effective as the bass roar in urging the Barons." She flippantly remarked that silence did not work in baseball or voting, hoping that men might understand why women wanted a voting voice.

The suffragists offered prizes for the best female and male fans. The stands were full of people rooting for the home team by waving balloons and suffrage twirlers and blowing horns. The suffragists sang, creating suffrage lyrics for traditional baseball songs, and a film crew shot footage of local movie star, Cora Gregg, cheering the home team from the stands.

After eleven scoreless innings were played, the umpire called the game on account of darkness. Some suffragists, always concerned about labor legislation, feared that the players would not get paid for overtime. Many male fans groused that the game would have been more conclusively resolved if the players had more time to play and thus score instead of waiting for the girls game to finish.

For the most part participants on and off the field considered the suffrage day at the ballpark to have been successful financially and promotionally as well as a pleasant and cheerful event. One suffragist remarked that "the cause is going to be better off financially because of the game as the baseball people have been so nice and generous in every way."

Jacobs wrote up the game for the newspaper commenting that "the score by innings of the game at Rickwood yesterday reads like the house journal of the Alabama legislature with the suffrage bill under consideration. It was a goose-egg result, neither side getting a decision." Using baseball terminology she explained that, "There were strike outs, some errors, a few assists, sacrifices, a wild throw or two, rotten decisions on the part of the umpires and at certain stages of the game the players were left on the bases." Jacobs narrated somewhat good-humorously that "some unparliamentary language was indulged in, also a little chloroform was temporarily administered." She stressed that the sexes could not be easily divided in social or political matters and emphasized that "women were as good fans as the men."

When the nineteenth amendment was passed in 1920, guaranteeing American women the right to vote, the Alabama Legislature refused to ratify it for several reasons. They did not want women to serve on juries or to give black women the right to vote. The legislators also feared that political empowerment of females might destroy the traditionally acceptable qualities of family and womanhood. The issue of federal imposition of legislation versus a state's right to rule itself, a theme common throughout southern history, was also a consideration. Despite the state legislators reluctance, and empowered by the federal decision, the first Alabama women to vote participated in Birmingham suburb elections on September 20, 1920. The Alabama Legislature finally ratified the nineteenth amendment in 1923.

ANNE WARD AMACHER, Ph.D.

1923 -

For Everything There is a Season And A Time.

Anne Amacher paraphrases Ecclesiastes 3:1-9 as her words of wisdom, emphasizing that she has "tried everything but <u>marching</u> for water quality." These Bible verses echo her feelings about the diversity of approaches that she has embraced in her volunteer work. There was a time To be vigilant, to study and learn, to verify, to correspond, to consult experts, to notify agencies, to publish, to serve on committees, to work with the League of Women Voters, to confront, to praise, to be grateful, to rejoice, and, ultimately, to relinquish. Through her persistence to protect Auburn's watershed, Anne has assured Auburn residents a source of pure and safe drinking water. Water pollution control and environmental quality have been League study issues since the 1950s.

Using her strong rhetoric, Anne has given voice to public concerns by asking essential questions and effectively communicating in a grassroots effort to demand protection of water sources. She has united community groups to pursue a common cause and has diligently devoted her time and personal funds to protect public water. Described by her admirers as intelligent and indomitable, Anne has proven to be a determined environmental sleuth, researching scientific studies and alerting government officials to potential public health problems. Refusing to accept the clichéd lament, "water, water, everywhere, and not a drop to drink," Anne took action to edu-

1

cate both the public and local and state government about environmental resources. She generously, however, credits other people for her successes.

Born Cordelia Anne Ward in Montgomery, Alabama, on July 9, 1923, the daughter of John Milton and Cordelia Scott Ward. Anne said, "they were perfect parents." She grew up in Verbena and Selma. Both of her parents were strong advocates of education. Her father, the son of a rural mailman, started to work after the seventh grade to support his family. A voracious reader, liking everything from Shakespeare to Karl Marx's works, he was "quite an independent thinker." He subscribed to the *Nation* magazine, and Anne says, "I think that influenced my liberal tendencies. To be exposed to it as an adolescent."

Her mother, the daughter of a photographer, had four sisters, all whom attended Montevallo. Anne enjoys telling how her mother once told an acquaintance that she'd had a sister at Montevallo for twenty years, and her friend asked, "Did she ever finish?" Anne's mother encouraged her to be musical by playing recordings for her and sending her to piano lessons. She also presented papers at her study club and was "a fanatic on health."

"I was raised in a very strict environment," being naive about many of society's ills. Enjoying an ideal childhood, she waded in a creek near Verbena with Sidney Lanier Gibson's daughter. A violinist, "Mr. Sid" was the nephew of the famous poet, Sidney Lanier, and he played the violin with Anne and "bought me a lot of music when I was growing up." She credits her teachers for influencing her, especially a high school teacher who boarded in her parent's home and who gave her books to read. Other mentors included her Presbyterian minister and volunteer youth leaders, including Elizabeth Mack Norton. "Selma for white people was a wonderful place to grow up," with good schools and cultural opportunities. There she became aware of race relations. Anne's family hired black cooks, and "they were on good terms." Her parents were "moderate and they could see the point of view of the black people."

When Anne graduated from the Albert G. Parish High School in June 1940, she knew that she wanted to major in English. She earned a freshman scholarship to Agnes Scott College in Decatur, Georgia, the school her mother had wanted to attend. Completing an A.B. in English in June 1944, Anne minored in history. Graduating with the highest grades in her class, Anne was elected to Phi Beta Kappa and Mortar Board. Living in World War II Atlanta was a exciting experience, and Anne had access to cultural activities as well as being inspired when her sociology professor, Dr. Mildred Mell, who taught a minorities class, took her students to listen to W.E.B. DuBois and Benjamin Mays speak, which Anne cites as her turning point in her intellectual grasp of race relations.

Anne completed her master's degree in English at Radcliffe in Cambridge, Massachusetts in June 1946. Her advisor warned her that she would never get a job north of the Mason-Dixon line unless she got help for her southern accent from the speech department. "I decided to prove her wrong, and actually my first job was in New Jersey."

She taught English at the New Jersey College for Women, affiliated with Rutgers University, where she joined the Urban League, helped integrate the swimming pool, and sponsored the debating society and student delegation to the Model United Nations Assembly. By 1950, she enrolled at New York University to attain a Ph.D. in American civilization. Anne enjoyed a summer session at Columbia University where she studied Fletcher Greene's American history course, examining the United States from the American Revolution through the pre-Civil War period. In addition to studying history, Anne witnessed history when she heard Paul Robeson sing and Eleanor Roosevelt speak. While working on her doctorate, Anne taught journalism at Hood College in Frederick, Maryland, and assigned students to cover Eisenhower's campaign whistlestop in that city, waiting with them at the depot.

Interested in international affairs, politics, and race relations, Anne incorporated these topics into her academic work. Funded with two university fellowships of $1,000 each, Anne wrote her dissertation about how a group of southern writers used their images of the south to fight against desegregation. This upset her. "I was in general mad at them," she said. In February 1956, she finished "Myths and Consequences: Allen Tate's and Some Other Vanderbilt Traditionalists Images of Class and Race in the Old South." She published several scholarly articles and book reviews in *American Literature, New England Quarterly, South Atlantic Quarterly, American Quarterly, The University of Kansas City Review, New Mexico Quarterly, and Saturday Review.*

Anne married Richard E. Amacher, who had also earned a doctorate in English. The year 1957 was a turning point for Anne. Auburn hired Richard to teach in the English Department, their daughter Alice was born on April 12, and the Auburn League of Women Voters was established. Anne, a member of other community organizations, including a sewing group, decided to participate in League work. She convinced other area women to join, including Charlotte Ward, whom Anne calls a "Renaissance scientist."

A gifted writer and photographer, Anne generously provided local newspapers articles and photographs about the League's activities. By establishing contacts with the local press, she acquired a forum for her future environmental essays. Recalling being catapulted by chance into the role of an environmental advocate, she says, "It was certainly fortuitous."

Although she lacked formal scientific training, Anne used her intellect as an English professor to interpret complicated technical documents and credibly convey the most essential aspects of these works to government officials and the public. In fact, while many scientists might have better understood the complex jargon, they might not have been able to communicate their concerns as effectively as Anne did.

Anne's awareness of the need for environmental protection was aroused by three people who played an important role in her life: her daughter Alice; her neighbor Bessie Sills whom she describes as a "homebred and natural-born environmentalist" who taught Alice to garden; and a German exchange student from the heavily industrialized Ruhr district. This young woman drank only bottled water and was awed by a sugar-white Auburn snowfall because she had only seen sooty black slush in her hometown.

Anne became immersed in controversy about Auburn's water after she wrote several newspaper articles about an oil spill that ran into the source of Auburn's drinking.

The oil spill had not been reported to the appropriate authorities. Since 1971, residents had complained of Auburn's water having a foul odor and oily taste. She began a quest to determine where the oily taste originated.

In junior high, Anne's daughter, Alice, had become especially motivated to preserve the environment. Anne accompanied her as an adult volunteer to a national Girl Scout environmental conference at the University of Wisconsin at Green Bay during the summer of 1972. They traveled with local Boy Scout Scott Goslin. The workshop required each participant to complete a project. "We decided to try to do something about Auburn's dirty water in terms of public education." Two projects resulted. When they returned home, Anne and Scott's father, William E. Goslin, approached Becky Smith of the Auburn Puppet Workshop to stage a production of the environmental parable Dr. Seuss' *The Lorax*.

Next, with sponsorship from the Scouts, the Auburn League, and the Soil Conservation Service (SCS) they presented an educational program. In November 1972, Auburn's first Watershed Workshop enabled a group of area students, teachers, and residents to tour Lake Ogletree, Auburn's primary source of water. This served to increase area residents' awareness of the need to protect the quality of Auburn's drinking water. Anne and Alice prepared handouts with the names of water and environmental officials and their addresses and phone numbers.

The workshop was held during a particularly rainy spell, and participants saw runoff soil pour into the lake. SCS and Alabama Cooperative Extension Service guides explained how the soil also transported chemicals and pollutants. A SCS official said that a "significant" oil spill had occurred at the Uniroyal tire plant in nearby Opelika, draining into Chewacla Creek and resulting in a fish kill on Lee's Lake, just upstream from Auburn's reservoir. Uniroyal settled out of court with Mr. and Mrs. Charles Lee, and although the county health department was informed of the fish kill, none of the appropriate state or local water and health boards were told.

"I had been suspicious of a different taste and odor, different from the one that had already been affecting water and which was more like vegetation. This one smelled like oil. So that was the signal to pursue Uniroyal. And we did a good bit of detective work."

Anne learned that there had actually been several fish kills. She was dismayed to discover that the Uniroyal plant had utilized a hay bale to filter effluents. After contacting James Gilbert, manager of the Auburn Water Board, Anne began to compile information about Auburn's city water supply, especially the possible effects of effluents from Uniroyal which emptied into Chewacla Creek ten miles above the confluence where the creek fed into Lake Ogletree.

Her investigation became a "consuming activity" of following up on leads and yearning for progress. In 1973 Anne wrote questions to Uniroyal, asking how they discarded waste water, and learned that they had no water testing procedures "partly because testing techniques were not as refined a few years ago as they are now, government agencies did not have the funds and staff and the laws had not been written" to implement more stringent control of water pollution.

She acquired technical documents and thoroughly read books about Uniroyal and rubber technology, attended water quality workshops, and subscribed to environmental publications. When proposed effluent guidelines and standards were published in the October 11, 1973, *Federal Register*, Anne and fellow Auburn resident, Carolyn Carr (who had a chemistry degree), were the only private citizens in America to comment publicly on the criteria.

Although the Environmental Protection Agency (EPA) had tested Auburn's water treatment plant in November 1973 and reported that no industrial organic chemicals were detected by gas chromatography, Anne tenaciously continued to press for more testing because Auburn's water still tasted oily and she was "afraid it was this oil spill that I knew about." She decided to go public with her concerns about industrial effluents polluting Auburn's water.

In a series of articles beginning on August 26, 1973, Anne reported Uniroyal's oil spill in the *Auburn Bulletin*. She credits editor Neil Davis for agreeing to print these controversial essays and journalists Judy Nunn and Martha Evans for writing additional articles. Her first article, appearing on the front page, urged experts to examine Uniroyal's discharge process because the plant would soon be receiving a new effluent permit.

This series "listed the questions that we hadn't got answered about this spill and what it signified as possible contamination on a recurrent or continuing basis of the process effluents and the drainage from the oil tank, an old storage tank which was the case in this accident, as something to fear, a continuing concern." She suggested that a public hearing should be scheduled regarding Uniroyal.

She estimated that the tire plant daily discharged 44.8 pounds of unspecified suspended solids and 11.2 pounds of undescribed oil and grease into Chewacla Creek. She insisted that a negative test on one day did not indicate Auburn's water would be pure on other days. Anne also complained that the Alabama Water Improvement Commission (AWIC) had not designated that Chewacla Creek be used solely as a drinking water source.

She wrote in her October 20 article that her requests for lists of toxic compounds used in the tire plant had been unanswered by the EPA's Effluent Guidelines Division and the National Institute of Occupational Safety and Health. She said that contaminated water would be difficult to purify. She noted the potential long-term health effects Auburn's residents could suffer if they consumed certain toxic substances. Alerted by the oil spill, Anne worried that pollutants were mishandled, importing residues into Auburn's water and that the Atlanta EPA office, unaware of this information, would issue Uniroyal a new permit.

Helped by an informal ad hoc environmental council developed by the Auburn League and Auburn chapter of the Alabama Conservancy, Anne organized study sessions and letter writing campaigns to raise questions about Uniroyal's disposal permit. Asking chemists to review her questions to make sure they were worded correctly, she frankly stated, "I would never have undertaken to do this at a place where I didn't have access to advice. I obviously was incompetent and untrained."

In a "ladylike fashion," she badgered the state, federal, and Uniroyal officials until she received the facts that she wanted. Finally, Howard D. Zeller from the EPA

Enforcement Division in Atlanta wrote her, "Because of your intense concern for the protection of the Auburn public water supply from industrial contamination, we are presently conducting tests of the supply and its source." Samples taken downstream from the plant revealed no industrial organic chemicals. Uniroyal, however, had been warned in advance, and another sampling taken within only two days of warning by the Alabama Division of Public Water Supplies, showed small concentrations of zinc and phenol. These were the first government-sponsored tests seeking synthetic organic chemicals in the effluents from the Opelika plant.

Auburn citizens became more concerned when a more sophisticated test in November 1974 revealed two highly toxic substances existed in Uniroyal's effluents. The Auburn Water Works decided to cooperate in the grassroots effort to protect Auburn's water and reputation. Addressing the issue at a public hearing in 1975, Auburn's citizens filled a room in the student union and spoke on behalf of Anne's work. Anne was surprised at the crowd. George Harlow, an impressed EPA official, told Anne "it was the best attended [meeting] he had been to," and Anne believed that it was the "people who came from the science and engineering fields who made a big difference."

After having been "embarrassed," Uniroyal volunteered to reroute its wastewater effluents from Chewacla Creek into Little Uchee Creek, which supplied no public water. Anne leveled, "Well, that was not great because it didn't require Uniroyal to do anything about getting the toxins out of the effluence, but it just helped our water supply. It didn't do any cattle on the other side or the fish in the other stream any good. But it got it out of our water supply." Soon afterward, samples taken from this creek indicated the presence of toxic substances.

At the time of the oil spill, no epidemics caused by contaminated water occurred, and so far Auburn's cancer rate has not deviated significantly, but long-term affects may not be known for years. The potentially catastrophic events that could have happened if the oil spill had not been publicized and Uniroyal had not diverted their effluents raises chill bumps. As her friend and fellow League member, chemist Charlotte Ward muses about the potential for water-borne diseases, Anne "bugged and bugged and bugged everyone to death but no one would have known" until it was too late.

"The best thing that could come from this undertaking is long-range awareness on the part of public officials, developers and all citizens, an awareness that before land is put to use for economic purposes or public utilities, detailed attention should be given to the potential affect on public health. I'd like to stress that one branch of government needs to let the other know what it has or hasn't done," Anne said that cooperation was essential to prevent ignorance of disasters such as the Uniroyal oil spill.

"Governments need to take advantage of the information and training some citizens—particularly in university communities—have." She said Auburn's city government did not always welcome advice from local experts and rarely cooperated with the League to disseminate information to the public during the planning process for city developments such as expanding sewer lines.

As a volunteer consumer advocate, Anne continued to observe civic meetings, collect data about Auburn's water supply, and inform area residents of events that might otherwise have been ignored. She was the League's representative on a citizen advisory committee that met quarterly with the Alabama Department of Environmental Management (ADEM) and served on the utilities subcommittee of Auburn 2000 to assure Lake Ogletree's ecological survival.

From 1987 to 1989 Anne was named state liaison for the Safe Drinking Water Project sponsored by the national League of Women Voters Education Fund. "The participation of the League of Women Voters, both in corresponding with the EPA and the fact that I met people at the state level in the League who were environmentalists, and that encouraged me." She was particularly influenced by Verda Horne and Weesie Smith, whom Anne met at AWIC hearings and state League meetings, as well as Charlotte Ward, who worked with both the League and the Girl Scouts. Anne interviewed Joe Alan Power, ADEM's chief of public water supply, and published an article in the *Montgomery Advertiser's* forum, "Alabama Voices," exhorting Alabamians to support ADEM in the quest for pure drinking water.

As part of the League's next study item on environmental management practices in Alabama, League president Carolyn Coker asked Auburn journalist, Judy Nunn, to include a summary of water quality issues in a study of Alabama environmental management regulations, for which Anne prepared questionnaires and interviewed the state soil conservationist. Part of her information was incorporated into the national League's report, "Crosscurrents: The Water We Drink."

The Auburn League focused on making the public aware of lead-contaminated drinking water. As the local League's city water board observer, Anne said that Auburn City engineer, Rex Griffin's interest in improving water was "a great joy." His "tactful and steady insistence that the water board pursue and deal with problems is the thing that has made the difference." Annie gave each Auburn Water Works Board member a photocopy of the EPA pamphlet, <u>Lead and Your Drinking Water,</u> which were distributed by the League. She also dispensed the pamphlet and <u>Safety on Tap</u> to interested citizens, and local newspapers printed excerpts. Anne urged Auburn officials to test water samples for lead contamination, and when such tests revealed that some samples yielded a higher lead content than the standard of 50 parts per billion, she demanded that they attempt to comply to regulations.

In the late 1980s, Auburn's water was again plagued by an unpleasant odor and taste. The *Montgomery Advertiser* reported that the obnoxious qualities lingered even after the water had been processed through the city water treatment plant. Attending water quality conferences at Auburn University and ADEM commission meetings regarding drinking water regulations, Anne wrote a flurry of letters, citing the Alabama Water Pollution Control Act in the 1975 Code of Alabama. She solicited written statements from Auburn residents to the commission about their concerns with local water contamination.

On October 7, 1989, Anne arranged another bus tour of the Lake Ogletree watershed, sponsored by the Auburn League. Significantly, Auburn's Mayor, Jan Dempsey, attended, "which showed that the city had come around to have a real interest in this which had been lacking. Nobody from the city or the water board testified at that 1975 hearing. They weren't interested."

Following presentations by public officials from ADEM and Auburn's Water Works Board, the health department's environmental officer, Auburn's city planner, and extension and SCS agents "who participated one hundred percent," League leaders urged Auburn officials to investigate and correct problems that endangered Auburn's water source.

Anne alerted Mr. Blevins, the Auburn Water Board's scientist who tested water, to a microscopic threat. "This is ridiculous since I have no science background." She was the first person to tell officials in the ADEM and EPA about the risk of cryptosporidium (which causes gastrointestinal distress) being in Alabama water.

Informed by a local veterinarian that cryptosporidium is endemic in calves, Anne urged Auburn to periodically test for cryptosporidium and increase filtration treatments to deal with it. One of the targeted pollutants was fecal material from a Lee County farm three miles upstream from Lake Ogletree. Since 1976, AWIC had warned State Representative Charles Whatley of Beauregard's Willow Run Farms to keep his dairy cattle (as many as four hundred) out of Chewacla Creek.

In addition, dairy barn personnel washed raw animal waste, averaging 260 pounds daily, into the creek. Sampling of nearby Lake Ogletree revealed the water's composition had changed, producing high coliform bacteria counts. This bacteria can cause death and have detrimental effects on humans, fish, and wildlife. For three years Whatley refused to comply with pollutant control directives until AWIC threatened legal action for polluting the headwaters of the city water supply. Building an animal waste lagoon to catch raw wastes, Whatley argued that the manure actually improved water quality and fishing conditions because it was biodegradable and killed weeds. As a member of the Sunset Committee, he tried to abolish AWIC.

In January 1980, Anne filed a complaint with the State Ethics Commission. Described by the press as a concerned "housewife," Anne asked the commission to determine if Whatley had violated the Ethics Act when he voted to terminate AWIC. Noting that Whatley's dairy was regulated by AWIC, creating a conflict of interest, she also mentioned that he had vocally sworn revenge against AWIC for levying fines on him for dumping untreated animal waste into Auburn's drinking water source. She filed the complaint because "I don't think he did the right thing. His motives were wrong and I wanted to see if it was legally wrong." Whatley's efforts failed, and ADEM fined him $2,500 in 1989.

Anne also followed a civil suit filed by ADEM against Opelika's Diversified Products Corporation in 1989 for failure to comply with water pollution control regulations at two wastewater discharge sites. She wrote to officials about local industry, Dexter Lock, emitting cyanide in discharges and wrote an article for the campus literary magazine, *The Circle*, challenging Auburn University students to advance her work. At the same time she was caring for her elderly mother, whom she had moved into her home. Anne devoted much of her energy to her.

In 1991, Anne won a W. Kelly Mosley Environmental Award for Achievements in Forestry, Wildlife, and Related Resources to honor voluntary work "which will result in the wiser use of renewable natural resources." Nominated by fellow League member Judy Aull, who wanted Anne honored "in appreciation of her years of diligent advocacy of improved water quality in Auburn and the State of Alabama," Anne donated her prize money to Auburn's League. "It was their money," she asserts, noting she had done most of her water quality advocacy with support from the League. Anne also received a limited edition print of a painting by Auburn University art professor, W.C. Baggett, Jr. Depicting a peaceful Alabama springtime scene.

Water quality remains a pressing issue in Alabama, which is one of the last southern states that has not yet developed a water management plan. In Auburn, League members, including Anne, currently promote protection of the watershed, observing public meetings and hearings regarding land use and zoning. The city's Planning Commission is only one of twenty-nine percent of water utilities surveyed by the League that pursues watershed management to protect water quality by limiting industrial development near the watershed. Spurred by Anne's work, city engineer and Water Works Board manager, Rex Griffin, Auburn research faculty, and the SCS have cooperated to reduce trihalomethane formation (THMs), carcinogens that occur if organic matter combines with chlorine during the disinfection process.

"With a Water Resources Research Institute and numerous biologists, civil engineers, and chemists on the Auburn University campus, with vigorous organization in Auburn like the chapters of the Alabama Conservancy and the League of Women Voters," she said, and "with water works which, according to Manager James H. Gilbert has two of the three Class I operators in Alabama, there is no reason why Auburn should not become a model city in protecting the watershed of its public water supply against improper land uses or other hazards."

In addition to her water work, Anne considers her most significant and satisfactory activity to be her enjoyment of music and foreign cultures. She and her husband are members of the Auburn Chamber Music Society. Richard, a gifted violinist, plays in several Alabama orchestras, and, as a student at the University of Chicago, he once performed at Hull House. Richard was a Fulbright scholar. Anne relishes hosting international students, welcoming them into her home and savoring musical presentations from a variety of cultures. Anne lived with a Turkish roommate when she was a graduate student at Radcliffe and lived in Germany for two years.

An ardent advocate of women's history, she is especially proud of writing a newspaper article about Marjorie Tyre Sykes, a former Metropolitan Opera harpist who founded the Auburn Chamber Music Society's concert series. She has also written about prominent members of Auburn's Afro-American community, including her neighbor Bessie Sills. She is proud of her daughter who continued her scientific interests by earning a medical degree and working as a pathologist.

When asked what she values most about her life, Anne said that in addition to music, "Having the chance to make friends of all races and countries. Having the chance to study how different government agencies, industries, and all of us in the public influence the quality of drinking water."

Her legacy to Alabamians is not only the pure water they consume, but her accumulation of resource materials that she hopes will be used to maintain the water quality that she has worked so hard to achieve. Anne has deposited her papers in the Auburn public library and wishes they "would be used by students of the environmental or politics . . . as a laboratory to study how the agencies interrelate and sometimes don't interrelate and as a case study of citizen involvement with water quality."

If she had not acted when she heard about the initial oil spill, Anne said, "I don't believe the discharge would have been removed from that creek that feeds our water supply any earlier than a few years after 1986 because I don't think anybody in the city really took note of the fact that discharge was there until we began to point it out after the watershed workshop." The EPA has since 1986, required that industries file assays of what toxins are present, locate toxic sources in plants, and deal with them "by treating them or getting them out or they could negotiate with their local sewage treatment plant about putting the effluent there."

"I have deduced about the possibilities of how you get some things done. I would say research, newspaper articles, correspondence to all the affected agencies and attempts to make them communicate with each other, recruiting or being sure that persons who would have an interest in this and who have more knowledge about it than you do participate, become involved, and make their contributions. That was the key."

"I've been trying for several years to get somebody else appointed by the League [to attend Water Board meetings] because I'm getting old and I just want to see other people get trained on it. I do still try to attend the meetings when I can." Anne is proud of local women who continue to be concerned citizens and environmentalists. For example, Dr. Cathy Solheim, the Auburn League's natural resources chair, has collaborated in organizing Alabama Water Watch, a task force to protect wetlands, recruiting citizens to test stream water. Anne delightedly asserts that this "shows that the League is continuing and really doing nitty gritty" environmental work.

Above all else, she credits her community with securing pure water. "The reason it succeeded, I think, really, was the participation of scientists, engineers, and others. They knew more about it than the EPA representatives did or the state folks, I think, and certainly more than I did. My hope from this is that it will encourage some other people to keep working on this." Intertwining her literary training and "watery work," Anne suggests this Shakespearean epitaph: "Too much of water hast thou, fair Cordelia, and therefore I forbid my tears."

written by Elizabeth D. Schafer

LEAH MARIE RAWLS ATKINS, Ph.D.
1935 -

You Don't Depend On Luck In Life,
You Depend On Preparation.

Dr. Leah Rawls Atkins, director of the Center for Arts and Humanities at Auburn University and an adjunct history professor, has heeded her father's advice. "I try to be prepared. Daddy used to say that you made your own luck." He also said that when "people were born, God gave everybody a little brown lunch sack full of luck and that what you wanted to do was go through life holding it very tight at the top. Daddy said that you should live your life so that you didn't have to open up that sack and reach into it to get anything out, because if you did it too often, you were going to reach in, and it was all gone."

Leah has energetically devoted her life to making humanities available to Alabamians. A renowned historian, she has secured $800,000 in grants to promote Alabama literature, art, and history from her office in Pebble Hill, the antebellum home of the Center for Arts and Humanities. She seeks opportunities for scholars, whether by arranging speaking engagements or funding sources, and has enabled Alabamians to have access to humanities programs across the state. Her primary ambition is to enrich the cultural life of every Alabama community. Carefully choosing her words of wisdom, her blue eyes sparkling, "I think you have to believe in yourself, and I think you have to push yourself, and I think you have to believe that, within reason, you can do what you're willing to pay the price to do and set out to do. I think you cannot blame your failures on other people. You can't say 'because I'm a woman I didn't get to do that.' Setbacks and other things come along, but you just have to overcome them." A world champion water skier, she was the first woman inducted into the Alabama Sports Hall of Fame in 1976. She illustrates her point with this analogy, "I teach a lot of kids to ski and they are often afraid of falling because falling is failure. Oftentimes people won't try to do something because they're afraid of failing and one of the things that I try to tell the young people that I work with is that they should never worry about failing because failing is just one step toward getting it right the next time."

Born on April 24, 1935, in Birmingham, the only child of Jack and Lena Margaret Jones Rawls, Leah credits two major influences for shaping her life, her extended family and growing up outdoors on the Warrior River. The descendant of pioneer settlers named Jones, Hawkins, and Roebuck who secured Jefferson County land after the Creek War ended in 1815 and battled bears and panthers on the frontier, Leah has documented her family history in *The Jones Family of Huntsville Road* (1981).

She explores her diverse roots, from her Michigan-born grandmother, Lena Florence Sheppard, whose family moved to Birmingham for her health, and her democratically-steeped grandfather, Charles Alfred Jones, whose marriage to Lena merged two traditions. Owner of the Charles A. Jones Company on Morris Avenue, Leah's grandfather sold "Happy Feeds," named for his disposition. She describes her grandmother as "a most unusual woman," who read voraciously, studied astronomy and Hebrew, and played the viola in the Birmingham-Southern College Orchestra.

Leah grew up very close to her mother's family. Near the Rawls's duplex, seven aunts and uncles and numerous cousins lived in her grandparents' and great grandparents' homes, where Leah Atkins delighted in playing and enjoyed family reunions and dinners. "I know that kind of large, extended, loving family had a very important part in my growing up years."

When she was about four years old, Leah recalls, "Mama was not well. And I don't know why she was not well. The story was that she was about to have a nervous breakdown. My mother was a very strong person. She wasn't about to have a nervous breakdown." The problem was, according to Leah, that the relatives kept traveling from domicile to domicile through her mother's kitchen. "Mama just got tired. She just wanted to get out of there. Daddy bought a little old fish cabin down on the Warrior River in Camp Oliver. We would go on the weekends. And that had an important impact upon me because of the water sports. I learned to swim and I learned to water ski."

"I love the outdoors. I was a Girl Scout." She hiked through the woods with her mother near their home in Edgewood and dug up wild plants, ferns, and honeysuckle, bringing them home in buckets. She went to camp every summer and rode her Shetland pony Rex, admitting, "I was a tomboy." As a child, Leah played hide and seek in an abandoned dogtrot, picked berries, built forts, climbed trees, waded in the river, and shot down mistletoe. She ate at barbecues, took lessons at the local riding academy, and fought fires during the dry seasons. Her social activities were important but never dominated her life. "What we did as a family was always more important." Remembering mentors, "My mother and my father, of course, were the greatest influence." She reveals that her mother's personality differed from her own, with Margaret being a "professional mother and homemaker" who was shy and never went to meetings alone or said the blessing. Leah's mother made clothes, sewed, and knitted, but "she pushed me forward and let me do anything I wanted to do."

Leah describes her father as retaining his generation's chauvinistic ideas about what women should and should not do, though "he never made me feel that I was inferior or different or there was something I couldn't do because I was female. I could pretty much do anything I wanted to do as long as I was willing to pay the price for it because there was always a price that had to be paid for anything that you wanted badly enough to do." He emphasized this point to her when she placed last in most events at her first water ski tournament at Cypress Gardens. Even when she was unsuccessful "he supported me in what I wanted to do."

"It was a very disciplined household that I grew up in. I was expected to be at the breakfast table somewhere between 6:00 and 6:30 every morning no matter what I did at night, whether I went to a dance or stayed up to study." Her father's interest in history deeply influenced his daughter. "He loved history and he loved the South and he loved Alabama," she recalls, crediting their talks about history, current events, and various ideas as important in forming her intellectual interests. She also enjoyed reading the comics in the conservative *Chicago Daily Tribune* which her father subscribed to when he became a Republican during Franklin D. Roosevelt's third presidential campaign. Leah explains that her father's switching parties could have been considered "quite a heresy in the South at that time."

Leah's historical career was also shaped by global events. "My growing up years were dominated by World War II." Numerous cousins and uncles went off to war, and she learned geography in her aunt's home on a map where pins indicated where family members were stationed. An uncle copied letters to distribute to the entire family, and welcome home reunions were looked forward to when the whole family would be together. Birmingham residents were concerned about Japanese bombing raids (the city was ranked as the second most important military objective in America), and her family retreated to a basement room during black outs.

At Edgewood Grammar School and Shades Valley High School she was "very fortunate to have good teachers who demanded a lot" and who "really pushed" her. Some of the women were devoted to their students and distributed ample amounts of both tender, loving care and discipline. Leah particularly remembers her English teacher, Miss Dennie Mae Mackey. "Miss Mackey was a terror to those who didn't do what she told them to do. And she was a very demanding teacher. She taught me a great deal." Leah also admired Dorothy Shirey Walker, her speech teacher, recollecting, "I just wandered into her class in tenth grade for an elective, and then I took speech and advanced speech and drama. She was a wonderful teacher and taught me a lot about literature, too, and about Greek plays and drama and theatre."

In 1950, Leah began to compete in water ski tournaments and she won several national and international titles. As she traveled outside the United States, she became more aware of how people throughout the world lived.

As a seven-year-old girl, she visited an older cousin at Auburn University. She slept with a pillow and a blanket on a desk in an Alumni Hall dormitory room. Listening to the Samford Hall chimes every hour, young Leah enjoyed her sleepless night and resolved to attend Auburn. In the fall of 1953, she entered Auburn University. She pledged Alpha Delta Pi, earned high grades and was selected for membership in the Alpha Lambda Delta and Kappa Delta Pi honoraries.

She had dated her childhood sweetheart, George Arthur Atkins, since she was in ninth grade and he was in twelfth. She married him on June 7, 1954. Although she had enjoyed social events throughout her teenage years, Leah admits that she was never boy crazy and that her relationship with George "had an impact on me in many different ways because I was very comfortable with my dating, and I could concentrate on my books, scholarship, and sports." Having had no strong history teachers in high school, "I didn't get turned onto history until I walked into Dr. Joseph Harrison's History 101 class at Auburn University. I fell in love with history and I fell in love with Joe Harrison." Leah describes her mentor as "just wonderful." She recalls, "I had never seen anyone who could talk about history without a note, making men and women live and breathe, and issues come alive." His history lectures were "as current as if it had happened yesterday." Leah said, "I thought I could do this the rest of my life."

As a sophomore, she took world history from Dr. Robert R. Rea whose different approach made her think, "my goodness, this is unbelievable." She considers her life-long friendships, formed in her freshman year, with these brilliant men as fortunate and important to her professional development. Her husband played football at Auburn until 1955 when he graduated and went to Detroit to play professional football. The Atkins' son George Timothy was born that year. Leah resumed her education in 1956 when her husband returned south to join the Auburn Athletic staff. She finished a B.S. in education in August 1958, and planned to teach American history at Auburn High School.

She admits "I never really thought about teaching in college," but Professor Rea encouraged her to apply for a graduate school fellowship. When she filled out the form, Rea advised her to note that she planned to use a master's degree to teach high school history because some faculty members did not think women should teach at the college level. "I wasn't sensitive to the gender issues at that time." There were no female faculty in the history department, and only a small proportion of the graduate students were women. Leah received the teaching fellowship. Her thesis, "Early Efforts to Control Tuberculosis in Alabama: The Formation and Work of the Alabama Tuberculosis Association, 1908-1930," was written because the association requested that the History Department have a graduate student work on the topic and provided money to pay for typing, "which was important."

After graduating with a M.A. in August 1960, Leah Atkins became an instructor in the department because of the large demand for lecturers for the introductory freshman American history series. Because Auburn did not have a Ph.D. program at that time, she investigated enrolling at the University of Alabama. She traveled with her father to Tuscaloosa about 1963 or 1964. Offered a fellowship, she considered commuting to the university every Monday and leaving for home on Thursday. She changed her mind, however, by the time she returned to Auburn because the roads between Auburn and Tuscaloosa were "awful," isolated, and heavily traveled by logging trucks.

Other priority considerations at home were her son, Richard Brian born in 1959, and her daughter, Laura Leigh born in 1962. Leah reconsidered. She continued to teach until September 1969 when she resigned her position to enroll in Auburn's new Ph.D. program. Although three degrees from the same school was "not the most desirable thing," Leah quips, "I didn't have a choice, because I couldn't leave with so much family responsibility. I just either went to Auburn or I didn't get the degree."

Dr. Malcolm McMillan, a prominent Alabama historian, directed her dissertation, "Southern Congressmen and the Homestead Bill," which analyzed the southern role in developing homestead legislation, an aspect overlooked by historians. Although she began her program after several other students, Leah earned the first Auburn Ph.D. in history in 1974. She finished her dissertation first because "I had to be so organized to take care of three kids and then I had a baby [Jack Raymond in 1970] in the middle of the process."

Briefly teaching at the University of Alabama at Birmingham, Leah joined the Samford University faculty, rising from instructor to tenured associate professor of history. Samford expected instructors each semester to teach an overwhelming load of five three-hour courses in American, Southern, Alabama, and local history. Writing when she could, Leah published several articles and A Manual for Writing Alabama State and Local History (1976). Samford was a small school, so she had many opportunities to become well acquainted with her students, which was a "very rewarding experience." She directed the honors program and taught summers at Samford's Institute of Genealogy and Historical Research. Samford's London program was "one of the most fun things I've ever done." She says that there were so many questions to consider, "How do you service it? How do you have a strong academic program in London? How do you build it?"

She also enjoyed teaching in Samford's two week January term where she spent all day with students and visited local art museums. "I am convinced that the learning was strong as it was meeting two and a half hours a week for the semester. It was a wonderful in-depth course, literature, music, art, and theatre. You can do so much that you can't do in a semester. I taught two courses in Jan term that I just loved. I taught the Wild, Wild West where I covered outlaws, silver and gold mining, Indian battles, cattle drives, San Francisco. . . ." Leah alternated western history with a World War II course. She also taught a popular Samford After Sundown course on John Wayne, lecturing and then viewing a movie to discuss various historical themes. Her goal was to interest people in history and encourage life-long learning.

"History is so important because I think you need to know where your society and culture has been so that you're comfortable with who you are and where you're going. I think that it helps you be a better citizen because you can judge and vote better if you know what the problems of the past have been and how they've been solved and what the successes or failures were." History could help America retain its international power, Leah said. "We have the greatest country in the world. We've got lots of problems, lots and lots of problems, and we're not going to be the greatest country in the world over the long haul if we do not find the leadership to solve these problems. History is one of the most critical subjects. What I resent so much is that educational administrators believe that history can be taught by anybody, you just give them a textbook and if they've got a degree from college, it doesn't matter. So most of the time they're football coaches or basketball coaches. It's just ludicrous."

In 1985, Leah moved back to Auburn to become director of the Center for the Arts and Humanities at Auburn which was created to make the humanities come alive for Alabamians. Housed in Pebble Hill, the former home of Colonel Nathaniel J. Scott, an Alabama legislator who supported Auburn's original college in 1856 (secessionist William Lowndes Yancey once visited Scott's house), the humanities center is the nucleus of Auburn's cultural programs and serves as an outreach department of the College of Liberal Arts. Helping Alabamians plan and present public programs in their communities, the center "exists to help Alabamians understand how human creations and traditions enrich our lives, enabling us to understand the past and appreciate the present."

Enthusiastically assisting citizens and professors to form a partnership to explore and appreciate Alabama's arts, humanities, history, and heritage, the center, directed by Leah, is the catalyst in the bond between academics and local groups to nourish intellectual interest in communities' cultural legacies. Programs organized by Professor Atkins have included studies of religious and ethnic groups, cemetery tours, visits to old gold mines, voyages down the Chattahoochee River, oral history workshops, county sesquicentennials, musical presentations, agricultural history of the Wiregrass, the World War II history of Selma's Craig Army Air Base, and a state-wide exhibition of nineteenth-century weaving and quilts from east Alabama.

The center's first major program, featuring Mobile writer William March, foreshadowed "Read Alabama!" As a result of their determined drive and persistence, a group of scholars, including Jerry Brown and Leah, secured the largest humanities grant ever received at Auburn. The program funded by the National Endowment for the Humanities introduced Alabama authors to the public. She explains that "Alabama had a lot of fine writers that Alabamians didn't know about. We wanted Alabamians to read their writers - people who wrote out of their culture. Writers that came from an Alabama setting. Not all Alabamians write about Alabama but the influence is there."

"Read Alabama!" was a scholar-led, reading-discussion program where participants read books and discussed themes. Earning acclaim both outside and inside the state, the program boosted circulation rates of Alabama authors. In addition to helping readers gain a perspective of Alabama culture, Leah said that access to good reading material would improve writing skills. "The more that you read, the more you understand vocabulary and how sentences are put together and paragraphs are developed. The way you teach someone to write is to get them to read good writing. History is a way to read good writing and I don't think it's used in that way.

"I think literature should go hand in glove with history because novels can fill in gaps that historians can't find substantiation for. The humanities enrich our lives and are what really make us a good people." She said that the humanities represent universal experiences and "let us understand a broader picture of the world. I think a person's ethical being is influenced by their religion" which is another important aspect of the humanities.

Leah has secured grants from the National Endowment for the Humanities to direct the "Civil War: Crossroads of Our Being," "World War II: A Time Remembered," and "Reading Our Lives: Southern Autobiography." The recent addition of the Alabama Writers Forum to Pebble Hill increases the center's commitment "to offering enriching, meaningful programming on Alabama's past and contemporary literary culture."

In addition to routine professorial duties such as serving on journal editorial boards and presenting papers to a variety of audiences, Leah has published widely about Alabama history and people in *Alabama Heritage, The Journal of the Birmingham Historical Society, Alabama Review, Alabama Historical Quarterly, Birmingham Magazine, Alabama English*, and has written study guides for textbooks. Co-writing the *First Frontier: Viewer Guide* for Auburn Television, she also was a consultant for film projects about Virginia Durr and Julia Tutwiler. Her most significant work to date is the recent *Alabama: The History of a Deep South State* (Tuscaloosa: University of Alabama Press, 1994). Leah and her three co-authors - William Warren Rogers, Robert David Ward, and Wayne Flynt - have been nominated for a Pulitzer Prize. The work is the first comprehensive Alabama history written in sixty years and based on modern scholarship. Leah's advisor, Dr. McMillan, was working on a new history of Alabama in the early 1980s, and asked her to work with him. She began to compile bibliographies, collect articles, and take notes. After McMillan died, the four co-authors started a completely new work. Focusing on antebellum Alabama, Leah profiled state history from its native peoples through European exploration, the Creek war, and settlement of the frontier, to the growth of the cotton kingdom and life on the Civil War home front. She especially gave life to Alabama women, whose names and actions have often been obscured by history.

"I made a concerted effort to include something about little people and discuss the lives of common folk so I used a lot of manuscripts and diaries and people's own words as much as I could. Rather than me saying what happened, I let them say it. Women are hard to find in history in any period. Black women are almost impossible to find before 1865." In Alabama history, she said that, "Women have been totally ignored. White men have pretty much written Alabama history, and they've written it from a political and economic standpoint."

In the antebellum Alabama period she said, "Quite frankly, women were not important politically. Women did not vote until the twentieth century. And they didn't really control their property if they were married." She said that male historians considered women historically insignificant. Women "were more than relegated to the back the back seat. I think they weren't even on the bus."

The book won the James F. Sulzby, Jr. Book Award, the Alabama Historical

Association's highest honor. Leah hopes the book attracts readers who will gain "a love and appreciation for Alabama." She said that the book is not definitive but rather "is a survey to try to point you in the direction where there are other things" to consult. Touring the state with the book's co-authors, Leah participated in the series "Understanding Alabama: Capturing A State's History." They discussed the book and helped to celebrated Alabama's 175th anniversary.

Dr. Leah Rawls Atkins has written several books as a "labor of love," including *Blossoms Amid the Deep Verdure: A Century of Women at Auburn, 1892-1992*, a history of Auburn women (she was on the steering committee for the Celebration of the Centennial of the Admission of Women to Auburn University on October 28, 1992), and *The Valley and the Hills: An Illustrated History of Birmingham and Jefferson County* (1981), the first interpretive history of Birmingham which she dedicated to her father.

Counted among Leah's numerous professional achievements and honors, are serving as president of the Alabama Historical Association (1986-1987) and Alabama Association of Historians (1987-1990); and membership in the Alabama Historical Commission, Auburn Heritage Association, and the Birmingham Historical Society. In addition she has been president and board member of the Friends of the Alabama State Department of Archives and History and editor of its newsletter.

She has acted as a humanities consultant and scholar for Alabama public libraries, writers groups, and historic organizations and has been an academic referee and grant reviewer for both national and state humanities groups. Leah has been a historical expert witness and researched history for legal cases. She has presented programs for universities, civic groups, patriotic organizations, and genealogical and historical societies, and devised workshops to discuss resources for Alabama history teachers to use state and local history in the classroom. She lectured at Normandy, France, for the fiftieth anniversary of D-Day, and has led historical programs at Old Alabama Town and for Auburn's Elderhostel series.

Listed in numerous biographical volumes, including *Who's Who of American Women*, Leah has won numerous awards, most notably the Alabama Humanities Foundation Humanities Award and Alabama Association of Historians John Ramsay Award of Merit, both in 1993. She has benefitted the academic community by serving on a variety of committees and advising student groups. Leah is an inspiring role model for younger historians, particularly women in the still male-dominated field. The Leah Rawls Atkins Award is given in her honor to Auburn's outstanding female athletes. She belongs to Holy Trinity Episcopal Church and the Auburn Women's Club. She has donated money to Auburn's League of Women Voters to initiate the Phyllis Rea Award in honor of that former state League president. Of her work, she explains, "Auburn has given so much to me and if I can do one thing to make Auburn better, the effort will have been worthwhile."

In her soft Alabama accent, Leah underscores her personal philosophy that the world would be a better place if people would "wake up every morning" and say "I'm going to find somebody to do something good for today." She considers her most significant and satisfactory accomplishments to be raising her four children and teaching students. Leah enjoys helping others, especially young people. "I think reaching out and pushing them, demanding a lot from them and seeing the pleasure they get when they do perform" is rewarding.

Having spent her life recording history, Leah humbly thinks that she has not been part of any historic actions. "Raising a family and working full time - that's about all you can do." Leah sees a lot of turning points in her life, "You move, and you change in your life. Children are born. They leave home. There are just lots of things that go on in your life.

"Women have a tremendous advantage over men because women are used to change. I am absolutely convinced that women adjust to change easier than men do." She became aware of this when her father-in-law moved into her home and had a difficult time accepting old age. "As I began to look at him and look at my own life I could see that for women – Daddy looks after you and you do what Daddy says. Then you get married and you do what your husband says, and then the children come along and you do what they tell you to do. I'm being facetious, of course." She laughed. "A woman's body changes. You're tiny and then you get pregnant, and you get big. And you are a daughter, and then you become a mother. Your whole relationship with people changes your whole life. You have to adjust to this change, and I think men are more in control of their lives, with what's going on around them and their family, and so they don't like change. But I think women are just constantly changing. Women have so many more different lives than men do. I think it's a great gift, not a burden."

In her book-lined Pebble Hill office, Leah skillfully documents history's lessons, weaving the threads of many lives into an intricate tapestry. Congenially answering the phone, she welcomes inquiries from Alabamians who have heard that she can help them learn more about their state. Of the future, "I'm looking forward to retiring. I don't have any plans for doing that tomorrow or the next day, but I'll be sixty this year, and I've worked the greater part of my life. I really want to do some things that I have not had a chance to do.

"I want to write my autobiography, not so much for anyone else, but because there are a lot of things about me and about how I have viewed my world that nobody really understands. I want my children and my grandchildren to have this." "I would like to make my yard a garden. I love working in the soil." She also plans to write more historical essays, read, travel, and enjoy her seven grandchildren. "That is what I plan to do for the years that the Lord lets me stay in good health."

written by Elizabeth D. Schafer

Photo by E. Scott Barr

PHOEBE BAUGHAN BARR
1906 -

It's Not What I Can Do, But That I Can Share Dance.
Dance Has Lifted My Life To A Beautiful Spiritual Vision.

Phoebe Barr dedicated her long and "marvelous" life to concert dancing. She has performed and taught dance all over the country and been a prominent figure in the University of Alabama and Tuscaloosa area dance community for forty-eight years. She was a central figure in the formation of the Tuscaloosa Community Dancers and her campus dance group was the forerunner of the University Dancers. She has inspired many students to commit their lives to dance and many others to stay fit all their lives through exercise and dance.

One of the original dancers in the Community Dancers, Edith Lindsey, said, "Before Phoebe and Lou Wall began the Community Dancers in the 1950s, there was nothing in concert dance at all in Tuscaloosa. There was lots of theatre and music, but no dance." Lou Wall, the former director of the University of Alabama Dance Program, said, "If there is such a thing as a natural teacher, Phoebe Barr is one. She has an extraordinary ability to communicate her own excitement about dance to others."

Phoebe was born June 14, 1906, into a very interesting, exciting family. Her father, H.H. Baughan, was a civil engineer who had worked all over the world. As a young man he had worked his way around the world including exploring the frontier of the Klondike. The family was living in Carrolton, Georgia, when Phoebe was born, but moved to the next engineering project when she was six months old. This mobility continued for Phoebe and her only sibling, an older brother. They were exposed to many new things as they moved with their parents around the South. Her mother was a very articulate graduate of the University of North Carolina at Greensboro. She was a Bible scholar and loved to tell stories about her ancestors who were English royalty, an Anglican priest, and early settlers of America.

Phoebe did not see a dance performance, not even ballet, until she was in college. Dance was considered a "frivolous activity" by her parents and many of their generation. She was very familiar with music, literature and painting as art forms, but didn't know that dance was art, too. She began North Carolina College (now UNC-Greensboro) in 1923. One evening her first year she was looking for something to do and went to see a concert on campus given by the Denishawn Dancers. She didn't know that this performance would change her life forever.

At that time, the Denishawn Dancers were the best dance troupe America had produced. Ruth St. Denis and her husband Ted Shawn were pioneers in modern American dance. Ruth St. Denis and Isadora Duncan were the founders of the new the art form of modern concert dancing. Duncan pursued her career abroad while St. Denis stayed home in America. Before Duncan and St. Denis, dance meant ballet which had been developed over centuries into very formal movements for the entertainment of European royalty. The new modern dance was for everyone to enjoy.

St. Denis dance inspiration came from the exotic themes of Oriental, Egyptian, and East Indian cultures. She performed her first concert in 1906 to a shocked American audience with her sensual-yet-chaste dancing and elegant-but-revealing costume. "BOSTON GASPS, AS RUTH ST. DENIS DANCES," a newspaper headline read. Ted Shawn was eighteen years younger than his wife. Shawn's dance was grounded in ballet. He loved American and primitive themes. He was very theatrical and was called the most popular male dancer in America.

That evening at UNC watching the Denishawn dancers was the most magical one of her life. One dance still remains vividly etched in her memory. Dressed in a flowing white gown Ruth St. Denis danced a story of unrequited love to the music of Liszt's *Liebestraum*. "At one point in the performance St. Denis swept around the stage in a great circle and then pierced the heavens with an upturned gesture of reaching into the void that left me in tears." She sat in her seat for a long time after everyone left and the house lights were turned off. In the darkened theatre she realized that she had been changed. "I had been uplifted and transported into another world. I knew then that I had to learn about dance—to learn about that kind of dance, but not to read about it. I wanted to do it." She wanted to "learn what they did to make me feel so good."

The next day she was encouraged to find that the college had an excellent dance teacher. Helen Robinson was happy to teach Phoebe the highly-regarded dance techniques Margaret H'Doubler had developed at the University of Wisconsin. Phoebe also learned the experimental dance theories that Martha Graham was using at the Eastman School of Music. She couldn't get enough dance at college, so she applied to and was accepted by the Denishawn School of Dance and Related Arts in New York City. She was a senior in college and was elated by the prospects of studying with this internationally acclaimed group that had so fascinated her as a freshman. Her parents were not happy, but reluctantly gave their consent.

In the fall of 1928, the "sorta numb and some scared," petite, energetic, blue-eyed brunette arrived at Denishawn House at 67 Stevenson Place, Manhattan. The spacious Moorish structure was dominated by its forty-by-sixty-foot dance studio. Denishawn had moved there in 1924 from Los Angeles and had become a major cultural institution with branches in a dozen cities.

Denishawn's Los Angeles school had developed its reputation as a haven for dancers and other performing artists who wanted to be associated with the vanguard of modern American dance. D.W. Griffith sent his silent film stars to learn "emotional expression through movement." The stars included Mabel Norman, Lillian Gish and others. The new leaders of the first generation of modern dance—Martha Graham, Doris Humphrey, and Charles Weidman—also studied and performed there.

When Phoebe arrived in New York, the Denishawn School and Dance Troupe had already peaked. It must have been during this time in her life that "marvelous" became and remained her favorite word. She filled her days, six days a week, with classes. St. Denis taught Oriental dance and Shawn taught ballet. Guest teachers instructed students in Dalcroze Eurythmics, as well as Hawaiian dance, Spanish dance and other ethnic dances. With less experience than other dancers, Phoebe's practice sessions continued late into the night. "I knew so little, but all the students were good to me, and company members would help anyone who would ask. I asked."

The Denishawn students were the darlings of the New York art world and received free tickets to museums and art galleries. Sunday, their day off, was usually spent touring museums and art galleries. On Saturday nights they often were invited to parties where they mingled with the city's most prominent artists and art patrons. During the week the family of dancers gathered for dinner around Miss St. Denis and Papa Shaw in the Denishawn's spacious dining room. Phoebe soaked everything up and learned quickly in this warm, congenial atmosphere.

Phoebe's dance style changed to the one it would follow the rest of her life when a new teacher came to Denishawn. Margharita Wallmann had been the head of the famed Wigman School in Berlin. Phoebe was delighted to find that Wigman's techniques were compatible with her abilities. "It was wonderful for me. It fit me." Wallmann agreed with her and chose Phoebe and another Denishawn student to demonstrate her lecture classes at Hunter College and at other schools in and around New York City.

"This was an exciting time in the dance world. Work that was to refresh and revitalize dance was going on in small studios and lofts in New York. In light of history, I know that my time at Denishawn was during its decline. New approaches and forms were emerging with the work of Martha Graham, Doris Humphrey, and Charles Weidman." An unmendable breach developed as the new artist broke with Denishawn. Phoebe's eyes twinkle with mischief when she tells of the break. "Denishawn's were not allowed to go to their concerts, but we did." She said, "Dance was not an athletic event as it is now. Dance was powerful expressions in movement."

In 1929, after a year and a half of intensive study, Phoebe auditioned for Doris Humphrey's new production of *Lysistrata*. On the same day she was both accepted by Humphrey and asked to join Denishawn's dance company. She was stunned at first. The invitations were tributes and recognition of the achievements she had made in just a few short years with her dance talent and ability. She signed with Denishawn.

"I decided that I wanted to be associated with the ground that had enriched the genius of Humphrey, Weidman, and Graham, rather than go to the new ground that was being cultivated." She has never regretted that decision. She toured with Denishawn all over the East coast, often introducing modern dance to audiences who had never seen it.

She met Scott Barr, her future husband, during her first year in New York. She was visiting in Greensboro, North Carolina. Her friend Margaret had a big party for Phoebe and she spotted a tall handsome man in a beautiful white suit. Scott was working as the foreign representative for VIC Chemical Company and had traveled to China and Japan. He was about to be sent to Italy and other Mediterranean countries. They courted before he left for this long trip. He returned on May 5 and they were married on May 9, 1931.

That year, Shawn and St. Denis broke up the Denishawn company and their marriage. Papa Shawn asked Phoebe to continue with his troupe for the 1932 tour. It was her last professional tour. "Scott often came to see me rehearse at the beautiful studios."

Scott decided to study for a doctorate in physics at Chapel Hill, North Carolina. Phoebe continued her enthusiasm for dance by teaching dance classes and directing stage movement for the Carolina Playmakers. Her dance group gave concerts in Chapel Hill's indoor and outdoor theatres.

In 1936 the Barrs moved to New Orleans where Scott taught physics at Tulane. Phoebe taught at the Metaire Park Country Day School. She also introduced and taught a class in action analysis for art majors at Newcomb Art School. Her students caught her enthusiasm and some became professional dancers. One student, Walter Terry, became America's foremost dance critic. He dedicated his 1956 book, *Dance In America*, to Phoebe Barr, "the first to lead me along the pathway to dance."

When Scott Barr graduated from college in 1926, he took a ship through the Panama Canal to San Francisco, then on to Hawaii. He taught high school there for two years and fell madly in love with the islands. He wanted to share Hawaii with Phoebe, and the couple made many, many trips to all the Hawaiian Islands and Asia. They both speak of their islands with great love. Phoebe studied the hula dance in depth and learned about the Hawaiian culture. She incorporated this knowledge into her dance. She performed the hula and taught it to her students. They have traveled to many lands and Phoebe brought back as much of the cultures as she could to share with her classes and other dancers.

In 1947 Scott Barr joined the physics faculty at the University of Alabama. Phoebe taught in the physical education department at first. Then for a while she became the acting director of stage movement for the University Theatre. At the University, she choreographed an annual performance for the Speech and Theatre

Department. She also taught private dance and yoga classes to adults and children until well into her seventies, and still teaches a yoga class.

She led in the creation of the Tuscaloosa Community Dancers. The dance group that she established on the campus was the forerunner of the University Dancers. She was president of the University Women's Club from 1964-1965. She is very artistic and enjoys arranging flowers and has used this talent for many years as a member of the Altar Guild at Canterbury Episcopal Church. She is still active in the P.E.O. sisterhood.

John Ross, designer and professor of Theatre and Dance at U. of A., has known Phoebe since he was a student in the 1950s. Ross remembers Phoebe as a vibrant part of the Theatre. "Phoebe did a lot of choreography for the Theatre. I have a vision of her during classes or rehearsals as tireless, endlessly tireless. She was a tiny, tiny person. She is dedicated to dance and to Scott Barr in that order.

"In the 1950s, Betty Rose Griffin, a faculty wife, was Phoebe's perfect dancer. Whatever Phoebe conceived of in a dance, Betty Rose could interpret it. In one performance that I lighted called The Lord's Prayer,' we were supposed to time it, but it was so moving that they had to dance it four times before the crew remembered to turn the stop watch off. Phoebe also has a social conscience. She choreographed and danced in a piece called 'The Lynching.' It was a stirring, passionate performance on the horrors of racism. It was inflammatory, strong stuff in the 1950s. At that time she was much older than most dancers and did more choreography than dance. She was very good at choreography."

Marian Gallaway was the powerful head of the Theatre until the 1960s. "Marian and Phoebe had an armed truce." John Ross said. "Since they were forced to coexist, they were perfectly pleasant, even relatively formal in public, but each thought the other to be outrageous. Marian often asked Phoebe to work on a project and then would alternately admire Phoebe's work or think it foolish. Marian was still demonstrating face front falls off stage in her sixties, but she would ask for Phoebe's help to choreograph fights, falls or a dance.

"Phoebe and Lou Wall became good friends after Lou came to campus in 1957. Lou first taught dance in the physical education department. With Phoebe's help, Lou was finally able to get recognition for modern dance on campus. It took many years to get dance moved to the Speech and Theatre and now we are the Theatre and Dance Department. Unfortunately Phoebe was never formally adjunct faculty. At first she often worked for no pay or for informal students' fees. She just loved dance.

"Around 1957 or 1958 Ruth St. Denis came to Tuscaloosa to visit Phoebe. This was a real tribute to her relationship with Phoebe. St. Denis was persuaded to lecture and demonstrate, which turned into a performance. I lighted her show, the 'Blue Madonna.' It required little movement by St. Denis, but was in full costume and was good. St. Denis admitted to being eighty-three at the time. Who knows how old she really was? One unforgettable afternoon I went with Phoebe and St. Denis to a local art patron and friend, Farley Snow's, for tea. The energy was incredible."

Another good friend, Alan Bales, Professor Emeritus of Theatre and Dance, has known Phoebe and Scott since 1947. "Phoebe choreographed many pieces for the

Theatre. Dance was an extracurricular activity then. She choreographed the dance for the Masque in Shakespeare's *The Tempest*.

"I remember she had a leading role in the play, *The Limbo Kid*. This was one of Marian Gallaway's premier productions and Phoebe did an excellent job as a smart, wise frontier lady. She also assisted me in directing *Emperor Jones*. She choreographed the weird spirits and the slave dance. Phoebe didn't like the way the drummer beat the timpani drums so she did it. At first the drum was faint, then louder, louder until it was unbearable. Phoebe has kept her hand in many productions of the University Dancers and the Theatre Department.

"Scott is a talented, patient individual," Bales said. "He was very concerned with his work in the Physics Department. Scott was always there for Phoebe, even when he was busy with his research and writing. He is well published including a biography of a famous physics. They have been married sixty-four years!"

When Phoebe moved to Tuscaloosa in 1947, she began to create a place for dance. Edith Lindsey said, "The Community Dancers began simply as a group of women who knew Phoebe. They all liked to dance, but none were professional. We met once a week for class and rehearsal. We learned modern dance techniques, Denishawn methods, folk dances (Jewish circle, Mexican, Hawaiian), Tai chi, and original dances choreographed by Phoebe or later Lou Wall. We didn't perform any big concerts. We danced at the high school, festivals at Capital Park or Kentuck, and a Christmas concert dance at Canterbury Episcopal Church.

"Dance was something we all enjoyed. We were very informal and didn't hold tryouts. So, some were much better than others, but it didn't matter. We enjoyed dancing and working as a group," Lindsey said. "Now Community Dancers has evolved into a more formal group that concentrates on ballet. They require auditions and perform big concerts like the *Nutcracker*."

"When Phoebe was a little girl in Greensboro, North Carolina, her parents' generation equated the stage with burlesque. It's really fabulous that she did what she did," Long-time friend and one of the original Community Dancers, Bettie Anne Cleino said. "The Christmas dances at Canterbury were so wonderful. We always danced 'Oh, Holy Night' sung by a beautiful voice and Phoebe would dance 'Silent Night' solo." For Phoebe's eighty-ninth birthday on June 14, Bettie Anne and other friends threw a big party at the University Club. "Over one hundred and fifty friends and family came. Phoebe loved it. She has lots of friends because she cultivates them."

Louise Crofton is a younger friend of Phoebe's. She is the director of dance at Shelton State Community College in Tuscaloosa and is one of only five Royal Academy of Dancing (RAD) Grades examiners in the United States. RAD is an international examining body operating in sixty-five countries to set the standards of classical ballet. She met Phoebe in 1975. "Phoebe has been a fabulous and valuable friend to me. She has been tremendously important and influential on the growth of dance in Tuscaloosa. She is always willing to give advice and help. She's an inspiration to all.

"She still comes to my classes to help with my adult and child students. She has a fabulous eye that she uses to watch the students and give them corrections. She can see what's wrong and mend it. She is a gifted, enthusiastic teacher. She conducted class until a few years ago. The students have the utmost respect for her. They adore her, and will run up to her at the mall or anywhere to say hello."

Her life long dedication to dance and her "ability to inspire students to try harder, to practice longer, and to be better than they think they can be," was honored in a story by Suzanne Wolfe in the Summer, 1983, Society for the Fine Arts' *Review* newsletter. The University Dance Program recognized her contributions in 1980 by establishing the Phoebe Barr Dance Award. The Druid Arts Award to a dancer was given to Phoebe in 1989.

In January 1990 the Newcomb College Dance Foundation of New Orleans gave Phoebe their first "Women In Dance" award. The award is in recognition of women who have a contribution to dance. Phoebe and Scott went to New Orleans to accept the award and Phoebe demonstrated underlying rhythms of dance at the ceremony.

In 1981 she was given the Heritage Honor Award by the Alabama Dance Council for her contributions to dance in Alabama. Then in 1995 the Council made Phoebe an honorary member. Laura Knox, founder of Southern Dance Works and first president of the Alabama Dance Council said, "The goal of the Council is to bring all the dance people in Alabama together—dancers, and dance teachers both private and at universities. We offer workshops, concerts and guest artists and teachers. Phoebe has been an important part of dance in Alabama and we appreciate her."

At eighty-nine Phoebe lives with Scott at Pine Valley Retirement Community where she teaches a Hatha Yoga class once a week and does yoga every day. She will perform when asked. Pine Valley Retirement residents and staff are still excited about her recent beautiful performance of the hula. Louise Crofton said, "When she danced we did not see an eighty-nine year old woman dancing the hula, we saw Hawaii. She held her audience in the palm of her hand."

" I have always looked for beauty outside myself. I think, what can I do to make a better place. Not as the younger generation seems to only ask—what's in it for me. Dance is one way for intimacy with the Almighty, and also with the devil. Ted Shawn studied and taught primitive dance. He would step hard to get God's attention, then reach up and pull power in from outside. This made a connection with the Almighty. He taught us to see and enjoy the things of the earth." Phoebe Barr has shared this strong connection with the earth and the Almighty in her dance and in her life.

written by Abigail M. Toffel

Photo by Paul Robertson

CAROLYN HOOD SELF BLOUNT
1925 -

Cast Thy Bread Upon The Waters
For Thou Shalt Find It After Many Days.

These words from the Bible best express Carolyn Blount's philosophy of life. She has given much to Alabama, the South, and the country. She and her husband, Winton Blount, gave new life to the Alabama Shakespeare Festival. Carolyn is on the board of the Alabama Humanities Foundation, Society of Fine Arts at the University of Alabama, and Art Council at Rhodes College. She received Auburn University's College of Liberal Arts Alumni Achievement Award in 1989. She also was named an outstanding alumnae at the centennial of women at Auburn University in 1992.

> "Age cannot wither her,
> Nor custom stale her infinite variety."
> Anthony and Cleopatra II.ii.240

These are the words her friend, actor Tony Randall, whispers to Carolyn Blount whenever they meet. Shakespeare's immortal poetry recognizes the depth of Carolyn's beauty, grace, intelligence, and magnetic personality. The first thing one notices when meeting Carolyn is her sparkling blue eyes and her warm, welcoming smile. Carolyn is eager to see you and embrace you. She is one of a vanishing breed of grand

Southern ladies with an outer shell soft as a magnolia blossom, an an inside of steely determination, and strong belief in God, which bolsters her strength and all those around her in troubled times.

As Carolyn speaks about her life, several themes emerge: her joy of life; her strong belief in God; her love of her husband, family, and close friends; and her willingness to give of herself. She has a strong feeling that she is responsible for herself. God gave her a life to fashion for herself and He is always there for her. "I can talk to God at anytime. I am responsible for my life but God is there to help me whenever I need him." She smiles radiantly as she speaks of her faith. "It is important for me as a Christian to witness by living the life God wants me to. I cannot tell you though how many times I have prayed for patience!"

Carolyn was born November 15, 1925 in Auburn, Alabama. Her father Leroy L. Self, Sr., was a district extension agent. She was very close to her brother, Leroy L. Self, Jr., who was killed in World War II. He was her "most precious friend." During WW II, Carolyn and other Auburn women dressed up as Mollie Pitcher and carried pitchers downtown to encourage residents to buy War Savings Bonds. Carolyn's mother, Anne Hood Self, helped shape her love of the arts, literature, and performance. Her mother believed that every young woman should be schooled in expression (known today as oral interpretation), dance, piano, and music. Carolyn won poetry reading contests, starred in dance recitals, and excelled in her school work.

She maintained a 3.9 grade point average and graduated a member of the Mortar Board and Phi Kappa Phi from Auburn University in 1947. She was a science and literature major, a member of Kappa Delta sorority and Sphinx coed honorary, and was selected a beauty at the ODK-Glomerate Beauty Ball.

Her appreciation of theatre did not develop until college because there were no classical theatres in the South at that time. Early in college, she found herself with a professor who looked like a spider. He sat on his desk with crossed legs and spouted the lines from Shakespeare's greatest plays. In Professor Hefner's literature class, theatre came alive and she fell irrevocably in love with the Bard. To Carolyn, Shakespeare movingly portrays the human condition - from the tragic nobility of Hamlet to the unalloyed villainy of Iago, the Bard reveals human nature without judgment - he leaves that to the audience.

Carolyn and her first husband, Judge Robert Edward Varner, have two children Carolyn and Ed Varner. After the children went off to college, Carolyn decided she did not approve of the way they were taught literature in high school; she went back to the university and got her teacher's certificate. For five years after receiving her certificate, she taught basic and honors literature at Sidney Lanier High School in Montgomery, Alabama. She was the sponsor of Future Teachers of America at Sidney Lanier. When she talks about her teaching career, her eyes light up with excitement and she leans forward to share with her listeners the joy she got from her students - eleventh and twelfth graders who were about "to jump out into the world." She says, "Teaching put more back into me than anything I've ever done."

For her basic literature students she had to devise innovative ways to teach Shakespeare, as mariy of them could not read well enough to understand the text. So she brought in records of Shakespeare plays for her students to listen to and learn. She recalls proudly the day her class discovered the meaning of Marc Antony's famous Brutus speech. "I pointed out to the students that Marc Antony used words of praise to punish Brutus. We then talked about how important it is to express yourself well and I asked who they knew today that used words to influence people. After a few far-fetched answers, one young man quietly said, 'Martin Luther King, Jr.' He saw through the words and internalized the meaning. It was so exciting! He later went on to become a sports writer for a major newspaper. I am so proud of him. As you can see, literature is very important in my life." Many of her former students keep in touch with her regularly.

Carolyn married Winton M. "Red" Blount in December of 1981, and acquired five step children: Winton, Tom, Sam, Joe and Kay (now Kay Miles). Winton was president of the U. S. Chamber of Commerce in 1969 and Postmaster General of the United States under President Nixon. He was the second Alabamian to hold a cabinet position. Carolyn now has two grandchildren, twelve step grandchildren and two step great grand children. Her son is Dr. Ed Varner, a GYN. at the University of Alabama at Birmingham (UAB) Medical Hospital. He is married to Dr. Pam Varner, a anesthesiologist at UAB. Her daughter, Carolyn Stuart King, is married to George King who works for Alabama's ABC Department. Anne Hood Self, her mother, died in July 1974.

The Blounts have a vacation home in Colorado. "I love to ski. I started right after we were married when I was fifty-six. I love to play tennis. I also love to travel with the grandchildren, but mostly without their parents. They are so much fun to be with alone. We have been to Carlsbad Caverns, Yellowstone, and we took four of them to Hawaii for ten days (Jay, Tom and Sam Miles, and John Blount). In Washington, we took Jay Miles and Kelly Blount to the grand opening of the Postal Museum in black tie and evening clothes. We were very proud of them. Stuart Ann and Duncan Varner spend time with us each August in Beaver Creek, Colorado. We go in a raft down the rapids of the little Colorado River, and we hike in the mountains."

One cannot speak about Carolyn without touching on the magnificent theatre named for her. When the Alabama Shakespeare Festival was located in Anniston, she and her friend, Jan Howard, went every year. They stayed in a run-down motel, saw three plays in a weekend and returned every summer. One day she sent the theatre a $50 check and wound up on the board of directors. When the Festival later began to have financial difficulties, she had just married Winton. A few key board members approached her about seeking help from her husband with the finances. She told them to go ahead, but she refused to talk with Red about it. She did not want to influence him.

An astute businessman, her husband knew that the Festival's financial problems were long-term and to solve them the theatre would have to attract a larger audience. He called Carolyn at home and told her to come down to the office because he was about to do something which concerned both of them. He offered to build a new theatre if the theatre company was willing to move to Montgomery. They were and the rest is history.

By donating land and money, and enabling the Shakespeare Festival to continue

29

functioning at a permanent base, the Blounts have built a performing arts center that is considered one of the best in the world. It is the only year-round professional classical repertory theatre in the Southeast. In his dedication speech, Winton Blount stated, "This theatre has been a work of love for Carolyn and me. I have been inspired by her interest and knowledge of Shakespeare and this has guided me in my developing appreciation. It is a privilege for both of us give this theatre to the people of the United States and to the generations of the future. It will stand as an enduring tribute of love to my wife, Carolyn, and it is my desire that it be known forever as 'The Carolyn Blount Theatre.'" Carolyn Blount hopes that the theatre enriches the humanities and enhances the quality of life in Alabama.

Staff members fondly refer to Carolyn as the First Lady of the Theatre, and she personally takes an interest in all the programs and people at the theatre. She and Red sometimes sneak into a SchoolFest performance with 750 high school students. "Our gift has been repaid many times over. Every time we see the children entranced by a play or a family picnicking in the Park, we experience again the joy of giving."

Currently, Carolyn is focusing on encouraging local artists and arts organizations through financial support. She and her husband sponsor the Montgomery Symphony and help provide scholarships for talented young people. They also support the Montgomery Museum of Fine Arts, the Alabama Humanities Foundation, and numerous other arts related causes.

They are planning improvements to the 250-acre Winton M. Blount Cultural Park. "We want to cultivate a love of beauty by making the Park a landscape and artistic paradise with sculpture, trees, lakes, and flowers. I want someone to turn a corner and find a nook of serenity where they can sit and commune with nature," she says with her eyes shining. "What country has been successful without an appreciation of art? People need the solace, serenity, and joy that art brings. Red and I feel it has been a privilege to be able to support the arts. We have been repaid so many times."

written by Kathy Yarbrough
further research by Elizabeth D. Schafer

MARY WARD BROWN
1917 -

A Backache Could Be Borne If The Heart Was Light.

Mary Ward Brown's fictional character, Willie Mae Boggs, said to sum up her philosophy in her Southern backwoods. Her Perry County creator incorporates these words of wisdom into her own life. "I try to be plain," Mary told *People* magazine soon after her debut collection of short stories about the Alabama Black Belt, *Tongues of Flame*, won the Ernest Hemingway Foundation Award. Mary, who began her writing career in the 1950s, earned acclaim for her first anthology in 1987. She is a widow who is dedicated to her family first and then her writing. Mary's use of plain language and simple settings to depict the complex changes experienced by Southerners during the last half century have greatly impacted Alabama literature.

Born Mary Thomas Ward on June 18, 1917, in Hamburg, Alabama, the daughter of Thomas Ira and Mary Hubbard Ward, Mary grew up on her father's 3,000 acre plantation in Browns, Alabama. She clarifies the traditional images of her home, insisting that "We had no great-columned house, just a good-sized farm." Her family never named their farm like many affluent Alabamians did. "It was not that fancy. We were just plain people and didn't think in those terms."

When she was five years old, her father built their sturdy home which was the heart of a small community. The community included a store, saw mill, dairy, and cotton gin. Mary has lived in this "plain" white-washed, two-story house, savoring its woody pine aroma, most of her life. She traveled the country road winding past her house to Blackbelt Consolidated Academy in nearby Marion. There she edited the high school newspaper, which sparked an early interest in a writing career.

Her father farmed while her mother tended the plantation store. Mary's early experiences with local black residents shaped her literary voice. She now admits that she was naive about race relations as a girl. "The black women taught me manners." Yet when she realized, years later, that they were not as affectionate toward her as she had believed, she was traumatized. "I never thought about what was right or wrong," she says. "I just had to have my eyes opened" and realize "how awful it was that we didn't call people Mr. or Mrs. because they were black."

After high school graduation she decided to be a boarding student at Judson College, a Baptist women's college located only six miles from her home. "The boarding kind of took the curse off of going to school at home." She enjoyed journalism and English classes, graduating with an A.B. in Judson's centennial class of 1938. Judson offered no creative writing courses, and Mary never met a fiction writer during her college years. "I think if I had, it would have changed my life."

Employed as Judson's publicity director immediately after graduation, Mary attended a conference for publicity directors in New Orleans. She rode the train because her father forbid her to travel by automobile with a group of male publicity directors that she knew. There she serendipitously met her husband-to-be, Charles Kirtley Brown, Auburn University's publicity director. Kirtley Brown was the son of a Judson alumnae, who had named him in honor of Ann Kirtley, for whom there is a monument on Judson's campus.

The couple wed on Mary Ward's twenty-second birthday, June 18, 1939, and settled in Auburn, living there seven years. They welcomed son Kirtley Ward into their lives. When Mary's father died, she inherited his estate, and the Browns moved into her family home. Kirtley managed her father's soybean farm.

She has always been interested in writing. "All my life, I remember wanting to write something, a poem, a play. I remember taking a story from a magazine when I was a girl and writing a play from it." She encountered obstacles mainly because "I did not know how to get along with it. I didn't know the technique."

During the 1950s her husband encouraged her to enroll in creative writing classes at the University of Alabama, studying with John Craig Stewart for one semester. Her husband insisted on driving her to night class because he "did not consider his wife a safe driver." She laughs, "That nearly killed us all" because he was exhausted from working all day in the fields "and some nights he wouldn't speak to me on the way home." She then took correspondence writing courses taught by Charles Edward Eaton of the University of North Carolina. Mary learned to make every word have a purpose in developing the plot. She wrote daily in an upstairs bedroom, penning short stories. She hired an agent to submit the stories to literary quarterlies.

Some of her earliest stories were published in *The University of Kansas City Review*, revealing the origins of her unique voice and insight into human nature. In October 1955, the journal printed "The Flesh, the Spirit, and Willie Mae," in which Mary's protagonist, a poor country woman named Willie Mae Boggs, leaves her husband Monroe when he buys a television set instead of the washing machine that she desires. Seeking refuge with her sister, Willie Mae discovers that her brother-in-law is a drunken wife beater. This story earned a Distinctive Story Rating in *Best American Short Stories of 1956*, edited by Martha Foley.

"People Like That" appeared in the June 1958 issue, exploring class issues and narrating how faculty wife Sara befriended her less-educated neighbor, only to be disappointed when her generosity was rebuffed. Publishing short stories became an "obsession" for Mary. She remembers that she began "to not want to do anything else."

Despite her personal enthusiasm, Mary was discouraged by friends who insisted that she should not write stories about simple poor people and blacks because few readers would be interested in such tales. She also felt guilty, trying to juggle farm and parenting responsibilities. She worried that she neglected her husband and son, explaining that "It was a matter of priorities. Here my husband was running the farm and I was upstairs with the door closed, writing. I got to be so stressed, trying to write and do everything else I was supposed to do." She admits that "some women can, but I could not be a wife, a mother and a writer."

The intellectual demands required to write well were tremendous. "The more I got into the writing, the more I realized to do good work—which is all I ever wanted to do—would take everything I had." She quit writing one afternoon. "I threw in the sponge." She did not finish another story until twenty-five years later. "I still thought like a writer," she said, "but I did not write." A busy housewife and mother, she "kept up by reading short stories" and "it was wonderful to know that such a writer like Flannery O'Connor was in the world, just over in Georgia."

After Mary's husband died in 1970, she rented out her land to local farmers and worked briefly as a secretary for the Office of Guidance and Counseling at Marion Military Institute. Having raised and educated her son, an attorney in Marion, she gradually began writing short stories, because "When you're a widow, you have to have a commitment in this world." By 1976 she decided to write seriously. "Then it was my time."

Realizing that "good work takes the concentration of a lifetime," Mary devoted herself to her craft. "It was ideal. Here I was alone in the country, and so I could do as well as I could do. It was up to me." She contacted an agent who, after several rejections, sold Mary's first major publication, a short story entitled "The Amaryllis," to *McCall's* magazine in 1978.

Sixty-one year old Mary was elated. "Before that, people told me I was crazy for staying home and trying to write." After her story about a lonely widowed attorney tending an amaryllis bulb appeared in a popular magazine, "people kind of gave me the right to write. They told me they liked the story because there was no sex or violence in it." Because of this encouragement, Mary committed to a writing career. "I wrote all that I could, more and more, every day."

She contributed short stories to literary magazines, publishing in *Threepenny Review, Ascent, Shenandoah, Grand Street, Ploughshares,* and *Prairie Schooner.* Mary wrote about the world that she experienced around Marion, Alabama.

"My stories are straight out of reality as much as I can make them. They all come from something that sticks in your mind. I don't start out with a story. I discover it." A story "starts with people, with characters, or a little germ of an idea." Mary then focuses on "giving form to experience." She explains that if her inspiration arrives in the shape of "characters, you've got to have a dramatic problem. If it's an idea, you have to make up the characters." She told the *Judson Cameo* that she usually is unsure of each story's conclusion when she begins to write. Once "the characters begin to live," Mary insists that she merely is a conduit, writing about the characters' conflicts until "they finish it. It's like you have a camera or you're in someone's mind."

She depicts her tales as "the simplest stories. They're not terribly dramatic. They're about small things in people's lives. I like simplicity. I like it in people. I like it in everything. I just think it's more beautiful than ornament. The older I get, the more I value something that's plain and genuine, like with people."

With her greying hair pinned back into a bun, Mary's hazel eyes flash enthusiastically behind her glasses as she discusses literature. She loves being labeled a Southern writer because the South is her home. "That's all I know to write about. But if you go deep enough, you'll touch a universal nerve." She also proudly mentions that other Southerners such as William Faulkner are considered to be some of the world's best writers.

Mary is interested in depicting how the Deep South has changed during the decades that she has lived so she incorporates racial and class themes into her works. "I've seen such changes, but I don't know where it's going. I wish I did. All I can do is show what I have seen and am seeing now."

Religion permeates her tales just as it does Alabama. Her stories reveal people's good intentions and misinterpretations of other people in a setting caught between the New South and its antebellum precursor. She discusses Old and New South themes of pain, loss, hope, honesty, suffering, aging, infidelity, and death. Through subtleties and idiomatic phrases, Mary emphasizes "what I really try to do is tell the truth." She eloquently gives voice to Alabamians who might otherwise be ignored by authors.

After her first literary agent died, Mary Brown carefully chose and called another agent. She recalls telling the woman that "I was not prolific; I was not young; and that if I could choose an agent, I'd choose her." This agent urged Mary to organize her stories into a collection. The eleven stories they selected were written over a ten year period. Each one was created individually, not with the idea that it would ever be included in an anthology.

Appropriating its title from the short story she that published in the Winter 1984 issue of *Prairie Schooner, Tongues of Flame* was published by Dutton in 1986. Well-received, Mary's anthology of vignettes, depicting ordinary people and problems, was appealing because readers could identify with her intriguing Alabama characters who faced universal issues. Set in Marion, these stories' sense of place strengthened their believability. She has put no inherent messages in her writing because "I don't think I know any answers in this world," yet "I try to write a fictional truth."

Her characters are typical rural Black Belt people such as farmers, preachers, attorneys, maids, businessmen, and doctors—rich and poor, black and white—encountering complex predicaments and trying to survive in a modern South that gives little credence to the Old South's unwritten rules. She notes that her stories are not autobiographical or about real people. "I run all my people through my imagination. It's only after I get them down that I sometimes see a resemblance to someone I know." Her characters' viewpoints of themselves, the South, and the world are mostly compassionate, although their behavior is not always proper. Tied to mores and expectations of previous generations, Mary's characters deal with dilemmas that seem ordinary but often carry deeper implications.

For example, in "Goodbye, Cliff," Mary tells about a widow, Miss Emma, buying a gravestone for her husband. Although he had abused her and saddled her with debts, Miss Emma feels obligated to purchase a marker. She was worried about his reaction when they would be reunited in heaven. Deeply religious, at first she is devastated then relieved when she learns that her deceased husband had kept a mistress and fathered an illegitimate child.

In "The Barbecue," a couple who own the local grocery store experience conflicting emotions when an upper-class customer is unable to pay his debts but expects them to furnish him food on credit for a party to which they are not invited. Although she did not intentionally incorporate a racial theme, Mary's "The Black Dog" reveals the role of race relations and the "limits of human responsibility" in the South. When a stray dog attempts to befriend a widow, initially she rejects it then begins to understand its efforts to survive in an antagonistic environment. The anthology's other stories explore the changing relationships and personal metamorphosis of fictional Alabamians.

Tongues of Flame received mostly positive reviews. Some critics compared Mary Ward Brown to such Southern writers as Flannery O'Connor, Harper Lee, and Eudora Welty. Calling her stories "often bittersweet and sometimes funny" with "attentiveness to word and gesture," reviewers complained that many of Mary's themes were trite. Mary good naturedly accepted the more critical reviews in metropolitan dailies like the *Washington Post*, humorously stressing that she got great reviews in the rural Alabama *Greensboro Watchman*. Most critics admired her "well written" tales "delivered in a measured, caring voice." In the *New York Times Book Review*, Kathryn Morton praised that "Brown writes like a woman offering warm homemade bread."

Because her small-town Southern characters seemed so familiar, some readers wrote Mary, telling her that they know who they are. *Los Angeles Times Book Review* critic Richard Eder described her characters as "clutching tatters of pride, passion, disappointment and fortitude" and seeming very realistic. "But they are no one I really know," Mary said. "They are a little bit of everybody."

In May 1987, *Tongues of Flame* won the Ernest Hemingway Foundation Award sponsored by the PEN American Center. Honoring an author's first book of fiction, many literary figures consider this the most prestigious award in the country for emerging authors. Mary's work was selected from one hundred entries. The judges explained their choice: "Mary Ward Brown writes quietly and forcefully about Alabama, where she has lived all her life and which she has observed during times of disarming change to Southern people, values and landscapes. She sees life as a whole, without prejudice, sentimentality or histrionics."

The award surprised Mary. When her publisher called her with the news, Mary politely told him that the award sounded "nice" but that she needed to return to her work. Busily writing her first story since the book's publication, she suddenly realized what her publisher had said. Mary tried to telephone friends to tell them, but nobody was home. Then she dialed her son's number (she had dedicated the book to him), and he answered but said he was too busy to talk. Eventually she was able to share her jubilation with her loved ones, and she traveled to New York to receive her prize of $7,500.

Astonished by her success, the modest Mary received widespread literary acclaim. Recognized at the age of sixty-nine, after laboring at her craft over several decades, Mary quickly became overwhelmed by the attention that she received. Inundated with interviews, she tried to keep her perspective by following her normal routines. She complained, "I've had enough of this fame business. It'll kill you." Mary took *People* magazine writer, Peggy Brawley, to a favorite barbecue restaurant for lunch to provide the reporter a glimpse of her simple life and to show that "I'm just what I was before." She also filled an envelope full of reviews, both good and bad, to remain objective about her work. "I am not seduced by any of the praise. I know that when I go to work it will be just as hard or harder and I may not be able to do this well again. You cannot feel anything but humble that you met with any success at all. I try to be a good craftsman. My thinking and attitude haven't changed a bit."

Demand for *Tongues of Flame* was so great that it sold out and was immediately reprinted in hardback. The anthology was also reissued as a paperback, with a cover Mary considered inappropriate. Preferring the burning church steeple on the hardcover version's dust-jacket, she dismissed the "sweaty-looking girl" on the paperback as unrelated to her stories' themes.

Deliberately writing stories, first in long hand, then tediously typing revisions on her electric typewriter, she produced about two short stories a year after *Tongues of Flame*. In 1988 "It Wasn't All Dancing" appeared in *Grand Street*, and "One Regret" was featured in *Redbook*.

She traveled to Washington, D.C., in May 1989 to attend a symposium of Soviet authors and editors, sponsored by the Quaker U.S.-U.S.S.R. Committee. The Soviets praised Mary's work. Preparing a joint publication of short stories, entitled *The Human Experience: Contemporary American and Soviet Fiction and Poetry* (1989), the committee encouraged literary contacts between the two countries. Mary's short story, "The Cure," was selected for inclusion, appearing with works by such prominent American authors as Joyce Carol Oates, Garrison Keillor, and Robert Penn Warren.

Boris Yekimov, a Russian short story writer whose work was also anthologized, called Mary a talented writer. "These are human and eternal problems that she writes about," he said. "They are absolutely universal." He admitted that the editors had a difficult time translating the regional idioms that Mary's characters used. Mary was excited and curious about the Soviets' interest in her work, especially because the Russians were unfamiliar with black people. She traveled to the Soviet Union in May 1990.

During this three week trip, Mary participated in a writer's conference and toured the country, meeting writers and publishers. Dr. Nancy Anderson, an Auburn University at Montgomery English professor who has studied Mary Brown's literature, stated that during the trip, Mary discovered that, regardless of ethnicity and other differences, she and the Soviets were "writing about the same people."

Mary returned home to chronicle the universal nature of the world through her Southern perspective. "A New Life," published in the March 1991 issue of *The Atlantic*, reveals Mary's fascination with the influence of religion in the South. She notes that many individual's identities are tied to their specific church membership (Mary herself is an Episcopalian). Intrigued by many Southerners' claims to know personally what God thinks about situations and people, she elaborated on this theme. Elizabeth, a grieving widow, is pursued by a religious group that believes it can heal her wounded spirit. Through her contacts with them, Elizabeth finally frees herself from her emotional paralysis.

Mary's powerful stories have been anthologized in such prominent volumes as the *Best American Short Stories* in 1983 and 1984. She was also selected for inclusion in *New Stories from the South: The Year's Best*, edited by Shannon Ravenel of Algonquin Books of Chapel Hill, in 1986, 1989, and 1992; *New Stories by Southern Women*, edited by Mary Ellis Gibson and published by the University of South Carolina Press in 1989; and *Stories: Contemporary Southern Short Fiction*, edited by Donald Hays of the University of Arkansas Press, also in 1989.

Mary writes daily even "on Christmas and Easter, the day our Lord rose from the grave," because "I'd rather do it than anything on Earth. I love to struggle with those sentences." Her day begins as early as 4:30 a.m. when she scribbles stories on tablets for several hours in bed. After a quick breakfast, she rests for awhile before getting up to review her work in her writing room where sunbeams dance across the polished floorboards. This quiet room, filled with overflowing bookshelves and scratched-out pages on Mary's desk, has witnessed her literary labor.

Typing to "see what the words look like," she stops only for a small lunch of meat and vegetables. With her German shorthair pointer, Boone, at her feet, she writes until mid-afternoon, then walks about two miles. Mary's evenings are devoted to reading. Asleep by 9 o'clock, she confesses that she frequently wakes up with ideas during the night. Jotting down her dreams, she explains, "Your subconscious is working on the problems and will sometimes hand you a solution in the middle of the night."

Calling herself "the slowest writer in the world.," she usually writes only two stories a year. A disciplined perfectionist, she rewrites and revises constantly, sculpting each word until she is sure that what she has said is exactly what she means and that "it's as good as I can possibly make it." She is careful in her use of detail and description. One year she wrote only one story because she "couldn't get the right handle" on it, and then it was rejected before a magazine finally published it.

She is committed to writing short stories, conceding that with her painstaking writing habits, "It would kill me to do a novel. I will settle for the short story," stressing, "if a short-story writer writes a memorable short story, that's enough." Mary does not believe that she has accomplished this yet and continues to perfect her craft.

"I'm just in love with the short story form," Mary told Don O'Briant of the *Atlanta Journal and Constitution.* "I can hardly wait to go to work each morning. I discover a story as I go along. I never know where it's going. I have to discover the people and get to know them by the end of the story, and I know what they will do and what they won't do."

Scholars consider Mary Ward Brown's stories an important part of Alabama's literary heritage and incorporated her anthology into the "Read Alabama!" program. Friendly and approachable, Mary attended meetings to talk to participants about her stories. Her writing schedule has also been interrupted when she presents papers and programs, serving as a panelist at Birmingham Southern's Annual Writer's Conference. Readings and signings at colleges, bookstores, and libraries also keep her busy.

The Alabama Library Association honored her with its fiction award, and the Alabama State Council on the Arts presented her the Governor's Arts Award and a $5,000 grant. She is glad that Alabamians like her works and recognize her characters, because "What I see is the life around me, and I try to reflect it in my writing." Before her book became famous, many of her friends did not understand why she wrote. She worried about their opinions of her book, but, when it was published, she discovered that even "People who don't usually read books say they read it. They think I've told the truth. And that's all I'm trying to do."

Although Mary is flattered by fans, she modestly states. "I don't like to be the center of attention." A private person, she would "rather stay at home and get some work done. When you write seriously, you don't have time for much of anything else."

Mary Ward Brown has donated her papers to the Auburn University Archives. The collection includes her worksheets, rough drafts, galley proofs, manuscripts, book reviews, newspaper clippings, and correspondence with agents and publishers. The collection is closed unless researchers obtain Mary's permission to consult it.

This outstanding Alabama author admits that she likes the Beatles and Bob Dylan almost as much as she admires authors like Chekhov and Tolstoy because they all tell "basic truths." Busy with her typewriter and chores, she calls herself a "non-political grandmother," treasuring visits from her granddaughters, Mary and Helen Brown, who are more impressed with their toys than the book their sweet "Ga-Ga" wrote. Mary, her son Kirtley, and his wife Susannah sometimes savor sleepy afternoons, sitting on the porch and watching the girls play with kittens.

Comfortable in denim skirts, oxford shirts, and practical pumps, Mary Ward Brown enjoys her family and home, serving hot tea and butter cookies leftover from an autograph party and proudly displaying paintings by her friend and critic, Selma printer Crawford Gillis. A quiet, elegant woman, she becomes animated and witty when talking about the South and its people.

For her profile in *Contemporary Authors*, Mary contemplated her future. "I marvel every day at the miracle of simply being alive. I think I write in an effort to celebrate that—to toast it, as it were, with such wine as I have." Mary Ward Brown's Southern roots have certainly yielded vibrant new shoots in Alabama's literary garden.

written by Elizabeth D. Schafer

MARY IVY BURKS
1920 -

If you work long enough with the environmental movement - it's discouraging-because the work is not an upper, it's a downer. You see all your good work and then something comes along, something political mostly, and sweeps it all away. These are not exactly words of wisdom and I don't want to discourage people, but it's the truth.

Mary Ivy Burks is the founder of the Alabama Conservancy and a nationally recognized champion of the environment. On the day when League of Women Voter's interviewer, Adeline Kahan, was finally able to catch up with Mary Burks and talk to her about her thirty years as Alabama's leading volunteer grassroots conservationist, she had just returned from Montgomery. Her trip there was not occasioned by an appointment with a state legislator, although she has done a great deal of lobbying for conservation causes in the past. This time she was invited by the Alabama Vegetation Management Society to speak at their two-day conference. Her topic, "The Alabama Wildflower Watch," was her most recent environmental interest. Since many of the 400 participants were herbicidal manufacturers, she said she felt rather like Daniel in the lion's den as she talked to them. But if overwhelming odds had ever daunted Mary, then most of her positive environmental achievements in Alabama would never have come about.

Adeline asked Mary how she became so ardently identified with conservation in Alabama. She said she thinks "she was born this way." She can remember herself as a small child coming into her mother's kitchen on Birmingham's Southside with small caterpillars or snails on her arm and saying "Mama, aren't they beautiful. Then my sister would screech and run upstairs." Mary fits the definition of the old-time naturalist who loves the world and everything in it. She feels that her work in preservation was a direct outgrowth of this love.

Of all her environmental work, she is most pleased with her work on the Sipsey Wilderness because "it is so tangible." When she initially started work on the Wilderness, she was told that "nothing in Alabama could qualify as wilderness." During the period from 1970 to 1977, she led ten organizations in a united fight to convince the Forest Service that the Sipsy met all qualifications for a "wild and scenic" area. Her forces grew to 100 organizations with 100 resolutions containing 23,000 signatures. They gathered biological field studies to prove the area's uniqueness. In 1975 the Sipsey Wilderness was dedicated. The Sipsy campaign was directly responsible for the passage of the Eastern Wilderness Bill.

Mary was born December 11, 1920 to Lorene and Earl Ivy in Georgia. Her family moved to Birmingham, Alabama when she was nine months old. She grew up in the tree-lined neighborhoods of Southside with one sister. Her parents also brought up a nephew and a niece, so the house was full of children..

She graduated from Ramsey High School in 1937 and then Magna cum Laude from Birmingham Southern College in 1941. She majored in English and French and studied Biology. She regretted that she didn't study biology until college, because she fell in love with it. Then she unsuccessfully tried to be allowed to earn a double degree - one in the arts and one in science. But her advisor feared for her health and would not allow it.

She worked for the telephone company and the federal government during World War II. Then she worked as a newspaper reporter for the old *Birmingham Post* 1944-1946. She took several journalism courses at the University of Wisconsin in Madison while her husband studied for a Ph.D. in chemistry.

In June 15, 1946, she married Dr. Robert Burks. Robert is called Bob by everyone. He is a chemist now retired from Southern Research. They have a son, Robert Ivy. Bob has supported and encouraged Mary in her environmental work. Their yard in Mountainbrook is a wonderland of flowering plants. Her many hobbies include gardening, reading, square dancing, traveling, hiking, canoeing, crossword puzzles, and backyard bird watching.

Although Mary is not a biologist, she could fool almost anyone. After 49 years of gardening and field study of plants all over the South, botanical names and ecological terms slide off her tongue with ease. She is one generation removed from the land. Her parents grew up on rural Alabama farms.

A person who was a tremendous influence on Mary's interest in the environment was Blanch Evans Dean. "Blanch was a remarkable biology teacher at Woodlawn High School. She was a teacher every moment of her life from the top of her head to the bottom of her feet. She wrote several books including *Wildflowers of Alabama and Trees and Shrubs of Alabama.*

"I met her when my son was small when we joined the Audubon Society for a family activity. We would go on field trips with Blanch as guide and she would teach us. My son used to say, Blanch is Mama's guru.'" Wildflowers and the wilderness have been a continuous interest to Mary since then. Mary said that Blanch influenced her through her meticulous teaching. "She taught you. She would not let you get away without learning all about a plant or flower."

Mary asked Blanch Dean if she had been born "this way." Blanch said that she had, and she loved all life. "Today a molecular botanist couldn't look out the window and tell you what a privet hedge is." Mary said. "They're not the same kind of people. We are naturalists and we love it all." What we need is bio-diversity. She said we need scientist like Dr. E. O. Wilson who is from Alabama. " Dr. Wilson has written a lot of splendid books." Mary has helped to bring Wilson to speak in Alabama many times.

In Adeline's interview with Mary for this book, Bob joined in, "People are important animals." "To other people," Mary adds. Bob continued, "But the whole of all biological life is important to all life. We need people to care for it." To encourage this care the Alabama Conservancy created the Bob and Mary Burks Award: Board Member of the Year. Mary and Bob received the first award. The Conservancy also set up the Blanch Dean Award: Outstanding Nature Educator.

With Bob's full support, Mary organized the Alabama Conservancy in May 1967. At that time the Audubon Society and the Wildlife Federation were the state's only environmental group. Mary said she realized that Alabama needed a group focused on saving and improving Alabama's environment after she took the Southeastern representative of the Nature Conservancy on a tour of the Dismals in North Alabama.

Mary relentlessly works on politicians until they see things her way on the preservation of land, and on improving the quality of the air, water, and life. She was the first chairperson, then president of the Conservancy from 1967 to 1970 and served as executive director for five years. She is currently the vice president for membership. The Conservancy was renamed the Alabama Environmental Council in the spring of 1995. They work on a broad range of environmental issues from recycling to establishing wilderness areas to help protect, conserve, and preserve the environment.

The Sipsy Wilderness was the Conservancy's first victory. Mary said, "We led the fight for the first Sipsey Wilderness, and got it, and that was sort of a historic fight, because the (U.S.) Forest Service was saying that there could be no wilderness areas in the eastern half of the United States."

"We went to Washington, a small group of us, to talk with the Forest Service," Mary recalls. When the Forest Service said nothing in Alabama would qualify as wilderness, Mary said, "Well, you know how Alabamians are. It made us so mad. We thought, 'We'll show you.' And we did. We got our Sipsey Wilderness and 15 others in the Eastern United States."

When Congress finally passed legislation in 1975 to protect 12,726 acres of the Sipsey River area, the same law created 15 others in the Eastern United States." Now the Sipsey Wilderness contains almost 26,000 acres, including the headwaters for Alabama's only nationally designated Wild and Scenic River, the Sipsey Fork, and its tributaries.

Former Senator Floyd Haskell said, "If it were not for the Alabama Conservancy, there would be no concept of Eastern Wilderness."

A long time chairwoman and founder of Friends of Oak Mountain State Park in Birmingham, one of Mary's priorities is in her own backyard. She organized the Friends in 1984 as a coalition of organizations interested in serving the park and promoting wise management of natural resources. In 1985 she directed a project for planting meadow wildflowers in the park as chairperson of the Blanch Dean Chapter of the Alabama Wildflower Society. She's convinced that preserving the natural quality of Oak Mountain State Park is critical to maintaining Birmingham as a livable city. "People need a place to go where they can hike, where there is solitude, and where there's beauty. Where they can watch birds and be a part of nature ... If we're not careful, we will destroy our life-support system, and we won't even know it until it's too late."

Today, at a time in her life when most people start to take life easy, she is engaged in a new project, the Alabama Wildlife Watch. Her vision is to restore native wild-flowers, grasses and shrubs to as many state habitats as possible. "Like many Alabamians, I have watched with dismay as our native roadside and meadow wild-flowers have disappeared under the combined attacks of mowing, herbicides, invasive aliens such as kudzu, grading, and other habitat destruction."

"Alabama Wildflower Watch proposes to help all the friends of Alabama's native plants to find each other and to work together to restore our natural heritage." It is a project of the Alabama Wildflower Society, LEGACY, and the University of Livingston. LEGACY is a group sponsored by the Alabama Department of Environmental Management (ADEM) to promote education about the environment especially in public schools.

As Alabama Wildflower Society's chairperson for Roadside Wildflowers, in February 1994, LEGACY gave Mary a grant of $27,000 to survey the variety of native wildfowers in every county in Alabama. Once they know what grows naturally, they'll know what to plant. The native plants will come up year after year. Non-native plants like the red California poppy have to be replanted every year. This is a big project and she is doing it as a volunteer with mostly volunteer help.

In other states like Texas, thousands of people spend thousands of dollars to travel to see the wildflowers every year. The Texas Bluebells are famous world wide. In addition to attracting tourists, wildflowers have been shown to reduce litter by 29 percent. Mary said, "They're somewhat reluctant to throw their trash when it looks like a garden."

"Before the advent of herbiciding, some of Alabama's most intriguing wild-flowers grew in sunny ditches and lowlands along our roads: pitcher plants, sundews, rein orchids, pine lilies, and many more. If allowed, many of the wetland species would return."

Mary said that Alabama has 103,000 state highways and many more city and county roads. "The potential for recovery of native flora along all roads is enormous. Where we substitute wildflowers for mowed and herbicide highway "lawns."" We can create artificial prairies with native spectacular meadow species which will renew themselves if allowed to produce seed. "There are also many sites—industrial plants, schoolyards, utility rights of ways, wildflower preserves, rails to trails, rural property of all kinds—many promising areas where native plants could be used or restored." Texas Bluebells won't grow here, but Mary said, "People don't realize what we have here. There are lots of beautiful native wildflowers like ruellia, native asters, and verbena rigida. In the forty-eight contiguous states, Alabama is number four in bio-diversity. We are only surpassed by the larger states of California, Texas and Florida. We can make a lot of this to benefit Alabama in money and other ways with nicely planted roadsides." Butterflies are attracted by the flowers, so restocking the wild-flowers will also yield a bonus of many more colorful butterflies.

She warns wildflower enthusiasts not to dig up wild plants. They should harvest only a few seeds and let the rest go to re-seed. They should try to beat the roadside mowers. It's OK to dig and transplant flowers that are in the way of bulldozers and other habitat destruction. She said, " Just give them a new habitat as close to the old one as possible." She recommends enthusiasts join a wildflower club and exchange plants, seeds or cuttings with other members.

Mary is one of twelve people in the U.S. to receive an award from the National Sierra Club, "For untiring, devoted, and effective labors in the cause of wilderness preservation in the Eastern United States." The award was given June 6, 1975 at the last Sierra Club Wilderness Conference held jointly with the National Audubon Society in New York City. That same year she received the Governor's first place Award for Conservation given by the Alabama Environmental Quality Association in recognition of the Sipsey Wilderness Campaign.

Mary has also fought for tougher clean air and clean water standards, and for cit-izens and industry to reduce, reuse and recycle all waste. She is a past board member of the Alabama Wildlife Rescue Board. She worked with the Conservancy and other Alabama environmental groups to create the Cheaha Wilderness and help protect Ruffner Mountain and the Cahaba River. She closely follows efforts to protect the Cahaba River and Little River Canyon and continues to comment on management practice in the Bankhead National Forest.

In addition to the new Wildflower Watch project and her duties as Vice President for Membership for the Conservancy, she lectures to garden clubs and schools. She is often interviewed by the press about environmental issues such as the importance of reclaiming strip-mined lands or the need to reduce the industrial use of toxic chem-icals. She actively serves on committees set up by EPA, ADEM and other state agen-cies dealing with hazardous and solid waste.

She lived in Mississippi from 1977 to 1983. As a member of the League of Women Voters, she served on the Mississippi State League Board. A former news-woman, every organization she has joined has ask her to serve as editor of their newsletter including the Mississippi League. She edited a local and the state League newsletter there.

She has also served on other boards including the Public Lands Institute, the Birmingham Civic Ballet, Civiettes, Friends of Bankhead National Forest, the Birmingham Audubon Society, and the Birmingham Branch of the American Association of University Women (AAUW). From 1949 to 1958 she held the post of newsletter editor, scholarship chairperson, recording secretary, membership chair and first chair of the night group for AAUW. She served on the board and as recycling chairperson for People Against a Littered State (PALS). At seventy-four, she has not slowed her fight. Her future plans include creating an organization of groups to work with state parks similar to the coalition that forms the Friends of Oak Mountain. She wants to get the numerous private and governmental agencies that are involved in planting wildflowers to cooperate with each other. She also plans to promote new wilderness areas.

Melinda D. Hollingsworth – educator, naturalist, and long time friend of Mary's – said, "I can't think of anyone who has had a greater or more continuous impact on the environmental quality of Alabama than Mary Burks. She has also had a very great impact on children by giving talks to them for all these years about the environment and the importance of loving it."

Interview and Research by Adeline Kahn
written by Abigail M. Toffel

Mrs. Durr with Ladie Bird Johnson at Martha's Vineyard
Photo by LaVerne D. Ramsey

VIRGINIA FOSTER DURR
1903 -

You Do It Because You Believe It Is Right.

Virginia Foster Durr will be remembered for stepping *Outside the Magic Circle*, as her 1985 autobiography is called. She was born to the privileges of aristocracy in Birmingham, Alabama, in 1903, to Dr. Sterling Foster, minister of the South Highland Presbyterian Church and Anne Patterson Foster. Her sister Josephine married Hugo Black, an ambitious young labor lawyer, who would eventually sit on the U. S. Supreme Court.

Virginia received what was considered to be, for a Southern girl, a liberal education at Wellesley. She married a fellow aristocrat, attorney Clifford Judkins Durr, in 1926. She was twenty-three. After Hugo Black won his race for the U. S. Senate, Cliff got the opportunity to interview for the Reconstruction Finance Corporation (RFC) in Washington, D.C.

Their first child Ann was born in 1927. As a young Junior League matron and mother, Virginia had been working with the Red Cross. A stint of unemployment for Cliff and her observations of the misery of the poorer classes had already started to form her compassionate view of the world.

Cliff went to work for the RFC in 1933. So the Durrs settled in the countryside near Washington D.C., and became staunch supporters of Franklin Roosevelt's New Deal. Because she had servants, Virginia, who was by 1937 the mother of three, was able to go into town to work with the Women's Division of the National Democratic Committee. This group worked to enfranchise women in the South by getting rid of the poll tax which had been instituted to disenfranchise blacks. It also affected poor white men and women, and Virginia had felt the sting of injustice when she had to pay back poll tax in Alabama in order to vote.

She associated with educated black women like Mary McLeod Bethune as they spoke together publicly against the poll tax. Virginia continued to renew acquaintances with other southerners who were committed to working for organized labor or racial and social equality. Clark Foreman, Joe Gelders, and Aubrey Williams held what most other Southerners called radical, liberal views about racial equality and were all branded Communists at one time or other, whether they were or not. At first Virginia was shocked by many of their views, but she held fast to the friendships and eventually became a victim herself of the anti-Communist hysteria that prevailed in the 1950s. During her service on the committee to abolish the poll tax, Virginia did not repudiate organizations that worked to repeal the poll tax even if they were Communists, opening herself up to charges of being a sympathizer, if not a Communist herself.

In 1936 Cliff went from the RFC to the DPC, the Defense Plant Corporation. This Corporation was Roosevelt's plan to prepare U.S. industry for the manufacture of armaments that he felt to be necessary for the inevitable involvement of the U.S. in WW II. Cliff went to the Federal Communications Committee (FCC) in 1941 for a seven year term. There he was instrumental in drafting laws that provided for public broadcasting frequencies for radio, then television. Then Cliff began moving the family around the country with different jobs until he developed a serious back problem. By 1951 the Durrs decided to move the family back home to Alabama to Cliff's mother's house.

The Durrs returned to a segregated South. They were more liberal socially, especially Virginia, than their neighbors. Their four daughters, Ann, Lucy, Lulah, and Tillah, had to adjust to life in Montgomery. Their youngest daughter Tillah, born in 1947, was twenty years younger than her oldest sister.

Cliff, who could not let poor blacks go without legal representation, got the reputation for representing poor blacks who could not pay. The Durrs suffered financially. Virginia kept a low profile in the early years after returning to Montgomery, becoming involved only inadvertently with the temporary mixing of white and black United Methodist Church women. That Christian effort at fellowship and cooperation was aborted by threats against the white women involved as well as financial blackmail against their husbands.

The anti-Communist hysteria brought about during the McCarthy hearings brought grief to many who had been associated with communists in any way. In 1955 Virginia was subpoenaed by the Senator James Eastland's Internal Security Subcommittee. This subcommittee corresponded to the Un-American Activities Committee in the House. Clifford Durr was suffering from angina, but he insisted on defending his wife until John Kohn, a Montgomery attorney, insisted on representing Virginia at his own expense. Virginia believed that long time friend and then Senate majority leader Lyndon Johnson intervened and prevented other committee members from joining Eastland in New Orleans as did Republican Congressman George Bender of Ohio.

An FBI informant and former Communist, Paul Crouch, was the backbone of Eastland's case against Virginia and her friend Aubrey Williams, the publisher of Southern Farmer. Crouch told impossible and easily disproved lies about Clifford Durr as well. Virginia, who was ready to testify that she was not and had never been a Communist, could not do so because she would have been forced to answer questions about other people. Instead, she insisted on standing mute rather than taking the Fifth Amendment against self-incrimination.

Clifford, who was given the opportunity to cross-examine Paul Crouch, then took the stand himself to testify under oath that he and Virginia had never been to Communist meetings in New York as Crouch had testified and to insist that either he or Crouch be charged with perjury. Clifford Durr had a heart attack during Crouch's later testimony that Eleanor Roosevelt had passed cabinet level secrets to Virginia to pass the Communists. Eastland, having nothing but the outrageous testimony of Crouch, never acted on the results of the hearings. Years later, Crouch's wife wrote to Aubrey Williams that her husband was glad that Aubrey had been cleared of being a Communist and asked for money.

When they got back home to Montgomery, the Durrs were treated well by their family and friends. However, many people associated them with the unpopular *Brown v. Board of Education* decision of the year before that had signaled the end of segregated schools in the U.S. Judge Hugo Black was vilified because he sat on the Supreme Court. Their family relationship with him, when added to the publicity about the Eastland hearings, brought social ostracism.

They moved into an apartment nearby to protect Clifford's mother from the threats they received, even though they did not take them very seriously. Virginia felt free to join the Council on Human Relations, which was the only interracial group in the city. At that time the White Citizen's Council was very active. This group was organized to fight integration every way they wanted. The United Church Women formed an integrated group. Virginia became acquainted with members of the Women's Democratic Club of Montgomery, many of whom were black college and public school teachers. There she also met Martin Luther and Coretta Scott King, E. D. Nixon, and Rosa Parks, who were to play major roles in the black fight for civil rights.

It was Mr. E. D. Nixon, Pullman porter and black leader, who called the Durrs when Rosa Parks, the black seamstress, was arrested for not moving to the back of the bus. Both went with Nixon to bail Mrs. Parks out of jail, and Clifford acted as advisor to Fred Gray, the black attorney who argued the case all the way to the Supreme Court. The black boycott of Montgomery buses, prompted by Mrs. Parks arrest, started in 1955 and lasted for a year. It was the *cause celebre* that thrust Martin Luther King into the role of the most prominent black leader in the United States. Many foreigners were guests of the Durrs when they came to Montgomery to hear King preach before he moved to Atlanta.

White outsiders who either supported or joined the freedom riders of the late 1950s and early 1960s found themselves depending on Clifford Durr to defend them in court and on Virginia for food and shelter. From the second floor office window of the Durr law office, Virginia helplessly witnessed a mob beating a busload of freedom riders in 1961. Her English friend, author Jessica Mitford, was on the street trying to get a story for a magazine article. Later, Mitford and a young student were in the black church that was surrounded by such an angry mob of whites that Governor John Patterson had to call out the National Guard. They had driven to the black rally in the Durr's car, which was burned by the mob. John Patterson, who was a cousin of Virginia Durr, had won the governor's office through his strong espousal of segregation.

During these turbulent times, other native Southerners stood up for integration of churches, hospitals, and schools. They left Montgomery as their jobs and businesses disappeared and they were treated as social pariahs. Grover Hall of the *Montgomery Advertiser* pilloried the Durrs after an article by Nat Hentoff appeared in the *New Yorker* in which the Durrs were quoted on the ills of Montgomery's race relations. They had spoken in confidence and Hentoff did little to protect their identities in his expose. Yet they remained in Montgomery, sending their four daughters north for school to escape the wrath of their classmates. Sympathetic friends in the North gave the necessary funds.

The Durrs gave food and shelter to civil rights activist members of the Student Nonviolent Coordinating Committee (SNCC) and Cliff eked out a living defending poor blacks. During the 1963 march from Selma to Montgomery they hosted a houseful of interested northern liberals. There they observed the split in the black ranks between Martin Luther King's leadership and that of the more militant SNCC. The writer Studs Turkel interviewed many of the famous and ordinary march supporters in the Durr household for radio coverage that was broadcast from Chicago.

Mrs. Durr is now 92 years of age and long widowed. Cliff died in 1975. She remains in Montgomery in a modest house in old Cloverdale avidly watching political and social developments. She is a member of the League of Women Voters of Montgomery. In addition to her many other affiliations, she spends much time visiting her four daughters, Ann Lyon, Lucy Hackney, Lulah Colan, and Tillah Durr. The four daughters and the grandchildren hosted a 90th birthday party at the vacation home of Lucy and her husband, Sheldon Hackney, on Martha's Vineyard. Hundreds of family members and friends from all over the world paid tribute to her long life *Outside the Magic Circle*. A video of her life produced at Auburn University was shown at the movie theater a few blocks away on the main street of Martha's Vineyard.

Although a victory can be claimed in the battle for civil rights, Virginia Durr is disappointed at the low level of voter participation in local and national elections. She is modest about her contributions of many hours of working against the poll tax, as well as her long years of providing food and shelter for front line troops in the civil rights battles. But she is proud of the years she was able to work beside her beloved husband Cliff. For Virginia Durr, it was a matter of conscience. "You do it because you believe it is right."

written by LaVerne D. Ramsey

The source material on Virginia Durr, aside from the author's own experience, is The Autobiography of Virginia Foster Durr, *Outside the Magic Circle*, an oral history edited by Hollinger E. Barnard, a Birmingham attorney. The University of Alabama Press, 1985

Photo courtesy of the Alabama Women's
Hall of Fame, Judson College

Hallie Farmer, Ph.D.
1891 - 1960

The Time Is Long Past When Alabama Can Afford Be Run On Only Half Its Brains, The Men's.

A n educator and an activist, Dr. Hallie Farmer said the above to all citizens. Hallie encouraged Alabama women to participate in government and to pursue legislative reforms. Although she believed that "Alabama was the most forward looking state in the deep South," Hallie acknowledged its shortcomings. As a history and government professor at the Alabama State College for Women in Montevallo, she enhanced Alabama's politics in a variety of ways. Her work was mainly to improve legislation, to streamline governmental processes, and to help legislators' increased responsiveness to citizenry. Devoting her life to helping others, Hallie's outspokenness made a positive impact on Alabamians.

Born on August 13, 1891, in Anderson, Indiana, Hallie Farmer was the daughter of Quakers Edgar William and Elizabeth Modlia Farmer. She and her brother, who was two years older (a younger sister was born when Hallie was 15 years old), enjoyed a happy childhood. Hallie sold vegetables with her grandfather, a truck farmer, and listened to her father quote Shakespeare.

Hallie often woke up early in the morning to read. Her mother had been orphaned at a young age and had to work for her foster parents instead of attending school. As an adult, Elizabeth Modlia wanted to be able to read. Her teacher, Edgar Farmer, fell in love with her, and they married. The Farmers wanted their children to be well educated and filled their home with books. Young Hallie learned that she could accomplish anything through hard work and by adjusting to, instead of resisting, uncomfortable situations.

Hallie Farmer graduated from high school in 1908. She taught school in Madison County, Indiana, for several years, then decided to go to college in order to become a better teacher like her father. She enrolled at Terre Haute Normal School (the precursor of Indiana State University), where she was president of the Women's League and graduated in 1916. She taught in several Indiana and Illinois high schools, then moved to Madison, Wisconsin, where she earned a master's degree from the University of Wisconsin in 1922.

Disappointed that she was not chosen history department chair at Ball State Teachers College in Muncie, Indiana, she returned to Madison to complete a Ph.D. in history in 1927. Renowned historian Frederick L. Paxson directed her dissertation on the People's Party movement. He had studied with the eminent Frederick Jackson Turner, who had formulated the frontier thesis. Hallie researched in the Topeka, Kansas, library, where thick files of newspaper clippings fueled her quest. She also taught undergraduates, gaining valuable insights into teaching methods. Few women at this time had earned history doctorates.

The Alabama State College for Women at Montevallo asked Hallie to become head of the history and political science departments. Interested in teaching women, she accepted, even though Alabama was far away from her home and family. Hallie, her mother, and her sister traveled to Montevallo, where they found an apartment and helped Hallie adjust to life in the Deep South. Hallie's mother was unsure whether her daughter had made the correct decision. Montevallo, a small town without sidewalks, seemed strange to her. She had never seen red clay, and people spoke with strange accents. Elizabeth Farmer was reassured when she met her daughter's colleagues at Montevallo, and they seemed intelligent and kind.

Hallie liked Montevallo immediately and enjoyed her students. The young women admired their jolly teacher, who always seemed happy. Being Quaker, Hallie dressed simply in dark dresses, but her smile decorated her plump face. A diabetic, Hallie had an unusually pale complexion, but she hid her illness and energetically pursued her work.

Enthusiastically she bustled around the campus, but she never was too hurried to stop and talk to her students. She also welcomed her students in her home to discuss personal concerns or to soothe them, as when Pearl Harbor was attacked. Professor Farmer hosted parties in which she encouraged her students to dress as famous historical figures. She enjoyed her friendship with fellow faculty member, neighbor, and Hoosier Josephine Eddy, a home economics professor who often cooked meals for visiting students.

Hallie told funny stories, laughing so hard that her glasses fell off and wisps of her hair escaped from her prim bun. She incorporated her energy into her lectures, making history come alive to her students. Although she assigned plenty of homework, students flocked to her classes to learn more about the past. Hallie believed that a sense of humor emboldened students to risk making mistakes and thus learn in the process. She laughed with her students, not at them, especially once when a student misspelled the word literate. Professor Farmer sought to improve academic standards, developing a history of civilization course that her students called "five-hour history." An intensive course, Hallie's class not only covered traditional topics but incorporated such aspects as art and music appreciation. She stressed that historians must make their work interesting, yet accurate, warning against sensationalizing, distorting, or propagandizing facts. Stretching a cord across the room, Hallie fashioned a timeline. Lecturing without notes, "she was one of the most provocative teachers I ever had," one student remembered. "She was most demanding but always fair."

Interested in exposing her students to more opportunities, Hallie told them about summer jobs and workshops that aided them in securing lifetime employment in public service positions. In 1934 she cooperated with the local National Federation of Business and Professional Women's Clubs chapter to establish summer career conferences for high school girls. For several decades, prominent college presidents, deans, and professors visited Montevallo to discuss vocational options.

Hallie also taught government classes. She urged her students to apply knowledge and be imaginative, not simply memorize facts. Expecting them to think deeply about their roles and responsibilities in the world, she challenged them to respond to difficult hypothetical questions. Instead of asking them what the Alabama governor did, Hallie would query, "If you were the Governor of Alabama, what would you do?" Encouraging her students to study and form their own opinions, she revealed her beliefs about such controversial issues as the Scottsboro Boys trial, but did not insist that her students accept her values. Hallie, however, expected her students to be able to defend their reasoning intelligently.

Hallie most wanted her students to become active citizens interested in their government. In addition to reading textbook assignments, her students visited government buildings and politicians in Montgomery in order to experience firsthand politics in action. At the Alabama State House, Hallie instructed her students to listen to lawmakers discuss money and then to consider different ways to reduce the government's budget. Often when Hallie and her students arrived at government buildings, legislators reprimanded them, "Young ladies should not concern themselves with the world of politics."

Professor Hallie Farmer responded that women could enhance politics, offering an applicable analogy. "Many women are in charge of their households," she said, and "the state of Alabama is just like any household. You have a certain number of things that you need to pay for. And you have a certain amount of money in your cookie jar. It is the same idea in a state government. The government of Alabama has a certain number of expenses. And it has a certain amount of tax money in its account. Women already understand these things."

By meeting and conversing with their legislators, Hallie wanted her students to realize that politicians were not "far-off," but ordinary people who worked for citizens. She instructed her students to canvass their hometown's neighborhoods to take surveys in order to understand that residents' opinions about government were important. She also said that everyone should be involved in government, even teachers and students.

To prove her point, in 1937 she ran for Montevallo's town council. Elected to two terms (no one would oppose her for reelection in 1941), Hallie served her adopted hometown. A staunch Indiana Republican, Hallie switched parties in Alabama. She explained that she became a Democrat because she was liberal and because Alabama endorsed the one-party system. Admired by her constituents, Hallie was asked to consider running for Congress, but she refused, believing that instead of being a politician, she should devote herself to studying politicians at work.

In the summer of 1941, Hallie established the School for Citizenship at Montevallo. Teaching women how laws are created, she guided her students through the legislative process, from the idea, bill, debate, and revision to approval. She encouraged the women to discuss issues important to them, such as improving laws protecting children and bettering schools. A scholar, Hallie published skillfully worded journal articles, book reviews, and more than fifty profiles for the *Dictionary of American Biography*. Well versed in professional literature, she grounded her research with standard political science treatises and articles from the *Annals of the American Academy of Political and Social Science*. She was especially interested in understanding the South, and her article, "The Economic Background of Southern Populism," in the January 1930, *South Atlantic Quarterly* described the detrimental impact of war and reconstruction on the region.

Holding the charter meeting in her office, Hallie helped organize the Alabama Historical Association in 1948 and served on the editorial board of its journal, the *Alabama Review*. She also joined national professional organizations, including the American Historical Association and the Southern Political Science Association.

Her best known works were published during the 1940s. She examined all available materials, attended legislative sessions, and testified before capitol committees. Hallie talked to as many elected officials as possible, including the governor (Kissin' Jim Folsom bussed her on the cheek once). She also communicated with clerks, reporters, and private citizens. Hallie realized that many Alabama legislators lacked fundamental knowledge of how their government worked.

Her first work, *A Manual for Alabama Legislators* (1942), was written specifically to help state government officials understand how to make laws more efficiently. By outlining the appropriate steps to create laws, she hoped this guide would reduce duplication of work and eliminate wasted time. Many state legislators consulted her book and asked Hallie for assistance because she seemed to know more about how state government functioned than most politicians. Serving as legislative counsel, Hallie also wrote the bill to establish the Legislative Reference Service which efficiently assisted officials to research and write legislation.

Ironically, Hallie, a pacifist who promoted world peace, next edited *War Comes to Alabama*. This was a collection of articles written by state officials, including Governor Chauncey Sparks, about the war's effect on life in Alabama, addressing demographics, public welfare and health, education, highways, crime, agriculture, business, and local government. Assisted by Lillian Worley, assistant professor of history and government at Montevallo, Hallie arranged the articles.

She wrote chapter 15 on "Postwar Prospects," warning that post-war life would be difficult as defense industries closed and farm prices fell. Recalling conditions in the post-World War I era, Hallie urged Alabamians to begin preparations to mitigate conditions in the future, especially women who would be fired so that returning veterans could be hired. She stressed that the government should be streamlined to become more manageable. She recommended an overhaul of the tax system and limited state spending. Hallie advised Alabama's officials and citizens to plan ahead for solutions and to conserve surpluses and build up reserves.

She then embarked as a research associate on The Legislative Process in Alabama series of pamphlets, sponsored by the Bureau of Public Administration at the University of Alabama. She cited Alabama constitutional law, provided basic legislative information in appendices and tables, and analyzed Alabama's government. She hoped legislators would benefit from her suggestions. Hallie also lobbied to eliminate obsolete and superfluous governmental committees and positions.

In her 1944 pamphlet, Local and Private Legislation, Hallie focused on how Alabama law making had changed as the state shifted from being rural to industrial. She was especially concerned with the pressures of "powerful political groups" and corporations. "The evils of local and private legislation in Alabama are obvious," she stated. Examining how the 1901 Constitutional Convention attempted to restrict local legislation, such as granting divorces, chartering corporations, and exempting property tax, she showed how the legislature, in fact, had more power than counties and municipalities over local affairs.

She described how legislators could be swayed by factions lobbying for specific local programs, and, as a result, focus on local problems, not state issues, in order to be re-elected. She declared, "It is the Legislature, not the law, which, by its defiance of the State Constitution and by its mockery of its own rules, makes possible that travesty of the democratic process which is called `passing local bills.'" She suggested that encouraging home rule would reduce local and private legislation at the state level and would help solve this problem.

In her next pamphlet, Legislative Apportionment (1944), Hallie declared that one of Alabama's major political problems was "securing an equitable arrangement of legislative districts" with demographic and geographic flexibility. Comparing Alabama to other states, Hallie outlined how Alabama's constitution used the census to determine legislative apportionment and fix the number of representatives and senators. Noting that the legislators were required to reapportion the legislature according to demographic shifts, she showed that South Alabama had gained representation, and controlled state politics, even though it had lost population, and that North Alabama was not adequately represented. She recommended either a constitutional amendment or convention to reapportion the legislature.

Hallie's Standing Committees (1945) pamphlet discussed how the Alabama legislature was overwhelmed by too many committees (many of them duplicating work), resulting in legislators being overworked and unaware of crucial facts. She continued to publicize the inadequacies of Alabama's legislature in scholarly journals. In the August 1947 Journal of Politics, her article, "Legislative Planning and Research in Alabama," analyzed legislative reforms.

Having once criticized the Alabama legislature because "too few of its members had caught the vision of the legislature as the great servant of all Alabama's people." Hallie had then sarcastically suggested, "If Alabama is to change a great deal, we are going to have to have a few well chosen funerals." She softened, "Laws have ceased to be broad general principles demanding from a legislator only integrity and a fundamental common sense. Alabama has established the machinery for effective legislative planning and research. The problem now is to develop legislative confidence in that machinery, and to increase legislative skill in its use."

The University of Alabama's public administration bureau compiled Hallie's pamphlets into the book, *The Legislative Process in Alabama*, in 1949. Considered a classic and pivotal work, this comprehensive book analyzed Alabama's legislative process since the 1901 Constitutional Convention. Hallie provided additional information on the legislature's organization and procedure, detailing the chief executive's power. Filled with statistics, tables, and documents, her work is a useful source for political scientists and citizens.

Hallie hoped that by monitoring politicians' work habits she could offer suggestions for improving their performance and assure Alabamians that their elected officials were honest and working for the citizenry who elected them, not pursuing personal goals. "Who gives these big, important lawmakers all the power that makes them big and important?" she asked. "Ordinary people, that's who! The lawmakers must listen to what the people want."

Writing thousands of letters to politicians and newspapers and presenting hundreds of speeches to organizations, Hallie began demanding changes in Alabama's political system. She challenged politicians to be more responsible to their constituency. She also crusaded for a state merit system to disable the spoils system that had enabled poorly qualified political appointees to attain crucial administrative positions.

Hallie demanded an improved jury system, mainly the inclusion of women. "There is only one problem with juries," Hallie declared. "Juries are always made up of men only. Women are never allowed to serve on a jury." To publicize her frustrations, Hallie contacted newspapers and spoke to church congregations, explaining why women should serve on juries. "Why on earth are there no women helping judges?" Hallie protested. "Women are in charge of teaching our children the difference between right and wrong. All those judges once learned about right and wrong from their own mothers." Women were finally allowed to serve on Alabama juries in the 1960s.

Hallie also wanted to eliminate Alabama's poll tax, which many Alabamians were unable to afford. This cumulative tax required citizens to pay certain amounts every year, including retroactive payments for previous years in which the person had not voted. Poll taxes could add up to exorbitant amounts. She and many others considered this an unfair method to prevent voting. She complained, "It is wrong to have so many people who are not allowed to vote. You should be able to vote whether or not you are poor. Our government needs to hear the ideas of all its citizens." She told her audiences that politics was controlled by a small group of rich, white men and that ordinary people, denied the right to vote, had no input into choosing their lawmakers and influencing political decisions.

Speaking against the poll tax everywhere she could, Hallie even protested it in her classes. Warned by friends that she might be fired by the college's administrators, mostly powerful white men, Hallie chose to risk dismissal. Governor Benjamin Meeks Miller's niece was in one of her classes, and Hallie's friends worried that the student would tell her uncle, an ardent supporter of the poll tax, about Hallie's fervent public protestations. Instead of concealing her opinions, Hallie worked harder, convincing her students, including the governor's niece (who expressed her concerns to her uncle), to abolish the poll tax.

Speaking to women's groups, Hallie inspired women to hold bake sales to pay their poll taxes and advised League of Women Voters members and home demonstration clubs how to set up booths to remind voters to pay their poll tax on time to validate their vote and to collect money for poor women's poll taxes. People began to speak out against the poll tax and voted for lawmakers who would nullify it. Eventually the cumulative feature of the poll tax was ended, and many newspaper articles credited Hallie for this success. She commented, "Half a loaf is better than no loaf at all."

Hallie also targeted the Alabama Board of Registrars for misusing the reading test to prevent people from voting even if they could pay the poll tax. Especially used against illiterate black and poor residents (mostly women), the board failed applicants whom they considered unfit to vote by administering extremely difficult tests. They justified this restriction by suggesting that anybody who could not comprehend reading materials could not understand politicians and thus should not vote. Hallie organized groups to protest this practice, and in 1949 the board of registrars was ordered to cease reading tests.

Prison reform was another major concern for Hallie who described Alabama prisons as a "stench in the nostrils of the nation." She campaigned for female superintendents at the Julia Tutwiler Prison for Women in Wetumpka. Despite Governor James E. Folsom's veto of a committee to study prison reform established by the 1947 legislature, Hallie convinced the speaker of the house to reinstate the committee. Even though they received no funds, the committee members studied and decided that Alabama's prisons were in dire need of reform.

"We put people in prison so that they will become better citizens. We put people in prisons so they will learn not to hurt other people," Hallie said. "But our prisons are horrible places. Guards beat men and women. Prisoners are being hurt, not helped." Protesting corporal punishment and violence in prisons, Hallie targeted whipping. In 1950 Alabama's governor forbid floggings of prisoners with whips, and a public bonfire of Alabama's prison whips was held. A state Board of Corrections was created to oversee reforms. Hallie's friend, Edwina Mitchell, was named superintendent of Tutwiler Prison in 1951. In addition to supplying better prisoner clothing, Hallie was also concerned with the implementation of fair pardon and parole systems. She took her students on tours of the prisons to alert them to this social problem.

Although she had good intentions, Hallie was ridiculed and denounced for pursuing political reforms. Conservative legislators considered her a nuisance and, to discredit her, hinted that perhaps she had communist tendencies. Alabama newspapers published cruel political cartoons, labeling her as an intrusive Yankee female teacher who should stay out of men's business in politics.

Hallie coped with these insults by maintaining her sense of humor and remembering that some state senators considered her a "forward looking" scholar. Hallie continued teaching at Montevallo and traveled across Alabama to talk about her ideas. She did not drive and rode the bus, grading papers and planning lectures. Often, the hotels where she boarded were filthy or crowded.

One of her favorite tales was about spending the night on a lobby couch. Feigning sleep, she overheard a conversation between the hotel proprietor and the local doctor. The pair gossiped about everyone in town, then suddenly remembered Hallie was on the couch. She emitted snores to assure them that she was "asleep." Hallie said that pretending to sleep that night was more difficult than delivering any of her political speeches. "I almost burst out laughing when that lady was listening to my snores."

She often spoke to women's clubs and church groups. She said, "Come on now, ladies. Think about it. Half of the people in this state are female. So half of the brains in this state are female. You'd better join in, ladies. Get involved." Hallie explained, "You can't expect Alabama to solve its problems using only half of its brains. Get to work. Write some letters. Express your views. In no time at all, you'll be helping write new and better laws."

"Feminist though I am," she once said, "I have always thought that if there is anything men can do alone, let them do it. But every major social and economic issue inevitably becomes a matter of government and citizenship. Women should have a more vital role in them." Serving as a charter member of Montevallo's chapter of the American Association of University Women (AAUW), Hallie was also a national officer. She praised the group as a "wonderful organization. It is made up of women who are not just ordinary women. They are wonderful women. They are they leaders. We have ahead of us a great future."

She also was a charter member of Montevallo's Business and Professional Women's Club. Hallie motivated women in these groups to unite for successful reforms. She promoted the establishment of the Women's Joint Legislative Council, consisting of a variety of women's groups, to strengthen and coordinate women's efforts to secure specific legislation. Although the council did not sponsor legislation, it prevented duplication and served as an information nucleus.

Dr. Hallie Farmer believed in improving educational opportunities. She recorded programs about government for radio station WAPI in Birmingham and taught extension courses in small Alabama towns. She joined Deep Thought and Studiosis, two local discussion groups. When Montevallo's Division of Social Sciences was formed in 1949, she became chairman. She was one of the founders of the Southern Regional Training Program to train students attending state universities in Alabama, Tennessee, and Kentucky for public administration positions.

She assisted her students to establish Citizenship Day at Montevallo, during which seniors are "formally inducted into citizenship in the locality, state, and nation." She also sponsored the Student Government Association and Young Women's Christian Association. Hallie promoted integration, taking her students and colleagues to desegregated meetings. She served on college committees and supported administrative positions, although she readily voiced her concerns and opinions. In 1941 Montevallo's students dedicated their yearbook to Hallie.

Hallie Farmer was also committed to civic duties. During summers she often returned to Anderson, Indiana, to teach Sunday School at the Mt. Oak Methodist Church (she also built houses to supplement her salary). A member of the first board of directors of the Alabama Hall of Fame, she also served as woman's coordinator for civil defense in Shelby County. Hallie advised and corresponded with League of Women Voters members about various political issues. Her letters are included in the League's papers in the Auburn University Archives.

In recognition of her contributions, Dr. Hallie Farmer received numerous honors, including being listed in *Who's Who of American Women*. She was named the Business and Professional Women of Alabama's first "Woman of Achievement" in 1954 and was selected as a Distinguished Alumna by the Indiana State Teachers College. Hallie received honorary doctorates from Alabama College and Iowa Wesleyan College.

Dr. Hallie Farmer retired in 1956. Her former student, Lucille Griffith, who had earned an history Ph.D. at Brown University, succeeded her as chairman. Tired by her vigorous speaking tours and diabetes, Hallie missed her mother and sister, whom she had only seen every summer. Before she left Montevallo, she gave friends copies of her books, which they valued because of her informative annotations penned in the margins. She returned home to Indiana to relax, play with her dogs Sam and Butch, and read mystery novels on the front porch.

Although retired, Hallie also continued to speak out for her beliefs and causes. On June 2, 1960, she traveled to Washington, D.C., as vice-president of the AAUW, for a meeting. When she exited a taxi, she collapsed, dying of a heart attack. While she was lying on the sidewalk, a thief stole her purse. When an ambulance took her body to a hospital, no one could identify her. Eventually, her name was determined, and the hospital notified her family of her demise. A determined leader throughout her life, Hallie died in pursuit of her goals to improve her society.

In 1971 Dr. Hallie Farmer, Helen Keller, and Julia Tutwiler, considered" Alabama's three most outstanding women," were the first women inducted into the Alabama Women's Hall of Fame at Judson College. Dr. Kermit A. Johnson paid tribute, stating that Dr. Farmer showed that "a woman could be brainy as well as charming and that the aspirations of good citizenship [could] walk hand in hand with the dignity of womanhood." He praised saying that, "her level head and her healthy sense of humor helped her and her coworkers through many a difficult situation" and that "All Alabama citizens, and especially women, are able to enjoy many privileges because Hallie Farmer came our way."

Two biographies about Hallie Farmer have been published. Patricia Sammon's *Hallie Farmer: Teacher and Leader* (Huntsville: Writers Consortium Books, 1989), is a children's book, while Carolyn Hinshaw Edwards' *Hallie Farmer: Crusader for Legislative Reform in Alabama* (Huntsville: Strode Publishers, 1979), was sponsored by the Huntsville AAUW.

At Montevallo, the student union center is named Hallie Farmer Hall. Each year a social science student receives a scholarship established in her honor. Funded by her students and friends, the biennial Hallie Farmer Lecture in Social Science series brings eminent scholars, such as former Secretary of State Dean Rusk in 1985, to campus. Nationally, the AAUW supports the Hallie Farmer Memorial Research Endowment for work promoting female education.

Dr. Hallie Farmer's determination gave Alabama's disenfranchised people hope. Although she was forthright and demanding, Hallie was also humane. On the flyleaf of her Bible, she explained her philosophy that guided her relationships with others as she campaigned to better her community. She wrote, "it seems best to be very careful how we try to do justice in this world, and mostly leave retribution of all kinds to God, who really knows about things; and content ourselves as much as possible with mercy whose mistakes are not so irreparable."

Hallie's students speak of her with great love. They vividly remember her lectures, friendship, and encouragement. Both women and men throughout Alabama welcomed her inspirational words and benefited from the reforms she initiated. Although some legislators were offended by Hallie's criticism, other politicians accepted her wisdom. Senator John Sparkman recalled, "I consider Hallie Farmer as one of the most active and able persons we ever had in Alabama. I knew her quite well and felt she had a great influence for good in the State."

Described as "coldly logical, intelligent, reasonable, and at the same time passionate in her belief," Hallie Farmer, "undisputed champion of this state's politically minded women," believed that it was her duty as a concerned citizen to improve Alabama, and she performed admirably. As her friend Josephine Eddy lauded, "We drew strength from Hallie."

written by Elizabeth D. Schafer

*Photo by Julie Lopez
for Habitat for Humanity*

LINDA BEVERLY CALDWELL FULLER
1941 -

A Decent House In A Decent Community
For God's People In Need.

These words of wisdom are the motto of Habitat for Humanity International. Through her co-creation of and dedicated service to Habitat for Humanity, Linda Caldwell Fuller has significantly improved the quality of life for many Alabamians, as well as people around the world. By forming an interdenominational Christian group that builds sturdy housing for the poor, Linda Fuller and her husband Millard, have empowered both the homeowners and the homebuilders to make the world a better place. She has proven that individual sacrifice can nurture the global community and that "Love should not be just words and talk; it must be true love, which shows itself in action." (1 John 3:18)

Born in Tuscaloosa in 1941, Linda Beverly Caldwell, the daughter of Paul and Wilma Caldwell, grew up respecting and helping other people. Her altruistic philosophy caused her to encourage her peers to become more involved in their community. Tall and slender, like their father who managed the Caldwell Electrical Shop, Linda and her older sister Janet attended Tuscaloosa High School.

Serendipitously, teenaged Linda met her soul mate and future husband. After Millard Fuller graduated from Auburn University, he enrolled in the University of Alabama's law school where he became business partners with fellow student and

59

now acclaimed civil rights attorney, Morris Dees. Avid entrepreneurs, Fuller and Dees pursued a variety of fund raising attempts to earn tuition money and gain riches. They sold mistletoe and birthday cakes and initiated a mail-order business, making substantial profits.

One day in 1958 Millard visited a local movie theatre to sell advertisements on desk blotters. He was smitten by the girl in the ticket office, but when he finished his sales pitch to the manager, she had left for the day. Wanting to ask her out, he was frustrated when no one at the theatre would give him her phone number or address. He remembered that her surname was Caldwell and began dialing numbers from the Tuscaloosa phone book. He failed to locate her with the first and second numbers, but on his third call, a young woman responded that she did not know who the girl was but that she understood his dilemma and would sincerely attempt to help him find her.

As Millard talked to this helpful woman, he thought that she sounded like a nice person and asked her name. She told him, "Linda Caldwell." He forgot about the theatre employee. During their discussion, they realized that they shared mutual friends. Suddenly, Linda asked Millard how tall he was. He told her that he was 6'4". She responded happly, that because she was 5'10", many men were often too short for her. Charmed by Linda, Millard asked if he could visit her. Linda gave him directions to her home, and they had their first date in the University of Alabama Student Union Cafeteria. They fell in love with each other at first sight.

The couple dated for a year. Much of their courting included trips around Tuscaloosa securing business orders. Linda often rode in Millard's unheated paneled business truck. They laughed about the rusted holes in its floor. She enjoyed encouraging her fiancé and his business partner and assisted them as much as possible.

After her graduation from Tuscaloosa High School, Linda Caldwell and Millard Fuller married at Alberta Baptist Church on August 30, 1959. Linda joked that she was so busy helping Millard and Dees with their business pursuits that she did not have time even to wash her hair before the wedding. On their wedding night, Linda and Millard signed an agreement to "outlove" each other, promising that they would keep no secrets from each other and that as a couple they would nurture a relationship with God. They hung this covenant over their bed.

Linda spent her early married life, typing envelopes for promotional mailings. She helped Millard and Dees sell everything from toothbrushes to cookbooks. The Fullers invested their profits into real estate near the University of Alabama campus. After Millard's graduation from law school, they moved to Montgomery in 1960.

As a young bride, Linda doted on her husband, but she quickly became isolated in her new Cloverdale home as Millard devoted his energy to making money. Busy with business deals, Millard neglected Linda who often ate meals listening to her husband and Morris Dees devise new financial strategies for the Fuller and Dees Marketing Group, Inc. Unhappy with her joyless marriage, Linda also became disenchanted with her community. When salesmen rang her doorbell, they asked her for her mother because she was so young. Linda spent much of her time pushing her son in a stroller at a nearby shopping center until she felt tired enough to sleep. She also attended classes at Huntingdon College to fill her lonely hours.

Profits from subleasing their Tuscaloosa property as well as Millard's direct mail and publishing ventures with Dees resulted in great affluence for the Fullers. Millard had become a millionaire, but Linda felt that he valued her only as a possession, as a beautiful wife that he could show off when he wanted. Linda lived in a luxurious home, with plans for a new mansion to be built outside Montgomery. She wore elegant clothes and drove sporty cars. The Fullers had horses and livestock on thousands of acres, and they also had boats at their lake cabin. A maid cleaned up after their small children, Christopher and Kimberly. Despite their material wealth, Linda felt a spiritual emptiness. She realized that possessions did not make her happy.

Her faith in God had always been important to Linda. She turned to her faith and decided to organize a United Church of Christ in her home. Millard occasionally attended services with her, but business was his priority. As he worked long hours and weekends, his health worsened. He neglected himself, his wife, and his children. Every night Linda hopelessly looked at the covenant over their bed, and by 1964 she told Millard that he had become a stranger to his family and that she did not love him anymore. She left him in November 1965 to decide if they had a future together. Her exodus was the catalyst for Habitat for Humanity.

Linda flew to New York City to talk to Dr. Lawrence Durgin, the pastor of the Broadway United Church of Christ. She and Millard had heard him speak on a previous visit to the city, and she hoped that he could offer her wise counsel about her future. Linda discussed her relationship and her fears of estrangement, remembering how she and Millard had committed to their "outlove" covenant and to cherish a relationship with God.

When Millard called, asking to come to New York to confront their personal crisis, Linda agreed to talk to him. At home, Millard had been agonizingly heartbroken, he feared that he had lost his wife due to his materialism. He admitted that money did not make him happy or provide much meaning to his life and that Linda was the essence of his being. Millard arrived on a cold day, and his future looked bleak as he worried that divorce was imminent.

After watching "Never Too Late" at the Radio City Music Hall, Millard and Linda sat on the steps of Saint Patrick's Cathedral steps under a full moon and cried. They had embraced the movie's message and they began confiding in each other about what was wrong with their relationship. Walking around the city, the couple experienced an epiphany in a Fifth Avenue doorway where they emotionally told each other how they had betrayed the marriage and revealed their personal regrets and pain. Through tears, they pledged their love and admitted that future togetherness was possible. That night they talked, sang, and prayed, healing their rift.

After much soul searching about why their lives had gone astray, they reconciled and agreed to sell all of their property and businesses and give the money away to the poor. Then they would renew their love by serving Christ. Linda trusted that God's love would guide them in the future as they sought a new life.

The Fullers returned to Alabama, singing "We're Marching to Zion" in the airplane to bolster their commitment to each other and to God. They took their children to Florida to celebrate their family's love and to look for the new path that they should follow. They desperately wanted to change the way they were living but were clueless to how they could accomplish this. They experienced a spiritual crisis and disheartened began the trip home. As they drove through Georgia, they visited their friends Al and Carol Henry who were living in an integrated Christian community named Koinonia, the Greek word for fellowship. During their brief stay, they were inspired by Clarence Jordan, the community's spiritual leader.

Linda and Millard decided that perhaps they had discovered their calling as disciples of God. Between December 1965 when they first saw Koinonia and 1968 when they returned to the community, the Fullers had several life-altering experiences. During the summer of 1966, Linda accompanied Millard to Africa on a church-sponsored mission. As a missionary, she visited schools, hospitals, and agricultural projects, familiarizing herself with the plight of refugees. Returning to the United States, she described the conditions, especially the lack of adequate housing, in Africa to as many people as possible, hoping to obtain relief resources.

To fulfill their ministry, the Fullers moved to New Jersey where they lived in a small, rustic apartment. Despite their good intentions, the Fullers were rejected by local church members who judged them as being inferior due to their dilapidated home. Combined with their African experiences, Millard and Linda had a vision of helping the poor have nice houses, not only to provide suitable shelter, but also to increase human dignity and give a sense of worth. After he had graduated from Auburn, Millard had spent his summer vacation as a construction worker in Michigan and had learned the fundamentals of building structures. This experience provided the Fullers a foundation for their dream.

In 1968 the Fullers returned to Georgia and moved into a house at Koinonia Farm. Millard and Linda utilized their business expertise by helping with the community's pecan, candy, and fruitcake sales. Unfortunately, the Koinonia community was at a low point, reduced to only two families because of persecution, harassment, and an economic boycott by opponents of interracial neighborhoods. Millard realized that relying on selling agricultural goods to angry area residents during the height of the Civil Rights movement would not be wise.

They needed a new plan. Millard, Linda, and Clarence Jordan discussed how they could improve the world. They focused on being partners with God to build low-cost homes for impoverished residents and rural sharecroppers. They decided that through a grassroots effort they would construct simple but sturdy houses financed by a Fund for Humanity. Home owners could make a small down-payment and pay a no-interest, twenty-year mortgage. Money for building materials would be acquired from gifts, loans, and profits from pecan sales. The first house was built for Bo and Emma Johnson in 1969.

All new houses were built on community land. Angry white residents committed acts of violence, hoping to prevent additional housing for blacks, but Millard and Linda persisted, and shacks were replaced by sturdy structures. For their ministry, known as Koinonia Partners, Linda typed correspondence, filled orders for pecans and the community's cookbook, and prepared copies of Clarence Jordan's Biblical "Cotton Patch" texts, translations of the New Testament into southern jargon, to distribute to rural Georgians in the hope that they would understand and embrace religion. Linda also organized the community's crafts shop, where community women sewed items for sale, and the Koinonia Child Development Center, a day care for community children. Having given up cars, she enjoyed bicycling with her four children. The family had grown with daughters Faith and Georgia who were born after her reconciliation with Millard. She spruced up their home at 603 E. Church Street by stripping off old paint, sanding the wood, and refinishing the walls. She fixed windows and shelves, sewed curtains, and painted used furniture. Millard organized a nearby office to handle paperwork.

In January 1973, the Fullers decided to apply their building houses idea to an African community. They chose to create a housing project in Zaire, a country that had gained its independence from Belgium in 1960 and consisted of squatter villages and a quickly expanding population creating a desperate need for housing. Residents suffered almost 50 percent unemployment and lived in flimsy cardboard houses and mud shacks, which were often destroyed by frequent tropical storms. The Fullers immersed themselves into six months of orientation, including a sojourn in Paris to learn French.

They arrived in Mbandaka, Zaire, a city on the equator, in July 1973. Initiating a local Fund for Humanity supported by a variety of religious groups, the Fullers began plans to build simple, sturdy concrete block houses for the poor. The first house was begun in March 1974, and the Fullers started a church too. Their children helped paint homes, and workers built parks, a playground, and a community center. Their goal was to offer a sense of hope and opportunity to the villagers.

For three years, they were frustrated and discouraged by prevailing cultural clashes and local conditions and prejudices - primarily ignorance and superstition. The Fullers also withstood theft, inflation, shortages of essential goods, and diseases indigenous to the region. Linda struggled to feed her family and volunteers, make their home liveable, and insure that her children had adequate schooling. Language differences created some problems. Millard was falsely arrested on trumped up charges, and bureaucratic red tape paralyzed their progress, but finally the Fullers convinced the Zaire government to permit them to build homes on an acreage in the center of town. This buffer zone between white European settlers and blacks was called Bokotola, meaning "man who does not care for others."

Linda helped Millard dedicate the new community on July 4, 1976. The area was, renamed Losanganya, meaning "reconciler." Although the homes they built lacked such standard American amenities as electricity or running water, their inhabitants considered them blessed gifts from God. By the summer of 1976, at least 114 houses were in progress and land for 56 additional homes had been purchased.

During their stay in Africa, Linda and Millard found strength in letters written by friends and visitors who proffered encouragement to confront such problems as machinery malfunctioning, work crews refusing to work, or inclement weather. Linda endured loneliness and isolation but overcame obstacles such as feelings of helplessness and frustration through her belief in the power of God. Despite their struggles, the Fullers enjoyed learning about new cultures and people, traveling in the countryside and picnicking in native gardens.

Although they wished to stay and help build, Linda and Millard realized that they needed to return to Georgia to raise money because of the great demand for more homes and expansion in Zaire. They also acknowledged that local leadership was capable of monitoring construction during their absence. In Georgia they recruited volunteers and collected money and old eyeglasses to distribute in Africa. Some of the money was used for the Rise Up and Walk program, where artificial limbs and crutches were given to disabled individuals to aid their employability and bolster their personal pride.

Soon after coming home from Zaire, the Fullers were approached by preachers to assist the Morgan-Scott Project of improving rural, low-income housing for an impoverished Appalachian area. They quickly realized that housing projects were welcomed throughout America and in developing countries. The Fullers believed that global harmony could be achieved through improved housing and living environments. They chose to honor Jesus, who had been a carpenter, by building better habitats for people to live and work in with dignity and to reach their full potential. In addition to dwellings, their plans incorporated beautification efforts such as planting trees and flowers and implementing erosion control methods.

In September 1976, the Fullers and their friends organized the non-profit Habitat for Humanity International, establishing the organization's headquarters in Americus, Georgia. The organization's purpose was to make the world a better habitat by tearing down shacks and replacing them with new homes that served as symbols of Christian love. Millard was named executive director and Linda his assistant on the executive staff, and together they promoted "The Economics of Jesus," where the more affluent individuals donated money and labor to help poorer people acquire decent housing. The Fullers emphasized that Habitat for Humanity was not a charity and that volunteers would not impose their cultural beliefs on homeowners. Builders would help only if future homeowners were willing to join building crews and invest "sweat equity."

Habitat for Humanity building crews replaced inadequate housing with sturdy buildings always taking into consideration local conditions. For example, in Central America, workers made cement blocks from indigenous ingredients, sun-baking them in a form, to replace houses constructed of mud, sticks, and cornstalks. The new houses were weatherproofed and reinforced against earthquakes. Racial cooperation at building sites flourished, and homeowners agreed to work both on their home and for other projects. Houses were also constructed for migrant workers in Florida and Texas.

Habitat for Humanity insisted that three criteria had to be met for a successful project. Each group had to have Christian leaders who could abandon materialistic standards and embrace Jesus. Selected families must live in substandard housing to qualify and were required to participate fully in building their new homes. And a sense of "love in the mortar joints" must prevail. This quality was defined as a genuine Christian love toward the recipients of the home being constructed.

According to Habitat for Humanity guidelines, some housing projects were fully sponsored while others were financed by local committees which raised funds and monitored volunteers. Often, new homeowners placed Bibles in the cornerstones of their houses. The homes were built according to specific standards designed by experts to insure their stability to house God's children. Habitat for Humanity homes in California and along the Gulf Coast have survived earthquakes and hurricanes. In 1979 the Fullers visited the Zaire community that they had helped. Inspecting ongoing construction, they were happy to view the community's progress and growth, dedicating the housing project. Linda joined the jubilation as people enthusiastically praised the Lord for their new homes, dancing, singing, and shaking hands. Three years later the Fullers also financed a project in nearby Ntondo to rebuild the entire jungle village of three hundred homes, one for every family. At a celebration, Millard and Linda were serenaded with songs and drums in tribute to their efforts to elevate the world's consciousness about poverty and the need for improved housing worldwide.

Linda and Millard decided that the best way to get Americans' attention about poor housing was to walk from Americus to Indianapolis, Indiana. After several weeks of preparing for the walk by exercising and praying, on August 3, 1983, Linda and Millard left the Habitat for Humanity office and strolled through Americus, singing the hymn "We're Marching to Zion." The same hymn they had sung when they decided to change their lives twenty years previously. As they walked, Linda was proud to see the streets lined with houses built by Habitat for Humanity. She waved at homeowners whom she had helped.

Former first lady, Rosalyn Carter, and her daughter Amy, residents of nearby Plains who were interested in the Fullers' work, escorted them to the edge of town. At an emotional ceremony, the Fullers and fellow marchers yelled "Habitat Oyée," a supportive cheer developed in Zaire. Millard and Linda spoke about why they were walking, to raise funds and consciousness. They pointed to shacks by the highway, reminding people that there was plenty of work yet to be done. Linda hugged her children and friends goodbye, balanced her backpack filled with lots of socks, a canteen, and trail mix, and began walking north.

The Habitat for Humanity marchers walked in the mornings and rested at noon during the hottest part of the day. They continued their march during the afternoon. On the way, people joined them and offered them water and food for sustenance. Churches provided them places to worship and sleep, and in return, the Fullers told congregations about their work. The walk was grueling, and Linda, like the other volunteers, endured the intense heat and suffered sunburn and bad blisters that had to be lanced and bandaged.

On the morning of September 12, the Habitat for Humanity walkers reached Indianapolis. Linda gratefully received flowers sent from Americus and a poem from her daughter Georgia that expressed how proud she was of her mother. Linda, Millard, and their supporters celebrated at the Roberts Park United Methodist Church, thanking concerned Christians for the $100,000 they raised to build more homes. They have since walked to other major American cities, raising millions of dollars to meet their goals.

Habitat for Humanity gained international publicity when former president Jimmy Carter worked with Linda and Millard on a Habitat project in New York City. Linda appliqued the Habitat logo on a pair of bib overalls for Carter to wear and rode the bus from Georgia to New York with him. The press closely covered Habitat for

Humanity's work, including a shocking discovery Linda made. While tearing up floorboards in the tenement building, Linda found bones. An expert examined them and determined, much to Linda's relief, that they were not human.

During this time, Linda and Millard saw the movie "Back to the Future" which reminded them of the crisis they had undergone in New York twenty years before. They sat again on Saint Patrick's Cathedral's steps and reminisced about how their despair had miraculously borne hope when they decided to change their lives. They vowed to strengthen their efforts to help others.

Linda and Millard Fuller have devoted their lives to being missionaries to slums in North, South, and Central America, Asia, and Africa, preaching "Jesus economics" to raising more money and volunteers. They have sponsored several thousand projects in the United States and abroad in more than fifty countries all over the world. Habitat for Humanity projects in impoverished Third World villages have uplifted populations by reducing their burdens and giving them a means for independence and a sense of hope. Americans living in Habitat for Humanity homes have gratefully praised God, the Fullers, and Habitat for Humanity for believing in their value as human beings. In July 1989, to celebrate paying off the mortgage of the first low-cost house sponsored by the Fullers and their ministry, the Johnson family burned their mortgage.

Linda and Millard Fuller have had a rewarding marriage and life since their reconciliation. The source of their happiness is their love for God, each other, and people. By shunning material goods and dedicating their energy to helping others, they feel that they have embraced the true meaning of life. Millard values Linda's "invaluable partnership in Habitat's ministry." He said she often types letters and manuscripts late at night and on weekends after devoting her day to fixing up houses for volunteers to live in and refinishing Goodwill furniture. He especially respects her role as a mother to his children, admiring the guidance that she has given each child. Linda has raised their children to respect and be kind to other people and to do whatever they are capable of to make the world a better place.

Linda has helped Millard prepare several books, researching, reviewing, and typing manuscripts for *Bokotola* (1977), *Love in the Mortar Joints: The Story of Habitat for Humanity* (1980), and *No More Shacks! The Daring Vision of Habitat for Humanity*, written with Diane Scott (1986). With her husband, she wrote *The Excitement is Building* (1990), chronicling their Habitat for Humanity work. Millard Fuller dedicated his most recent book, *The Theology of the Hammer* (1994), "To my precious wife, Linda, my best friend, partner, and sweetheart for life."

Linda was awarded an honorary doctorate from her alma mater, Huntingdon College in Montgomery in 1994. The Fullers have received numerous other awards for their work, including an honorary doctorate of public services from Presbyterian College in May 1995. Linda humbly acknowledges this praise. She realizes that her projects have made a significant impact on communities all over the earth. She prefers that attention focus not on her but on her humanitarian achievements and their beneficiaries. Friend Marlene Muse, wife of Auburn University's president, admires Linda for "leading a kind of life that Jesus asked us all to lead—to care for other people's needs and not to store up treasures on earth."

Linda Fuller lives a busy and full life, traveling to Habitat for Humanity projects across the United States and around the world. She has painted and hammered on all-women-built houses sponsored by Women Accepting the Challenge of Housing (WATCH) and Girl Scout troops. She has worked side by side with American presidents, religious leaders, celebrities, famous athletes, prominent politicians, and even Miss America. Thousands of houses have been built as a result of Habitat for Humanity. Linda and Millard Fuller enjoy attending dedication ceremonies and seeing the joy of new homeowners.

Linda frequently speaks to regional and college chapters, covenant churches, and civic groups about her work, encouraging others to embrace Habitat for Humanity's goals and to join in the fellowship to build an earthly Kingdom of God. She ask them to work for others despite this materialistic society's incessant demands to acquire wealth and possessions. Her message is clear, that everyone can help "faith-activated house, community and people building," whether by digging a foundation, mixing cement, or buying construction materials. Linda hopes to ease suffering in the world and to spread love for humanity and Christ as evidenced by altruistic actions not merely empty rhetoric.

The Fullers often return to Africa where they began their life's work to renew their commitment to each other and God. Linda enjoys visiting her children, grandchildren, and widowed mother who lives in Tuscaloosa. Her family and her work have given Linda the most satisfaction as she plans and dreams for a future where everyone on earth has a decent home and faith in second chances.

The United Nations cites homelessness as a major international problem; one-fourth of the world's population lacks adequate shelter, either living in substandard shacks or having no dwelling at all. If you would like to volunteer your time or make a financial contribution to make the world a better place, you can contact Linda Fuller by telephone at 1 (800)-HABITAT or write Habitat for Humanity International, Habitat & Church Streets, Americus, Georgia 31709.

written by Elizabeth D. Schafer

ILA NEWELL GLYNN

THE MAIDEN FROM MILLEDGEVILLE

There once was a maiden from Milledgeville town
Who went to New York to live.
Then she came down
To live in the South and at last to begin
In old Tuscaloosa with her husband Glynn

She taught the piano to girls and to boys;
Inspired them to music's pleasures and joys;
She spread understanding
In music and arts,
Played organ at Hunter's to fill Christian hearts.

But we know her best for her glorious past
In helping Community Singers to start.
Salute her for singing
For twenty long years
Join us now as we give her three great long loud cheers
Singing
I—la—N; I—la—N;
Ila N. Glynn!
Three great loud long cheers!

The foregoing cheerful little song was written by Lois Pyle for a very special occasion. On March 31, 1990, The Tuscaloosa [Alabama] Community Singers presented the Maiden from Milledgeville with a certificate:

> In Appreciation for Outstanding Contribution to the
> Tuscaloosa Community Singers as a Founder and Continuous
> Participant and a Dedicated Supporter in the Advancement of
> Musical Culture in the Community.

Beyond being recognized in Tuscaloosa, the subject of the song and the certificate, Ila Newell Glynn, is loved and admired by people all over the United States. Some are her former music students; some have sung hymns to her organ accompaniment at various churches. Others have served with her on the City of Tuscaloosa Board of Education or lunched with her at a League of Women Voters meeting. Each one recalls some particular incident, some special treasured memory of Ila Glynn; but all remember her as the gracious, impeccably dressed lady so remarkable for her unassuming intelligence and quiet dignity.

Ila Newell was born in Milledgeville, Georgia. When she was very young, her parents separated. Her mother moved with her to New York where they both were welcomed into a large, extended family of uncles, aunts, and grandparents. As an only child, she naturally felt her mother's influence strongly, but all the members of this outgoing, loving circle of relatives were supportive and concerned with Ila's growth and education. In fact, Ila's early aptitude for music was first discovered by her grandmother who observed that whenever Ila went out to play in the yard, she carried some pan or basin to beat on with a spoon or stick. Quite obviously the child wasn't simply making noise. She was definitely finding variations in tone and rhythm and was using them to produce simple music. "That child wants to play music," her grandmother said. "She should have a piano." Ila's first piano was given to her by her grandmother.

Along with private piano lessons, grade school and high school were completed in New York. Ila returned home to Georgia to Fort Valley for her college degree. Every summer, however, she was back in New York to study music – history, harmony, and theory – at the Juilliard School of Music while still continuing her private piano lessons.

With an excellent musical education and a college diploma, Ila went South again in 1939. Her first position was church organist at St. Mark's A.M.E. Church in Montgomery, Alabama. She also taught public school music at Booker T. Washington High School. There she met the man who would later become her husband. Robert Glynn was the principal at Booker T. Washington High. Since the city school system in Montgomery had an established prohibition against husbands and wives teaching in the same school, after their marriage in 1942, the young couple moved to Tuscaloosa, Alabama.

For a little while it looked as though the move had been a bad decision. There were no openings in Tuscaloosa for a public school music teacher, and Ila began teaching academic subjects in Maude Whatley's elementary school. The housing problem, however, was even more serious than the employment situation. The only houses they could find for sale or rent were in neighborhoods where living conditions were untenable. Sleep was interrupted by noisy drunkenness at night and the daylight hours were made equally disagreeable by loud contention and fights. For a time, Ila feared that even her marriage was at stake and that she would have to go back to New York to live with her family.

Ila's supervisor from Montgomery suggested that she give private piano lessons, and Tuscaloosa proved to be a productive field for her talents. Meanwhile, Robert had decided that the only solution to their residential difficulty was to build a home in an area that provided suitable surroundings. Accordingly, he secured a lot on Twenty-ninth Avenue and had a comfortable, spacious home built with one room especially for Ila's lessons.

Soon all Ila's time was filled with classes – youngsters after school and adults during the day. In addition she began playing organ at Hunter's Chapel A.M.E. Zion Church on Sundays. The pastor's taste in music differed somewhat from Ila's, and he was not above making occasional comments from the pulpit about the selections she had chosen for the services. One Sunday morning, Robert Glynn said to his wife, "Today I'm going to take you to a new church where we are not known, and no one will ask us for anything. All you'll have to do is sit and enjoy the service."

That was true for only a short while. Robert Glynn was entirely too modest both about his as well as his wife's accomplishments. They were *well* known by many of the members at the First United Methodist Church for, by this time, Governor George Wallace had appointed Robert to the Board of Trustees of Alabama State University in Montgomery. He also had become head of public housing in Tuscaloosa. Ila's musical reputation had preceded her as well. She began playing the organ every Sunday for one of the Sunday School classes and the piano for the noonday, midweek worship service on Wednesdays.

Ila has never been an activist in the common conception of the word. Preferring to let her music speak for her, she has never participate in marches or demonstrations. "We are all God's children," she says. "I know no man that I hate. Many people have been good to me; and I try never to do anything to anyone that I don't want done to me. What we have in our hearts and what we make of ourselves by our own efforts are things of greatest importance."

In spite of her denial of activism, various community causes both in areas of music and academic education have succeeded because of Ila's loyal, but always quiet, support. In 1949 Ila learned that the Tuscaloosa League of Women Voters had been organized. They met in the homes of members to discuss and plan numerous projects. It was an exciting time and the newspapers reported on the League activities. "We read about all the things going on in the League," Ila remembers, "and we wanted to be a part of it. We tried to organize a League of our own, but were not able to do so because the National League charter specified that there shall be only one League in any given community." Thus the Tuscaloosa League of Women Voters was integrated from its very inception. Ila and her friends were welcomed into the membership and immediately began to participate in numerous programs.

Although the Alabama legislature had ruled that public kindergartens should be allowed, most municipalities, Tuscaloosa included, did nothing to implement their creation. Establishing a K—12 school system was one of the League's projects, and Ila became chair of the Kindergarten Committee. Under her leadership, the Committee convinced the City Board of Education to add kindergarten to the school curriculum. Later on, Ila herself became a member of the City of Tuscaloosa Board of Education and served as its secretary for 15 years.

She has been just as effective in promoting music. In 1968, Doris Leapard, a well-known Tuscaloosa music lover and Ila's longtime friend, organized a children's chorus composed of youngsters from all over the city, many of whom were Ila's students. Because churches were segregated at that time, the children were not permitted to practice together; but Doris solved the problem by having them practice separately to sing an antiphonal hymn. Their Holy Week performance at Christ Episcopal Church was sung with black children on one side of the church and white children on the other. Ila perceived how effective music could be in achieving interracial harmony, and she proposed to Doris that the chorus be expanded into a multiracial, interdenominational, adult chorus. Together the two women organized the Tuscaloosa Community Singers which continues to the present giving several concerts during the year, each one more impressive than the last.

After her husband died in 1983, Ila chose to stay in Tuscaloosa in the house he had built for her, and she continues to give piano lessons in her special music room. Even though Ila is considerably older now, she would like to continue teaching as long as possible. She believes that contact with young people keeps her youthful and interested in what goes on in the world and will increase the length of time that she can preserve her own independence. "If you stay alone, the world will leave you alone," she says. In substantiation of this belief, Ila maintains active membership in The League of Women Voters, The Tuscaloosa Arts Council, and The Tuscaloosa Music Club. She also participates in an exercise group and continues on a regular basis to play piano and organ at The First United Methodist Church.

Mrs. Ila Glynn has taught hundreds of young people to love and to perform music. Former students from all over the country remember how she inspired them to love music. They keep in touch with her regularly informing her where they are and what they are doing. Her strong influence extends beyond music. It is no surprise to learn that Ila's pupils were motivated toward higher academic education. Her former students have taken degrees from The University of Alabama, Talladega, Tuskegee, Fiske, Stillman, Howard, Spellman, and Columbia Universities. Some have earned their doctorates in music. Her students are represented in various churches and schools all over the country. Two currently teach music in the Tuscaloosa School system. Several are teaching music in California. Leon Dodson, who has his doctorate from Columbia, is in New Jersey and James McCullough is in Alaska.

All over the United States there are musicians who developed self-confidence, dignity, and integrity at Ila Newell Glynn's piano. She inspired pride in excellence, in truth, and in The Golden Rule. Because of her and her musical talents, there are musicians all over the United States who salute "The Maiden from Milledgeville" with "three great, loud, long cheers."

written by Joyce Mahan

Photo courtesy of Auburn University Archives

JANE TERESE LOBMAN KATZ
1931 - 1986

We Should Congratulate Ourselves On Our Victories, Console Each Other On Our Defeats and Persevere!

Jane Katz's rallying cry was a familiar refrain to Alabama League of Women Voter members. As Alabama League lobbyist, legislative chairman, and editor of the Capitol Newsletter, Katz capably represented the League in the state legislature. She also was the League's first vice-president. Her expertise on state legislation enabled her to voice civic concerns and to command respect among state officials. League members fondly called her their "watchdog on the Hill."

Born on February 12, 1931, in Montgomery, Jane Terese Lobman was the daughter of Bernard and Dorothy Merz Lobman. Jane's paternal grandparents, Nathan and Carrie Pollack Lobman had moved from New York City to Alabama in the mid-nineteenth century, joining the large Jewish community in Montgomery after the Civil War. Jewish families, relocating primarily to escape religious persecution, were influential in Montgomery businesses and politics. The Jewish community provided friendly moral support to its members. Nathan Lobman, a prominent merchant, operated the wholesale Steiner-Lobman Dry Goods Company at the corner of Commerce and Tallapoosa streets near the riverfront. The building now houses attorney's offices, but the Lobman name is still carved in its elaborate stone facade.

Although Jane never knew her grandparents, their values and beliefs impacted her.

In addition to being a diligent entrepreneur, Nathan Lobman served on Montgomery's city council, chairing the finance committee. He also was active in the Chamber of Commerce and community and civic groups and devoted service to the Jewish temple where he was on the board of trustees. Jane's grandmother, Carrie Pollack Lobman, a graduate of Hunter College, served on the board of directors of the Anti-Tuberculosis League and the Montgomery Infirmary and was president of the Ladies' Hebrew Benevolent Society.

Jane's parents encouraged their daughter to be civic-minded and altruistic. Her father, Bernard Lobman, a graduate of the Harvard Law School and a World War I veteran, was a prominent bankruptcy attorney, representing the firm Sternfield and Lobman. He promoted cultural growth in Montgomery, striving to bring talented musical groups to the city. Bernard Lobman also chaired the public library board and was president of the Montgomery Jewish Federation. Jane's mother nurtured her daughter and two sons, Arthur and Walter, at their 109 Bankhead Avenue home. The extended Lobman family in Montgomery was large, with grandparents, uncles, aunts, and first cousins providing a supportive family atmosphere and influential role models.

Jane Lobman graduated from Sidney Lanier High School in 1949. Active on the business staff of the school's yearbook, the *Oracle*, she also participated in the Spanish and Dramatics Clubs. Wearing a sash emblazoned "Marshall" over her clothes, Jane proudly served the Marshal club "to help run the school in an efficient manner by welcoming visitors and by keeping order in the corridors." Her classmates described her as being "versatile" and "cultured" with "pretty eyes."

After graduation, Jane attended Syracuse University and Huntingdon College. She married Warren Katz and worked as an office secretary for the Royal Liverpool Group. They had three children; Theresa, Laura, and Daniel. An active leader in a variety of community organizations, especially the Montgomery Mental Health Association and Alabama Conservancy, and religious groups at the Temple Beth Or, Jane enjoyed playing tennis and the piano and served as president of the Montgomery Chamber Music Society.

Interested in politics, Jane joined the Montgomery League of Women Voters in 1964. She immediately impacted the group statewide. The Alabama League had debated its effectiveness in monitoring the state legislature because there were too many bills that the League supported and opposed in each session. To insure adequate attention to pending bills, the League decided to establish the position of legislative chairman to lobby the legislature. League leaders hope that one person would accept this position so that legislators would become familiar with this individual and respect her input.

In November 1964, Norma Brewer, the League's legislative chairman, resigned. Alabama League president Alice M. Hastings wrote Jane that Brewer had "strongly recommended" Jane as her successor. Brewer had already asked Jane to accept the position but Jane had been unsure, Hastings reassured her that many times "your name has been given me enthusiastically and without reservation as being the RIGHT person for this most important job." Hastings expressed admiration for Jane's aunt, Dorah Sterne, a "staunch and devoted Leaguer," in Birmingham. That if she was like her aunt, "YOU must be a person of real League mettle."

Hastings advised Jane that she would be supported by committees and individual members. She told her not to worry about being a recent League member, insisting that the League needed new leadership. Hastings predicted that Jane would "make League history in Alabama glow bright. League is essential for Alabama, . . . As Legislative chairman, you would be leading through [the] legislature those hopes we, as Leaguers, have for good and responsible government for our citizens . . . and for proper education for our children." Jane accepted the position, and the February 1965 *Alabama Voter* announced, "Jane is a very bright addition to the state board and has started off her new job with a Bang!!"

Jane reported to the council that Norma Brewer had been a "tremendous help" in orientating her to legislative responsibilities. From November to February, Jane read resource material and prepared herself and the League's legislative committee for the regular session in May 1965. She wrote in the February 1965 *Alabama Voter* that "Your Legislative Committee hopes to be able to keep up with all of the hundreds of bills which will be introduced, to select those pertaining to our program for support or opposition, and possibly to get legislation of our own into being." She foresaw "tackling" such issues as absentee voting, tax reform, and reapportionment. "We must have your support at the local level." She represented twelve Leagues throughout the state with over 800 members.

When Governor George Wallace called a special session in February to discuss education, Jane experienced sudden "total involvement." Thrust into action, the poised Jane performed well. In March 1965 she testified before the Senate Finance and Taxation Committee about the proposed textbook bill. She stated the League's position against political censorship in textbook selection.

The bill was amended and passed both houses after debate, incorporating League suggestions. Jane had practically lived at the capitol lobbying and one senator had warned her, "Young Lady, if you spend so much time here, you will have a crop failure." Jane had a sense of humor about her introduction to lobbying. "Representatives from the Klan, DAR, Women for Constitutional Government, etc. were around constantly," she reported. "I got into some very funny situations and kept wishing somebody would take pictures."

On a more serious note, "This primary experience in the Legislature has been very productive in making many valuable contacts, gaining some friends, laying the ground work for good relations with the press, and gaining a much greater appreciation of the law-making process and some of the very real problems of fair legislation." She asked local leagues to keep her informed of their positions to enable her to communicate more effectively with legislators. "I am terribly impressed with the LWV," Jane stressed. "I think the time has come for this organization, already well established, to move more into the field of action. Sometimes we will not receive proper credit for our deeds but the important thing is the deep satisfaction that will come from having an active part in building toward a better world and toward the realization of the American Dream.

"In case there are any doubts this is the most demanding job I've ever had and the most stimulating." Studying between sessions and informing League members about legislative processes, she honed her lobbying techniques, signing letters "Exhaustedly but optimistically yours." In addition to keeping track of hundreds of bills and reporting about them in the *Alabama Voter*, Jane edited the *Capitol Newsletter*. A bi-weekly publication issued during the regular session, the newsletter analyzed selected bills, focusing on public interests such as education and consumer protection in the legislature.

Descriptions including bill number, sponsor, status, and League support or opposition with an explanation of potential effects were provided to educate the "well informed, effective citizen." Jane humorously commented on the demands of her volunteer position: "Frankly, I could easily utilize a larger budget. Couldn't we all? A personal secretary would be a great convenience."

Jane contacted as many legislators as possible, interviewing them by asking for information and advice on specific issues. She dispersed League publications to every legislator, outlining League interests and describing community service activities. Jane clipped and stuffed newspaper articles about legislators in their mailbox, explaining "most legislators find this hard to resist. Once you have established this relationship, the opportunity for pushing League's position becomes more readily available."

Jane attempted to be extremely polite when meeting with legislators, apologizing when she felt that she had taken too much time to inform them of the League's position on bills. "Time is one obstacle to communication. It's difficult to reach the legislator to whom you want to speak in the time available to you and him." A familiar sight in the capitol's halls, "I don't like to lobby by calling a legislator out of a session. I prefer to talk to him either before or after the session."

It was difficult not to get personally involved in every legislative item. "It's all so interesting and I become involved so easily." It was difficult to determine the League's exact effect because other groups actively lobbied the legislature, Jane concluded that "it is easier to kill a bill than to pass one." She noted that few bills opposed by the League actually passed, and "Our batting average is 41% which is very respectable. Our communication trees are working and definitely have had an impact."

In 1966 Jane represented the League supporting a resolution for equalization of assessment of property taxes. During the next year, she lobbied for increased appropriations for education, criticizing legislators for not funding growing enrollments. She urged them to seek new funding sources to improve public education and explained that conditional appropriations limited administrators from adequately staffing and equipping schools.

Jane considered the legislative sessions exhilarating but also disappointing due to the influence of special interests. "It has been a frustrating experience," she described the 1967 regular session, "caused primarily by the antagonism between rural and urban forces. Hopefully this antagonism can be called 'growing pains,' and the future will bring greater harmony." The legislators were well aware of Jane's presence in the chambers, and when the *Alabama Voter* reported about the 1967 League Legislative Day, it noted "Our attractive legislative chairman, Mrs. Warren Katz, took some cheerful ribbing from Rep. [Pete] Matthews when he spoke of recent committee hearings on education and schools and commented that Mrs. Katz 'was always there, of course—and always made a statement, of course.'"

Jane tenaciously followed the legislature. "All in all the 1969 session saw much of the LWV program enacted into law. Because there was such heavy opposition to much of the educational program, it seems obvious to me that most legislators had heard from you Leaguers." Two years later she reported that "the 1971 regular session of the legislature is being designated a failure because it failed to pass several vital pieces of legislation, i.e., the general fund and education appropriation bills, ad valorem tax equalization, redistricting, and reapportionment.

"There is not a simple answer to the question, 'Why?' Acceptance of legislative reform would certainly help. However, the basic struggle for power will go on as it is part and parcel of the political process." She elaborated that the "power struggle during this session was accentuated by the smallness of the governor's mandate, his concern with national politics, the push for legislative independence, and a jostling for power among possible 1974 gubernatorial contenders.

"In spite of these obstacles, some accomplishments should be noted. This legislature did begin to act like an independent branch of government! They did demonstrate greater fiscal responsibility. The seeds of concern for Alabama consumers and the mentally retarded and ill have been planted and are beginning to grow. And they did pass some significant legislation!" The air pollution control bill, which Jane had testified for, was one of these successes.

Katz spent the early 1970s training a lobbying corp to address the legislature. She often spoke to Alabama Leagues and university classes about her experiences at legislative sessions, labeling herself a professional but unpaid "lobbyist." Her volunteer work as legislative chairman prepared her for the legislative challenges of the 1970s. In 1973 with League State Election Laws Chairman Olivia Harrison, President Phyllis Rea, and an American Civil Liberties Union attorney, Jane Katz drafted election law reform bills.

The bills provided employees time off from work to register and vote as well as preserved the rights of absentee voters, better defined residency and eligibility to vote, and required frequent re-identification of voters. "Local Leagues are going to have to stress to the legislators how very important it is to us that Alabama have an election system that facilitates registration and voting, that is as fraud-free and as uniformly administered as possible." The League's attempts at election reform were not immediately successful, but were eventually incorporated into state law.

Jane's next major lobbying issue was the Equal Rights Amendment. "Lobby your legislators and your friends for ERA. This is an issue where quality counts and thousands of regularly sent letters, etc., reminding your legislator to vote for ratification will make a difference! Equality of rights under the law regardless of sex is a broad and basic principle which should be a part of our constitution." She told legislators that opposition to ERA was "based on fear of radical judicial interpretation and a total lack of understanding of how judicial interpretation is developed.

"League members are, for the most part, homemakers and mothers—a few of us also work outside our homes," Jane stated. "We fully realize that discrimination because of sex will not immediately disappear with ratification of the ERA, but we are directed to the dream that our children and grandchildren (be they girls or boys) will be able to face life with, at the very least, an equal opportunity under the law."

At an ERA Rally on April 28, 1973, Jane stressed that "the reality is that the law of this nation is not always for all because it is not always equal and the administration of the law is not always equal. Our Constitution and Bill of Rights are truly remarkable documents, . . . but the constitution was not perfect; it treated black people as property and women as non-legal persons. I do not expect miracles. I know that the opposition to the Equal Rights Amendment comes from men and women who are comfortable with inequality. They are use to it. It's a habit and habits don't disappear easily or quickly."

She testified in support of ERA before a senate committee in 1973. The Alabama legislature, however, voted against ERA. Disappointed because she believed that ERA would have opened educational and employment opportunities, Jane also thought "It would [have added] dignity to the homemaker and mother because she could choose to be in the home, and the ERA would point in the direction of that American dream of recognizing each person as an individual."

Jane refocused on other issues before the legislature. She was especially irritated that the legislature failed to pass so much important legislation in 1973, primarily because it would be two years before the next legislature met. She especially centered her criticism that no strip mining controls, consumer protection, or election law reforms passed, noting "on one hand we appropriate money to Auburn University to find ways to grow food, and on the other hand, ravage the land making it unsuitable to support growth."

Angry that not even simple election reforms passed, "Constitutional revision, I'm afraid, is going to take a constitutional convention. There are those who believe that the only insurance against an irresponsible government is constitutional restraint. This method of control has proved self-defeating in that it has prevented state government from meeting the needs of a dynamic society. Is it not better to give government the power necessary to meet its obligations and keep it honest through an informed and concerned citizenry?"

She considered the passing of the ethics bill to be "amazing," stressing that legislators need to know more "about where the state ought to move and who the people are" instead of concentrating on reelection and networking within the political system for votes. Labeling the session a "disaster" because so many legislators campaigned for governor and reelection, Jane pushed for annual legislative sessions to handle the plethora of bills. "Industry uses the legislature as a tool. They're afraid if they meet more often, they'll have more time to consider issues."

Jane Katz considered the League's careful study of select issues crucial for gaining legislative respect. "As legislative chairman, I find that when I go into the legislature and I speak on an issue, I speak with a whole lot of background because we've done that study, the material is there, and I speak knowing that there is a real consensus in the League,"

She also empowered the League with her biweekly newsletter and an annual legislative report, the *Voter Record*, compiled at her Laurel Lane home. Published at the end of each session, the *Record* listed every legislator and his or her action on selected bills which represented statewide interests. It listed many controversial bills such as the death penalty and ethics legislation. Not only did it inform constituents of major legislative issues and how their representatives voted, but it also provided vital information to legislators. "Even legislators find out how they're voting. Sometimes it's shocked them." Legislators from areas in Alabama without a League gained positive contact with League members through this service.

League President Phyllis Rea affirmed that this publication prodded legislators to consider the League more seriously. Sarah Cabot Pierce, who also presided over the state League, called the *Voter Record* "one of [Jane's] most valuable deeds for the people of Alabama." Distributed to public libraries and individuals, the legislative *Voting Record*, was totally objective with no analysis or commentary. It helped citizens evaluate legislators' performance and understand legislative processes. It also aided citizens in making voting decisions for future elections. 77

Disgruntled with the legislature, Jane decided to run for public office. In January 1974 League president June McBride announced Jane's candidacy for State Representative James Harris's seat for House District 81. As required by the League, Jane resigned from the board of directors and challenged well-entrenched ideas about women in politics. Alabama politicians, traditionally dominated by the white male "big mules" of the Democratic party, had been condescending to the few women legislators who entered the chamber. From the first woman legislator in Alabama, Hattie Hooker Wilkins in 1922, through the 1970s, the press labeled women legislators as "lipstick lawmakers," "Democratic darlings," and legislative "sweethearts."

Jane, however, had the self-confidence to challenge the "good old boys" system and attempted to change the state through the political process to accomplish her goals. She stressed that she was running for office because too many legislators were representatives of narrow special interest groups and that she thought the state needed an issue-oriented candidate who promoted state not local goals. Jane described herself as a "consumer-oriented housewife with no conflicts of interest."

She considered her most effective tactic to be door-to-door campaigning: "I thought I could get to every house in my district which turned out to be an exaggeration of my walking ability." In addition to making meaningful personal contacts, she also distributed letters to collect financial and voter support as well as using personal notes, yard signs, campaign cards in local business, and radio and television advertisements. She accrued enough primary votes to be in the run-off with incumbent Harris, but she lost by 102 votes of 8,000 votes in the election. "After spending $8,000 and wearing out several pairs of shoes, probably the most concrete thing that I got out of it is that I'm almost never asked how to spell Katz."

The *Alabama Voter* lauded Jane when she decided to run again. "She is a believer in practicing what she preaches. . . . Twice she has campaigned for a seat in the legislature and it is a real loss to her district that she has been defeated twice." After her second unsuccessful legislative campaign against Larry Dixon, Jane returned to her portfolio as League legislative chairman. She frequently lectured about her legislative campaigns.

With Auburn League members, she discussed the pros and cons of women campaigning for political office in Alabama. Jane stressed that candidates for political office must sincerely like people and be totally committed to their campaign, which she noted often seemed to usurp twenty-five hours a day, requiring great amounts of energy and excitement to keep going. Jane warned that a candidate's entire life revolved around the campaign and that support from the candidate's family and spouse were essential. She did not regret her decision to run and encouraged other women to contemplate political campaigns to publicize crucial statewide issues.

Jane spoke at workshops and on Alabama Public Television, narrating how political campaigns function and serving as a panelist for a special on legislative effectiveness. She also visited Leagues and women's groups to discuss lobbying techniques, describing it as the art of persuasion. According to Jane, "almost everyone has a special interest of some kind. All public officials need us. They need our opinions." Jane advised lobbyists to "develop a case and analyze your opposition" then seek support because "all public officials want some sort of justification for making any change."

Most importantly, lobbyists should present information in an understandable format and "assume a total lack of knowledge" from the legislator—explain jargon and abbreviations. She promoted using public relations techniques because "the fact that information on your issue is in the newspaper or radio [broadcasts] automatically makes it more important in the mind of an official." She advocated that lobbyists should acquire committee assignment lists and a legislative phone book with home, office, and Montgomery numbers.

The best way to sway legislators is personal contact."You may talk to a legislator anywhere you can get a hold of him. And don't apologize. After all, they ran for the job." Lobbyists should acquire a legislative magazine with photographs of legislators or ask pages and "ladies of the rotunda" to identify legislators. She also advised lobbyists to become familiar with legislature rules, such as when legislators can be called off the floor "but use this sparingly because this might make him miss the boat on voting on an issue."

Jane noted that committee meetings were excellent opportunities to achieve personal contact with representatives because "Here you get a feel for the people." She recommended that lobbyists wear name tags, identifying their organization too, and introduce themselves every time they contacted a legislator to make him or her more comfortable. "Try to say something nice, if at all possible—even if you are furious that they raised their pay on the first day of the session."

"Be as brief as you can and to the point. Try to talk on one issue at a time even though you have a laundry list of things on your mind. And for heaven's sake, smile." Initiating conversations with a question about a legislator's opinion on an issue is "good psychology and good use of time." During the lengthy, complicated process as a bill becomes a law, Jane urged lobbyists to follow the bill and utilize "telephone trees" to achieve "mass contact" with lawmakers. Lobbyists and their telephone contacts should write legislators about the bill especially at crucial moments such as when it is in committee or on the governor's desk. Although quantity influenced legislators, at least one "nice thoughtful letter" should be sent to a legislator, "so, when he decides he supports your issue, he'll know why."

Jane lobbied in the Capitol's hallways and chambers so much that she was on a first-name basis with many Alabama legislators. She believed that many of the legislators valued her because they often asked for help from the League to resolve political issues. Sarah Cabot Pierce insisted that, "They respect Jane particularly because she knows as much as they do and she's got a very bright mind." Albert P. Brewer, when he was speaker of the Alabama House of Representatives, thanked Jane for sending him League publications and suggestions, praising her, "I invite your attention at any time you are interested in pending legislation, and I look forward to working with you during this regular session."

Jane's sense of humor and diplomatic manner also won her friends in the statehouse. When a "particular League group accosted" Senator Larry Dumas, Jane wrote him a letter, enclosing a bottle of aspirin. "I thought they were out of line and have been looking for an opportunity to apologize," she wrote, assuring him that the League respected and valued him as a legislator. In return, Dumas apologized for a facetious remark he made: "I spoke before I thought. I should not have done so, and I apologize for any innuendo of disrespect. I am happy to have the League of Women Voters whisper to or counsel with me at any time."

"I've been there a long time, . . . the fact that I'm there for so many years has helped some; they don't have to worry about who is the legislative chairman this year. Everybody knows me." The abundance of bills to support and oppose decreased her effectiveness in the legislature. "I've tried to get the League to cut down to one or two issues," but the seriousness of much legislation prevented this. Also, the League often made a difference when two strong lobbying groups such as the AEA or Farm Bureau supported an issue. "If someone's pushing" a legislator, and they "have no [financial] axe to grind, I think he's responsive to that. I think we are amazingly effective considering our numbers and considering the number of things that we put our noses into." The League represented the positive aspects of lobbying for all citizens.

As a result of her legislative activity, Jane received numerous awards. In 1973 the Montgomery County Bar Association named her the first woman finalist for the Liberty Bell Award, recognizing her encouragement of the community to better understand and respect the government. Two years later, the Alabama Women's Political Caucus designated Jane Katz as Outstanding Political Woman for the year. The awards ceremony celebrated her lobbying, especially for women's issues, including ERA, that promoted gender equality. The *Alabama Voter* praised, "Congratulations, Jane!! You bring honor to us all."

In 1980 the Mental Health Association of Montgomery honored Jane for her "outstanding service," specifically for educating the organization on how to lobby for which it received national recognition. Serving her hometown throughout her life, Jane was appointed to the Montgomery County Board of Equalization in 1980. She also was a member of the Governor's Council on Libraries and Information Services. Jane was active in the Montgomery League, serving on several committees, including publications, constitutional revision, consumer protection, and voter service. Jane's community involvement often influenced the issues she lobbied on behalf of in the statehouse; she testified about the Department of Youth Services in 1976, stating "We urge you not to recommend its termination. However, we realize some changes are in order."

By 1979, when newly elected administrators and legislature ushered in a new group of politicians, Jane demanded that League members send her ideas and recommendations because "This new legislature needs input from the citizens of Alabama. It especially needs input from Alabama Leaguers."

She described the new legislature to League members. "A vigorous, young, lieutenant governor sought changes in the Senate, and, while maybe the Senate did not run like clockwork, it ran with relatively little squeakiness and grinding. The new governor came with 'new beginnings' a 'war on illiteracy' and the 'politics of unselfishness.' He was not overly successful, but he will certainly learn from experience. The House leadership was not new and the House ran pretty much as it has always run."

Jane Katz promoted the League as social advocate. "You have to be very careful because what happened with the early League in Alabama," she suggested, "they were taking positions and passing resolutions on everything and anything and when you're spread way too thin you can lose your membership support." She also noted, "the League is always ahead of everybody else practically and the little delicate problem is, that's fine to be ahead of everybody, but if you're too far ahead, you lose them. You look back and there's no one there."

Alabama League members recognized Jane's valuable input to the state League, and many leaders such as Sarah Cabot Pierce believed Jane should have been on the National

Board and guided national League policy. Although she never was named to the National Board, Jane did participate in national activities, such as attending the national council with state delegates.

She continued to devote her energy to observing the state legislature, especially crucial special sessions regarding school prayer and textbooks. She complained that "the 1983 legislative session was unusually frustrating" when a federal court ruled that every legislator would have to campaign in 1983. "Suddenly everyone is a candidate, and they have hardly had time to learn how to be an elected official. Because of vast inexperience and because most legislators felt that the less they voted, the less ammunition they would give opponents running against them, the leadership in each house had pretty tight control."

Jane promoted reforms such as full disclosure of campaign finances, a two party system, a strong press, and involved citizens. "You've got to stop reelecting those who are using their positions to line their own pockets or to lobby for their own interests. You've got to really get angry about it." She also defended the legislature, "Alabama citizens think a lot more is withheld from them than actually is. I have found the Legislature, by and large, to be a very open-minded body. There's always someone in the League keeping an eye on what's going on."

At the 1985 regular session, Jane supported Voter File Maintenance legislation, designed to prevent duplication on the rolls, to remove voters who had moved out of state, and to require deletion of voters who had not voted for four years unless they were re-identified. She lobbied for amendments regarding background checks of child care providers, regulation of political action committees, enforcement of ethics legislation, protection of environmental issues, and entrenchment of pro-equality legislation.

"I, myself, breathed a huge sigh of relief that the session was over!" Jane remarked after the 1986 regular legislative session, riddled with delays and stalled bills by legislators hesitant to handle legislation while attempting to get reelected. Despite the long hours and irritating filibusters, Jane enjoyed her lobbying. She especially treasured acquiring new insights and knowledge about people and politicians. "I empathized with Governor Wallace when he said, `I've been around for a long time, and I find out something new every day.' Me, too, governor, me too!"

Throughout her service as legislative chairman, Jane endured a heart condition and diabetes. Fifty-five year old Jane Katz died on August 18, 1986, in Birmingham's University Hospital after open heart surgery. Her sudden death was a shock to the community. It also occurred during a time of political turmoil in the state when the Democratic party split, enabling the first Republican governor since Reconstruction to be elected. Jane would have enjoyed following that development.

The August 1986 *Alabama Voter* eulogized, "As League leader and friend, she will be missed beyond measure," and promised that memorials to the League would be used "to carry on Jane's lifetime commitment to good government in Alabama." The League of Women Voters Papers in the Auburn University Archives contains many of Jane's letters and legislative statements, preserving her warm and witty sense of humor and passionate but often acerbic insights about Alabama politics.

written by Elizabeth D. Schafer

MARY EUGENIA MARTIN
1878 - 1963
I Would The Gods Had Made Thee Poetical.

Mary Eugenia Martin best wish for her college classmates was a talent to be poetical. A life-long admirer of literature, Mary devoted her life to promoting enhanced cultural opportunities and to providing better library services in Alabama. As president of the Alabama Library Association, she campaigned for expanded library facilities. She established county library systems to make books available to rural residents. A suffragist, she also supported equal opportunities for women. The building on Auburn University's campus where she worked as head librarian was named in her honor.

Born on October 5, 1878, at Easley, South Carolina, the daughter of C.Y. and Eugenia Martin (the family called her mother Jenny), Mary and her siblings—Charles, Ben, James, and Beryl—were educated at home and in private schools. In addition to selling insurance, Mary's father, a native Alabamian of Scots-Irish descent, edited the town's newspaper and had a knack for writing a good feature article.

At age eighteen, Mary took examinations to enter the junior class of Winthrop Normal and Industrial College at Rock Hill, South Carolina. Established in 1886, this state institution offered both undergraduate and graduate courses for female students. Mary studied traditional classes such as history, English, Latin, French, pedagogy, physical culture, domestic science, and sight singing, as well as such scientific fare as chemistry, geology, astronomy, and solid geometry.

Obeying rigid school rules regarding behavior and dress (the college uniform varied according to seasons), Mary attended church every Sunday and never missed her classes. Such strict standards extended to campus cultural activities, including lectures, concerts, and the Star Course entertainment series.

Named her class's poet, Mary joined the Shakespeare Club and literary society, assisting with the group's magazine. Winning numerous friends with her gregarious manner, Mary was elected to a term as school treasurer. Underneath her yearbook portrait, the following verse memorialized Mary Martin:

> We wonder why
> She is so shy
> When teachers are around;
> While any day,
> With classmates gay,
> No merrier maid is found.

The senior class prophesied that Mary "will for a short time contribute her poetical gems to the leading papers, but later her sphere will broaden and she will edit a paper of her own." Proud of their fellow classmate, the girls predicted, "A brilliant future lies before her, which is only the climax of her former successful attempts."

Surrounded by her senior class flower, the rose, and crimson bunting (another senior class favorite), Mary graduated in 1898. Participating in a commencement program from June 5th to 8th, Mary listened to the baccalaureate sermon and concerts and enjoyed a literary society celebration, receptions hosted by her teachers, and class day exercises. South Carolina Attorney General William A. Barber was the speaker. Her high grades earned her membership in Phi Kappa Phi.

From 1898 to 1905, Mary taught elementary classes in the public schools of Greenville, South Carolina, serving as principal for five of those years. She enrolled in the Southern Library School in Atlanta, Georgia, and completed library training in 1905. School principal Delia Foreacre Sneed annotated a list of graduates, commenting by Mary's name that she was "good, able." Sneed was not as complimentary with other students, whom she described as "impossible" and "light weight" pupils who "just scraped through." The library school was incorporated into the Carnegie Library School, the precursor of Emory's library school, in 1907.

Mary returned to her alma mater. She was employed as assistant librarian at Winthrop's Carnegie Library for six years, from 1906 to 1912. She was particularly skilled at cataloguing, and performed this work during summer sessions at the Guilford and Hollins college libraries. A talented scholar of French and German, Mary specifically catalogued works written in those languages.

In July 1910, Mary wrote Winthrop's president, D.B. Johnson, that "Without any solicitation on my part, I have been elected first assistant in the Birmingham Public Library." She admitted that she was enticed by Birmingham's salary but would like to work at Winthrop at least one more year because "it will be better for me to stay on" at a place which "has grown to seem like home to me." She was hesitant "to give up college library work." Asking "to share the teaching" load with the head librarian, Miss Dacus, Mary stressed, "It will mean harder work for me but an experience which will be useful to me."

Two years later in 1912, the Alabama Polytechnic Institute's board of trustees sought an assistant librarian to replace recently married Lucile Virden. Recommended by the principal of her Atlanta library school, Mary was especially suited for the work at Auburn's Carnegie library because of her cataloguing expertise. She represented one of the few library school graduates employed in Alabama. Only approximately fifteen of the several hundred librarians in the state had completed an accredited program at that time.

Prior to that time, most of Auburn's librarians had been adjunct professors. Women filled clerical and assistant positions. Head librarians in the early days were usually English professors, such as Mary's supervisor, Dr. James R. Rutland, the grandson of Georgia's "lost poet" Dr. Thomas Holley Chivers, who allegedly inspired his friend Edgar Allan Poe to write "The Raven."

Hired on August 15, 1912, Mary Martin reported to Auburn's campus. By New Year's Eve she wrote Johnson, expressing thanks for "a Christmas gift which delighted me very much." Discussing a vacancy at Winthrop, Mary revealed that adjusting to life in Auburn was difficult. "In spite of my homesickness for Winthrop and some uncomfortable conditions at Auburn," she commented, "I am interested enough in the library and in my professional reputation to determine to stay there until I can leave it in something like the order which Miss Dacus and I were proud of having at Winthrop."

Because her father was in poor health, Mary stated that she had refused positions and tenure at larger libraries because the future was "extremely uncertain." Although she found Alabama to be bleak, "So far as I can see right now, I shall remain in Auburn two years."

Instead, Mary Martin spent most of her life in Auburn, improving Alabama's library services. "Miss Mary," as students and faculty called her, quickly became known for her no-nonsense, serious, business-like demeanor. Auburn resident Ann Pearson recollected Mary's stern manner, noting "to generations of Auburn students, Miss Martin maintained old-fashioned library discipline and earned a reputation of never being amused."

Mary rarely smiled, and students quickly learned to whisper in her presence or else risk a sharp reprimand of "Hush up!" Remembered as running a tight ship, Mary Martin quickly quieted noise makers. Dr. Howard Strong, who worked with Mary when he was a student, stated that "Miss Mary E. made herself pretty well known." He explained that "there were very few people who went into the library who didn't see or maybe hear Miss Martin." Despite her strict rules, "she was the only one who could make noise in the library. She could stamp around as loud as she wanted to." Strong joked that she "sounded like a race horse [and was] sometimes screaming for everybody else to quit whispering." Mary also carefully monitored student access to stacks, pouncing on one youngish-appearing female faculty member whom Mary mistook for a student because she was wearing bobby socks. Her offence? Not having put in a request to obtain admittance to the shelves.

According to campus lore, Mary knew every book in the library. Her extensive memory allowed her to have an almost encyclopedic knowledge of every title and author catalogued as well as of the precise location of materials. Such comprehension permitted Mary to be aware of books which she deemed inappropriate for young college students.

Restricting books with language she considered profane to the back shelf of closed stacks, Mary imposed her own form of censorship. Only she and student workers (coeds worked in the library for tuition money) could retrieve the books for patrons, and the library clerks gained many friends while guarding Miss Mary's banned books.

Mary had loved flowers since she was a girl. She planted a variety of flora around the library. She cultivated a large garden behind the library, and cut flowers to arrange in vases for the reading room. Considered "quite a horticulturist," Miss Martin utilized her coffee breaks, "digging around her iris and spider lily bulbs." She was not able to see well, and sometimes she accidentally planted one bulb on top of another. Her garden earned her public acclaim, inspiring one reporter to pen a newspaper article, "Librarian Mary, How Does Your Garden Grow?"

Mary also suffered as a result of her garden. Carrying on a "long running feud" with the ROTC cadets, Mary diligently protected her flowers. Every morning the boys, who lived east of the library, took a shortcut, straight across Miss Mary's garden, to the drill field on the other side (where the quad dorms are located now). At first she tried "to direct traffic," but the cadets boys divided "on either side of her," straight through her prized petals. Next, she erected a "barbed wire entanglement from one side of the lawn to another," but campus authorities asked her to remove the barrage.

"Still not to be outdone," Mary "stationed herself one day out behind one of the big bushes." Connecting a water hose to a nearby spigot, she asked the library's janitor to hide by the faucet. "Just as the wave of cadets started across the lawn," Mary signaled the janitor, shouting, "Okay, Hut, let them have it." Waving the hose, she "generously sprinkled about fifty cadets who had to report to the drill field dripping wet."

Mary became one of Auburn's favorite eccentric characters. Auburn journalist, Ann Pearson, portrayed Mary as the ideal "librarian of yesteryear—the high jabot and steel-rimmed spectacles." Far from being a clotheshorse, the blue-eyed, blond Mary dressed like a scarecrow with no sense of fashion, as her first cousin, Edna Neal, described her. Mary draped her svelte 5'9" frame with simple frocks. Every so often, Mary was known for writing Sears Roebuck and telling them to "send me a hat—your choice."

Mary, proud of her English heritage, habitually served tea in the library at 4 o'clock in the afternoon "whether her employees liked tea or not." One student recalled that many workers abhorred the taste and "sometimes some of the tea got poured" on her potted plants.

Mary developed a reputation as a skilled librarian, and succeeded Rutland as head librarian in December 1918 when he retired. The founder of the Alabama Library Association, Rutland served two terms as president from 1921 to 1922. Mary held offices and participated on the membership committee. For thirty-seven years, this professional organization not only gave her a forum to address library issues, but it also aided her in enlarging Auburn's library.

Twice president of the Alabama Library Association, Mary implemented vital programs. First elected at the 1931 meeting, Mary, as first vice-president, also served out the 1938 term of Mrs. Avis Dawson when she died. Campaigning for expanded library facilities in Alabama, Mary promoted county library systems which made books available to rural residents who lacked library facilities. During her first presidential term, the Rosenwald Fund granted Alabama $7,500 over a three year period to finance a library field worker to establish county libraries.

Mary voiced her interest in creating a state library commission to increase the availability of library books to more citizens. In 1939, she noted that only five states lacked a state library commission and that Alabama was the only southern state without a central library agency that could "bring library service to the door of every person in the state." According to Mary, a state library would offer direct book service until a community built a library.

She described North Carolina's library commission. "Here is a remarkable collection of books used for traveling libraries," which contains "mounted pictures and envelopes of clippings on every subject for debates and club papers." These resources were not only for use "at schools and post-offices, but ready for the call of individuals all over the state who need them for specific purposes." The Alabama Library Association members' efforts have provided a state library service in Montgomery for many years.

Mary Martin supported the Alabama Library Association when it presented library bills before the state legislature. She wryly commented about her qualifications as a public speaker, "Poor, but willing; not often asked." Mary also joined the American Library Association, Alabama Educational Association, and Auburn Public Library Association.

Despite the difficult eras in which she worked, during the Depression and World War II, Mary increased library services at Auburn. From 1929 to 1937, she directed the establishment of five branch libraries on campus. Two still exist: veterinary medicine and architecture. She also supervised additions to the Carnegie Library which were completed by 1940.

Seriously tending the library like her garden, Mary's collection blossomed from 15,000 to 100,004 volumes in 1944 when she resigned as head librarian (the position of library director was created that year). Since 1934 she had especially focused on acquiring Alabama materials and first editions written by Alabama writers. During her final five years at Auburn, she expanded this collection. These books are currently housed in the Alabama Room of Auburn University's special collections.

She left Auburn sporadically on one-month leaves during the winters to visit her ailing father. She never drove and always took the train home. When her father died in October 1939, she wrote Auburn President Ralph B. Draughon, from South Carolina, "Most sincerely I thank you for the message of sympathy." She elaborated, "My father was so discouraged over his helplessness and growing blindness that we feel he has what he so often implored his physician to give him relief.'"

Mary Martin continued her professional and scholarly pursuits. An avid reader, she enjoyed helping as well as challenging English instructors, including her former student worker Howard Strong. He recalled, "Miss Martin was a big help to me when I was teaching English because she was quite a good resource person," alerting him when new books arrived at the library.

She also corrected him one morning when he was teaching in a temporary building with low windows located behind the library. Lecturing to an American literature section on modern poets, Strong absentmindedly said one poet's name when he actually meant another. "As I did, this head popped through the window, and it was Miss Martin who was right outside the window eavesdropping as she dug around her plants," he narrated. Rebuking him sharply, she declared, "Howard, that was Robinson. It wasn't Frost at all." He invited her inside the classroom, and "It was the next best thing to having the poet come in because Miss Martin delivered quite a nice impromptu lecture." Other students and faculty members claimed similar memories of Mary. "I think Miss Martin was a rather remarkable librarian in that she was always extremely helpful to young students who had a desire for research and information," Draughon lauded. "I recall that she used to allow me to remain in the library beyond the closing hours at night as I worked on my thesis for the master's degree in history." He also noted, "She was greatly beloved by those of us who were fortunate enough to be in college or on the faculty while she served this institution."

Active in the Auburn community, Mary joined the Presbyterian church and was a charter member of the Auburn Women's Club. As president of the local Women's Christian Temperance Union, she chided her cousins for parking in front of Opelika's liquor store. She was afraid that someone might mistakenly think she was making a purchase. Mary also participated in Auburn's Little Theatre, the Business and Professional Women's Club, and Daughters of the American Revolution.

When the Auburn Equal Suffrage Association (AESA) was founded in August 1914, Mary was elected the group's first president. Meeting the third Wednesday of school months in members' homes, Mary often hosted the AESA in the college library. Also serving as secretary-treasurer, Mary lovingly recorded the AESA minutes in her distinctive cursive handwriting.

The women answered roll call with suffrage news or biographical sketches of prominent suffragists. Especially concerned with consumer and labor topics, mostly in regard to children and women, AESA members read the Woman's Journal in the college library. They planned their campaign to secure a federal suffrage amendment, discussing the protocol and parliamentary aspects of governmental and judicial systems.

In addition to researching Congress, Mary studied elections at the state and national level, compiling bibliographies of suffrage books to distribute at meetings. Mary practiced for debates with anti-ratification women, clipping newspaper articles. She presented papers about political issues and literary topics, being especially pleased with her report on the "Minimum Wage Law for Women."

Bedecked in yellow ribbons printed with the slogan "Votes for Women," Mary joined in humanitarian work, distributing garden seed to Auburn's black community to insure a supply of nutritious food. The AESA hosted a suffragette ball on April 1, 1916, with national suffragist, Lola C. Trax, visiting. The group staged the first public demonstration promoting suffrage passage in the South on April 10.

Decorating cars and a pony cart with yellow, black, and white streamers and pennants, representing the state and national suffrage campaign's colors, Mary rode in Auburn's suffrage parade. The procession circled the city before assembling in an open air meeting, where Trax and local members spoke, encouraging Auburn women to embrace their cause. A month later, on May 2, 1916, they celebrated National Suffrage Day with a symposium about why they were suffragists. Mary and other AESA members were selected to attend Alabama suffrage schools to learn more about the state's platform.

World War I presented the Auburn suffragists with a new set of problems. Trying to balance patriotism and pacifism, the women focused on attempts to relieve the hunger and pain of women and children in Europe. They compiled a book of wartime recipes to raise funds. The war overwhelmed the AESA. The group's last minutes are dated April 1918 when the national flu epidemic struck Auburn, and the women were engulfed with service work. Closing the library for one month, Mary volunteered as a practical nurse in the diet kitchens of temporary flu hospitals on campus. Although local suffrage work had been abandoned, she welcomed the Nineteenth Amendment two years later, dutifully entering the election box to mark her ballot in local, state, and national elections.

Mary roomed with several local women in boarding houses near campus, living at 118 North Gay St. with Mollie Hollifield who later donated this land for Auburn's public library. Several of Mary's relatives lived in the Auburn area, and Mary enjoyed visiting her nieces, nephews, and cousins, giving the children books for Christmas and birthdays and telling them adventurous yet virtuous stories.

Always a thin woman, Mary lost weight as she aged but insisted that her health was "fairly good" and that she had not "missed any time since Nov. 1939." On her campus personnel form, she stated that her only infirmities were her glasses and painful corns from being on her feet all day in the library.

She also proudly asserted her financial health, revealing that she had never declared bankruptcy or encountered any other legal problems. When she first came to Auburn, her salary was less than $1,500, increasing, with cost of living raises, to $2,520 when she retired. She invested most of these funds into real estate and the Easley Savings and Trust.

State regulations required that she retire at age seventy. Auburn's President Draughon told his secretary, "I'd like to do something nice for Miss M. I love her." He wanted "appropriate action" taken to express appreciation for her devotion to the college as a "faithful employee." He asked Clyde Cantrell, who became the library's first director in 1944, to consult with Mary's friends and co-workers about suggestions to honor her.

The committee considered continuing the garden which "Miss Martin has loved and tended so carefully during the years," giving her a set of matched luggage "which she needs very badly," binding a collection of letters from her "hundreds of friends," and having a portrait painted of her. They also suggested that the Carnegie library be named in her honor and that a collection of books, distinguished with engraved book plates, be added to the library, noting that she was especially fond of tomes about England during Shakespeare's time and children's stories. Mary was honored in most of these ways, although many memorials were not enacted until after her death.

At Mary's retirement reception on June 30, 1949, Draughon told her that Auburn would never be the same without her meticulous service. He reminisced gratefully, "I shall never forget the many kindnesses which you showed to me as a librarian." In particular, "you made me feel that the library was a wonderful place in which to work and learn."

Draughon recalled "with a great deal of pleasure the help that you and your staff gave to me in my efforts to set up reading shelves in Government, International Law, and Political Science." He humorously remembered, "I am sure that I, and my students, must have caused you an occasional worry" but "I believe that all of us always felt that you were a person who stood ready and willing at any time to help anyone who wanted to learn something." This, he concluded, "is the highest tribute that could be paid to a librarian," wishing her good "health and happiness."

Mary returned home to Easley. Contented to be home with her brothers and their families, she lived in a small house and rented office space to several doctors. Occasionally, she visited Auburn and examined the collections that she helped to establish. The library committee expressed its appreciation for her "excellent work through the years." They acknowledged that "against almost insurmountable difficulties and with very meager financial support which was common to all Southern institutions of the period," Mary "laid the groundwork for the library program as we have it today."

Mary's poor eyesight deteriorated, and glaucoma blinded her. Family members and friends read her beloved books to her. "Considering the uncertainty of my earthly existence," Mary, who never married, signed a will leaving her property – her father's farm, town lots in Easley and Clemson, Alabama Power Company stocks, and her personal effects and furniture – to her brothers and sister.

In her hometown, Mary Martin died on April 9, 1963, at the age of eighty-four, after suffering an extended illness. The July 1963 *Alabama Librarian* printed her obituary. Paying tribute to her "remarkable" service, librarians praised Mary because "her efforts have been far-reaching and significant." Draughon wrote Mary's family in South Carolina that he was "extremely saddened" to learn of the death of a "wonderful person" whom he "loved and respected."

Auburn founded the Mary Eugenia Martin Memorial Book fund, asking for donations of money or books to build the library's holdings. Designed "as a lasting memorial" to Mary "who loved Auburn so dearly and who worked for its betterment" by "improving the quality of the book collection and the services the Library offered," the Alabama Room's resources have aided scholars throughout the state.

"Eternally grateful" to Mary Martin, the University commemorated her by naming the Carnegie Library in her honor after the larger Ralph B. Draughon Library opened in 1963. Renovated into offices for the registrar and other administrators, Mary E. Martin Hall on West Thach Avenue was christened in a dedication ceremony on November 20, 1964. A portrait of Mary, elegantly attired in a pale blue dress, was presented to be displayed in the building.

In addition to being considered an influential woman in Auburn's history, Mary gained statewide recognition for her outstanding library service. In 1980 the Alabama Library Roll of Honor saluted her as a librarian who had significantly contributed both to the advancement of her profession and to the betterment of Alabama.

Auburn University's archives maintain Mary's suffrage, personnel, and library papers, and the Alabama Library Association's records are in the Alabama Department of Archives and History in Montgomery. Both collections chronicle aspects of Mary's life and career.

Mary Martin believed that good books and conscientious people were necessary for a library to thrive. By concentrating her efforts on enhancing both the quantity and quality of Auburn University's library, she contributed not only to scholarship of the campus's faculty and student population but to the strengthening of Alabama's cultural milieu as a whole. Her endeavors to improve and increase library services, public and college, throughout the state were perhaps her most notable professional achievement.

written by Elizabeth D. Schafer

EULA MCGILL
1911 -

Try To Do Something To Help Others. Be Politically Active. Do What You Want To, If You Can. Always Have Goals In Life.

Eula McGill, at age 83 is still physically strong in spite of using a cane. She is best known for her contributions to the union movement and her advocacy of workers' rights and responsibilities. Ironically, she was not even a union member when she was fired from her first adult job for what was perceived to be union activity. She had gone to Washington D.C. with members of the Women's Trade Union League. The publicity generated by an invitation to the White House by Eleanor Roosevelt led to the loss of her job in the cotton mill. She had first worked at the mill as a fourteen-year-old.

Thus began a forty-six-year career of union activity. She began as an organizer, which led to full time union work with the Amalgamated Clothing Workers of America, now called the Amalgamated Clothing and Textile Workers Union. Eula McGill's union responsibilities, which increased yearly, became her life work in a job that had been traditionally a male domain. She says that in her travels over the United States and Canada, the demands of the work and the need to be above criticism in her union contacts led her to avoid marriage. She had an early marriage that was brief. Then a marriage encounter at 43, but the best-loved man in her life died after twelve years of companionship without getting her to say "Yes."

For Eula McGill and her teenage peers, it was not unusual for them to end their education at junior high school, then marry at sixteen. For Eula, however, marriage was a brief and forgettable experience. Its only saving grace was her pride and joy in her son, Thomas Wilson McGill. Her parents, with her financial help, raised her only child with the same devotion that they always gave to her.

Joseph Hamilton and Mary Rachel Susann Wilson McGill moved to Alabama from Resaca, Georgia, after the mines "played out" and Eula's father needed work. Eula had been born May 15, 1911. She was five and had a sister seven years older when the family arrived in Gadsden. Her father worked as a carpenter until he was laid off at age 40. It was common at the time for a man of 40 to be considered over the hill for hard manual work, Eula says. Her uncle, a respected driller in Alabama, got her father a job on a dam project.

Hard times were taken for granted as the natural course of events. At fourteen Eula worked at the Dwight Mill in Gadsden. She had lied about her age. That summer she worked for six weeks as an unpaid trainee, and another six weeks with meager pay. It seemed natural that her early experiences with family, friends, and acquaintances' hard scrabble existences would lead her to spend her life fighting for other people's rights.

After having gone "on staff" with the union in 1937, she became the first woman business agent in 1943. This union job required her to negotiate and police contracts and grievances. It was not an easy job to get accepted by the local union members. She demanded that grievances be submitted with respect for the job that she was assigned. John Busby and John Carlton, attorneys, are given credit for instructing her in her early organizing activities.

Later, as joint board member, Eula used her experiences with workers and production lines not only to improve conditions for workers, but also to improve production for the plant managers and owners. She was always aware that higher pay and better working conditions resulted from workers taking responsibility for productivity. Joint board members were liaison between the union and management. Eula negotiated the rights and responsibilities of both.

Because Mollie Dowd of the Women's Trade Union League had helped organize the League of Women Voters of Alabama in 1920, Eula admired its goals. Eula had always wanted to join the League, but her travel and work took precedence. When she returned to Birmingham to live for the rest of her life and career, she joined the League and became a stalwart supporter, contributing both time and money. She has also been a strong advocate for a national health care plan. Finally retired, she can seldom be found at home during the day since she is still involved in political and community activity and encouraging others to be active also.

Eula McGill credits numerous people for helping her on her life's journey from her parents and teachers in her formative childhood years, to career help from the first president of the Amalgamated Clothing Workers of America, Sidney Hillman. She is very active, presenting her views and her memories of an exciting life in her vigorous, strong voice for all to hear.

written by LaVerne D. Ramsey

NINA MIGLIONICO

Keep At It, People Quit Too Soon.
Integrity and 'Stickability'
Are The Most Important Traits To Have.

Nina Miglionoco's lifetime achievements are unique for their quality and duration. After a public school education in Birmingham, Howard College (now Samford University), and the University of Alabama Law School, she is in her fifty-fifth year as a practicing attorney. Four other women were in the same law class. They all had lifetime careers in law while remaining supportive friends for each other wherever they lived. Elizabeth Johnson Wilbanks (deceased) of Alexander City was one. She lived in several foreign countries with her husband over the years while maintaining a law partnership back in Alexander City. She provided Nina with the opportunity for wonderful enriching visits during her vacations.

Long time friends Evelyn Keenon and Vivian Stanford are highly respected by the financial communities of Alabama. Evelyn Keenon was the first woman stock broker. Vivian Stanford was the first woman banker to become a bank officer without the benefit of family ownership. These three female pioneers belonged to Zonta, an international women's service club that, for women, was a counterpart of Rotary, Lions, and other clubs that were then exclusively male. In addition to contacts with the professional women of Zonta, they were a weekly threesome at lunch on

Saturdays for many years, a nurturing force for each other. Keenon and Stanford, now deceased, survived their husbands by many years. Even in retirement, they continued with Nina to offer encouragement to younger career women.

Her year of birth is guarded information. Miss Nina, as she is affectionately called by almost everyone was born to Mary Ann Marsicano and Marion Joseph Miglionioco on September 14. Her one sibling, Dr. John R. Hamilton, anglicized his name.

" Father said that I could do anything I wanted provided I got an education first. He went to the old First National Bank to borrow the money for me to go to law school. The bank president, General Persons, didn't think it was a good idea, but my father said, 'If I leave her money, it can be taken away, an education can't.'" Mr. Miglionico, without doubt, was a strong mentor for his daughter, encouraging a powerful mind housed in a very small body.

This diminutive dynamo is perhaps best known for her service on the Birmingham City Council. She was elected to the very first council in April, 1963. She was the first woman in many years to be elected to public office in Jefferson County and was reelected for five additional four-year terms. She was always supported by the votes of both black and white citizens, but in 1985 she chose not to run for reelection.

She had many other firsts. First woman president of the Alabama League of Municipalities, which serves all the elected officials of Alabama's cities and towns. In 1974, she was the first woman nominee of any party in Alabama for a congressional seat. In the Sixth Congressional District, she was defeated by the Republican incumbent in the general election. She was the first woman to be appointed and to serve on the Citizens Advisory Committee of the Commissioner of Internal Revenue. (1959-1961)

President John Kennedy appointed her as a member of the Committee on Insurance and Taxes of the President's Commission on the Status of Women. President Lyndon Johnson chose her as the only reappointment to serve on the new committee on the same subject during his administration.

The need for legislation to improve the lot of women and children was always a focus for Miss Nina. She made many appearances before the Alabama Legislature campaigning for better child labor laws, pure food and drug laws, and voting and ballot reforms. She was Vice Chairman for the Alabama Committee for Poll Tax Reduction and Elimination, Vice Chairman of the Alabama Committee for Jury Service for Women, and Chairman for Revision of Family Laws of Alabama.

Public service contributions resulting from her legal and political expertise were the presidency of the National Association of Women Lawyers, a two-year term membership of the House of Delegates of the American Bar Association (1959-61), committee memberships of the National and Alabama Leagues of Municipalities, the presidencies of the Birmingham and the Alabama Joint Legislative Councils, and the presidency of the Alabama Merit System League.

Included in her many years of community service to Birmingham, Jefferson County, the state of Alabama and the nation is leadership in numerous business, and professional associations and service clubs from the local to the national level. Organizations that have benefited from her membership are: Business and Professional Women's Clubs, Zonta International, League of Women Voters, YWCA, the Symphony Association, Birmingham Beautification Board, Children's Theatre, Jefferson County Mental Health Association, Family Court Advisory Committee, Women's Chamber of Commerce, Committee of 100 Women of Birmingham, Alabama Zoological Society, American Association of University Women, and Alabama Women's Hall of Fame.

Miss Nina has been a role model for participation in Alabama citizenship during her long career. She has spoken in almost every one of Alabama's sixty-seven counties and in twenty states on laws and issues concerning women. Women are now respected members of the legal profession, but it was the early career attorneys like Miss Nina who paved the way. After fifty-five years in the practice of law, she is still a dynamic professional and a civic activist.

written by LaVerne D. Ramsey

GLORIA NARRAMORE MOODY
1933 -

**My Love Affair With Music
Has Enhanced Every Part Of My Life.
And It Is Too Important Not To Share.**

Gloria Moody fell passionately in love with music as a child and this passion has inspired her life. The love of music has made Gloria not only a noted pianist, but a nationally known patron of the arts. In 1992 the Society of the Fine Arts presented her with their Patron of the Arts Award for her devotion to promoting world class music in Alabama through performances and scholarship. The Society of the Fine Arts is the University of Alabama's arts support organization in the College of Arts and Science.

Born in Tuscalooosa on December 27, 1933 to Benjamin and Coy Narramore. She has lived her whole life in Tuscaloosa. Her father worked for Gulf States Paper Company in Tuscaloosa. Gloria's parents were supportive of their daughter's precocious musical talents. Her father said, "She started playing before gammer school, when she was so small she couldn't even get up to the bench without help. I've always been proud of her."

When Gloria was eleven she was discovered by the chairman of the department of music at the University of Alabama. It was the summer of 1945 and Gloria was at

Girl Scout Camp Cherry Austin. She was accompanying her troop on a rickety upright piano in the camp's assembly hall. The chairman was there visiting his daughter who was singing along with the rest of the girls. He yelled over the music to ask Gloria her name, then her father's name. Without missing a beat, Gloria answered the questions.

Unknown to Gloria, "He went home, called my father, and said, I would like to see your child at the music department as soon as she gets home from camp.' So at the age of eleven I found myself entering the doors of the music building to study piano with Roy McAllister. That day marked the beginning of a lifelong love affair between me and the department of music at the University of Alabama."

UA music professor, pianist Amanda Ward Penick has known Gloria since they were children. "We both began studying with Roy McAllister as children. All I heard from Roy was about this talented younger student—Gloria. I didn't like hearing so much about her, but when I heard and saw her play, I understood why he thought her so special."

Just before she graduated from high school in 1952, her father bought her a Steinway piano. "My father went down to his friendly banker - who just happened to be a handsome young rake named Frank Moody (her future husband)." Much later after she and Frank were married he told her, "He was astounded by my father. Daddy's credit was solid, but Frank couldn't believe a man would pay that much for a piano. He told him, My goodness Ben - you could buy a new Buick for that.' Daddy has since told him he should have known then that I was expensive."

Although neither of her parents were musicians, they enjoyed their daughter's music. Her father said the Steinway and the lessons did not cause the family any great sacrifice because the house was always filled with his daughter's music. "It was a comforting sound, even to a poor fellow who was trying to sleep during enthusiastic practice sessions. I learned to hear it and not to hear it at the same time." There was other musical talent in the family. Gloria's two Narramore aunts enjoyed playing for the pleasure of it and for the enjoyment of Gloria and their family.

At the University of Alabama, Moody earned a bachelor's degree in music in 1956 then pursued graduate study. A petite, blue eyed beauty, she began teaching both privately and at the University. She also began a lifelong contribution of her talent as an organist to Christ Episcopal Church and other churches. Later after marrying Frank Moody, she went to New York City to study with Jeaneane Dowis.

In 1954 she married Hugh Rowe Thomas, the son of the Alabama's head football coach, Frank Thomas. They had two children, Hugh Rowe Thomas, Jr. and a daughter, Lee Thomas Walter who live in Birmingham, Alabama and Atlanta, Georgia. Hugh Thomas was in insurance and was a highly thought of state legislator. He was killed in a car wreck in 1967. The bridge was named for him that crosses over the Black Warrior River linking downtown Tuscaloosa to Northport.

Gloria was devastated by her loss. She turned to her music, her family and friends. Amanda Penick and Gloria have stayed friends through the years. They married about the same time and have children about the same ages. They were together after the tragedy as Gloria pulled herself together. Mrs. Penick said, "Gloria has the ability not to dwell on the tragic aspects of life and let it ruin her. She faces life with optimism for the future. This is one of her most outstanding qualities. She looks backward, but not to dwell on the bad. She doesn't let tragedies impact her optimism about life. Later when (her second husband) Frank died she prepared herself for his death, to be able to go on without him. He left her work to do and accounts to manage and she has taken them over and been able to go forward with all the projects.

"Her world and mine collect at points of time. We do things like perform together. I may not hear from or see her for six months then the phone will ring and it's like we were never apart. I miss not seeing her more often.

"She has a great deal of energy. I don't mean nervous energy. She may do twenty-four things in one week, but she never complains of being tired. I am a big admirer of her as well as a close friend. I support all her efforts. She is very diplomatic. She has learned the language of diplomacy. This is a struggle at times, but she always manages it. She is always nice to people when she speakes to them. She's firm, yet diplomatic.

"She is a very fine musician. She taught my two daughters when they were young. I just wanted the best for them and Gloria is the best!" Mrs Penick said.

In 1969 she married Frank McCorkle Moody, a banker. He was the fourth generation in his family to lead what for a long time was Tuscaloosa's largest home owned bank, the First National Bank of Tuskaloosa. Frank, a widower, brought four children into the marriage. He had three daughters: Sara McCorkle Moody, Louise Morrisette Moody, and Jane Hamilton Moody now all in New Mexico, and one son, Frank M. Moody, Jr. of Tuscaloosa. Gloria was a very active mother. She loved Frank and her big family. Frank, Jr. was only eleven when they married. She gave up her career to devote herself to her large family and to Frank, Sr.'s very active life.

In 1980 the Moody's spent the summer in Washington, Connecticut and decided they would spend the rest of their summers there. First they bought a condo, then a house. The greatest attraction was Tanglewood in Massachusetts about two hours drive from there, where summer is celebrated with beautiful music. It is the summer home of the Boston Symphony. Tanglewood and its musical family became a part of their lives. They often would see world famous musicians like cellist Yo-Yo Ma, pianist Emanuel Ax, violinist Itzhak Perlman and others. Frank retired as chairman emeritus of First National Bank of Tuscaloosa in 1987 after the bank was purchased by AmSouth Bank.

Later, Frank's poor health caused them to buy a home closer to Tanglewood. Their summer home in Lenox, Massachusetts is so close they could walk to Tanglewood. Since Frank's death in 1993, Gloria has become even more involved with the Tanglewood family. She takes seminars and piano class there. She enjoys the informal, casual, friendly atmosphere. She has also contributed financially. In 1994, the Foundation made a significant gift in support of the new concert hall at Tanglewood. The hall's upper balcony foyer was named in memory of Frank.

The Moody's decided they wanted to bring more classical music to Tuscaloosa. In the early 1980s, they began working with the University to improve the school of music. With their own money they helped revitalize the School of Music, pouring over one million dollars in funds, art, and musical instruments into the program. A beautiful $11.3 million dollar state-of-the-art building with an acoustically perfect concert hall was built through their generous fund-raising. The building was named in their honor. The works of art they contributed include two huge Roy Liechtenstein tapestries hung in the foyer of the concert hall. Gloria personally raised funds to provide much-needed pianos.

The building was dedicated in January 1988 with a concert. "That was one of the most thrilling nights of my life," Gloria said. "The excitement generated by the capacity audience, the glorious voice of Marilyn Horne with the Alabama Symphony, the fact that this was taking place in Tuscaloosa - well, it was a marvelous sensation, and I just did not want to let it go."

"And then I began thinking how wonderful it would be if we could do this type thing once a year. I would go every summer to Tanglewood, hear these incredible musicians, and think, I want Yo-Yo Ma in Tuscaloosa. I want Jessye Norman in Tuscaloosa. I want the city and the department that I love to have the same opportunities that people in other parts of the country have."

From the seeds of this dream in the spring of 1990 Frank and Gloria established the Gloria Narramore Moody Foundation. It is dedicated to helping the School of Music and other arts organizations to promote excellence and quality in the arts and performing arts in Tuscaloosa and throughout Alabama. The Gloria Moody Foundation has developed a reputation for planning and underwriting world-class musical performances in Alabama.

Gloria was inspired by her rich childhood in Tuscaloosa. She remembered that when she began studying in the department of music, the department had an outstanding concert and lecture series. She was particularly inspired by the Robert Shaw Chorale back in 1949. "That was a big turning point in my life." She said, "I realized that even if music was not to be a serious career for me, music would have a serious place in my life. And that's the impetus for this annual concert. Even though today's youngsters are preoccupied with so many different things, I think that what happened to me forty years ago can happen to them now.

"The appearance of Guarneri Quartet may not inspire them to become string players, but it may make music a part of their lives, it may excite them to know that such things exist in this world." She saw the Foundation as a way to realize that vision. The Guarneri Quartet is internationally acclaimed as the world's premier quartet. John Dalley, a member of the quartet, is from Tuscaloosa and used to perform with Gloria when he lived there.

The former director of the School of Music, Dennis Monk said in 1992, "For a musician of Itzhak Perlman's stature to come to a city the size of Tuscaloosa is almost unheard of. We will have him here because of the Gloria Narramore Moody Foundation. Her strong support of music in Tuscaloosa is without comparison."

"Artists brought to Tuscaloosa by Gloria Moody are of such stature that they rarely appear outside of major music centers of the world," David Durant said in 1995. He is the coordinator of music services for the University of Alabama School of

Music. "For music lovers within a 300-400 mile radius of Tuscaloosa, the Moody Gala Concerts truly provide a rare, if not singular, opportunity to experience world-class musical talent."

Frank Moody admitted that his motivation for establishing the Foundation in his wife's name was not based on the same sentiments as Gloria's noble ones. He was quoted in a *Tuscalooosa News* story in 1990, "I don't know that I ever told her that she had to quit teaching (when they married). She may have known intuitively that our busy lifestyle was not conductive to a full teaching schedule. I always felt a little guilty for divorcing her, in effect, from not only her career but also her first love—music. In setting up this Foundation, I wanted to do something for her—something that she would like to do."

Gloria said in 1993 as president of the Foundation, "It's a full time job. I didn't realize it, but I think Frank did. As always, I'm grateful to Frank for the imaginative, wonderful way he thought of others and for establishing the Foundation. It's wonderful, and it's what I plan to do the rest of my life."

In 1995 she started a new business with Janice Mayer. The company is called Janice Mayer and Associates, LLC and has an office on West 54th Street in New York City. It is an international artist management company dedicated to advancing and serving the vocal arts. Janice is president and Gloria is vice president.

In February 1992 Gloria gave a much anticipated performance. Her first performance since 1986. It was a benefit performance in support of the University of Alabama's School of Music scholarship fund. She performed in the Moody Music Building Concert Hall with music professors and friend, Amanda Penick—piano, Bruce Murry—piano and harpsichord, and with the Tuscaloosa Symphony Orchestra under the direction of Calton McCreery. They performed the Concerto for Three Harpsichords in C Major by J.S. Bach. They used pianos rather than harpsichords.

Paul Isom reviewed the concert in the *Tuscaloosa News*. "The most attention was focused on Mrs. Moody, who made an impressive and memorable debut in the hall named in her honor. The Bach piece was not only a great showcase for the musicians, but an appropriately stately work that lent an upbeat mood to match the occasion of Mrs. Moody's debut."

In March of that year Gloria was surprised to be named one of the Ten Best Dressed Women in Alabama by fashion designer Kelle Thompson of Haute Couture Maison, Inc. of Mobile. Thompson has been choosing the honorees for twenty years.

"I'm very flattered. I certainly never expected this," Gloria said in a *Tuscaloosa News* interview, "Especially since I don't dress in a trendy way. I try to choose clothes that are classic in style, because I wear them year after year." She said the beautiful white dress she wore to her debut at the Moody Music performance was six years old.

In March of 1994 the Moody Foundation planned a Gala to premier the newly written "Let Evening Come." The summer before, the Foundation and New York's Lincoln Center commissioned Pulitzer winning composer William Bolcom to write a piece for New York Opera singers soprano Benita Valente and mezzo soprano Tatiana Troyanos in memory of Frank Moody. The opera stars performed in Tuscaloosa in November 1992. Sadly, Tatiana Troyanos died in August 1993, so the performance was also dedicated to her memory. The premier performance was played to a standing room only audience. Later in April, it attracted the same attendance in New York later at the Lincoln Center performance. *The Birmingham News'* review called it, "A work of imposing power."

Balcom's wonderful "Let Evening Come" is a song cycle with three poems by Maya Angelou, Emily Dickinson and Jane Kenyon. It is a cantata for lyric soprano, viola and piano. The California-born soprano, Benita Valente performed with violist Michael Tree and pianist Cynthia Raim. Tree is one of the most widely recorded musicians in America. Raim performs extensively in the United States, Canada, and Europe.

The Moody Foundation is a vital cultural resource. The excitement generated by the Foundation's work keeps building momentum. Gloria has found that the work of recruiting the best artist has gotten easier as the reputation of the Foundation and the School has spread. "Just a few years back, when we were starting, they had never heard of us and had never heard of the Foundation. But time has shown we come through with what we promise and people are becoming familiar with us."

Gerald Welker, director of the School of Music said after the Yo-Yo Ma, Emanuel Ax performance in 1993 that the performers seemed pleased. "They have uniformly responded positively to our concert Hall, the facilities, and also to the warmth and hospitality of the people here. Itzhak Perlman went out and ate ribs at Dreamland Barbeque. He apparently had a wonderful time.

"We certainly hope Yo-Yo Ma and Emanuel Ax have a great visit . I've heard that they are fun people, very accommodating. We're looking forward not only to the performance, but meeting and chatting with them. It means a lot to the faculty and students when you can rub elbows with musicians of this caliber, to see these people walking up and down the halls of our school. The Moody family has done so much—we wouldn't be talking from this building if it weren't for the Moody family. On behalf of the school, we could not be more grateful.

"Both Frank and Gloria have taken a real interest in bringing outstanding, world-class people to this campus. It would be extremely difficult for the school to invite musicians of this caliber to perform, on a regular basis, without the Foundation. These artist are the kind who appear quite regularly in New York City, Los Angeles, Boston, Paris, London, but do not always get to communities of our size.

"There are any number of people who recognize Yo-Yo Ma and Emanuel Ax as two of the premier musicians in the world. In short, this is as good as it gets," Welker said.

Gloria works personally with artists and agents to bring the performers to Tuscaloosa. Other performers have been famous pianist Richard Goode who performed in April 1991. In October 1994 world class pianist John Browning performed. The 1995 featured performer was the internationality acclaimed top basso Profunda solist in opera today, Samuel Ramey. The March 1996 Moody Gala will feature opera soprano Dawn Upshaw and pianist Richard Goode.

In May 1994 Gloria established a scholarship in her parents' name. The scholarship supports top young men and women in their studies at UA's School of Music.

"This scholarship is mainly to honor my parents for the many sacrifices of time, money and energy they made toward my education. It means there will be Narramore scholars long after we're gone." She has also established the Frank M. Moody Memorial String Program Scholarship in honor of Frank.

In June of 1995, Roger Sayers, president of the University of Alabama said, "I think of Gloria Moody as the first lady of the arts in Alabama. Her contributions both as a performing artist and though her philanthropy have enriched so many lives. Gloria Moody is one of the University's most distinguished alumnae with a vision and love of music that is inspirational to us all. We are indebted to her for her contributions to the arts, for sharing with us her extraordinary musical talents, and for her enthusiastic service to our community and state as a patron of the arts."

James D. Yarbrough, dean of the College of Arts ands Sciences said, "Gloria Moody is one of the College of Arts and Sciences' most generous supporters. Her generosity to our school of Music has spanned many years and has been instrumental in our ability to offer high quality academic programs for Tuscaloosa and the state.

"We believe that education is not a private privilege, but a public responsibility to be shared and supported by all. As a public institution, we must rely on the contributions of private citizens to maintain our standing as one of the South's best universities. So we are indeed fortunate to have the support of such a farsighted Alabamian and friend as Gloria Moody."

Both Gloria and Frank's contributions were recognized by the UA's School of Music with a special celebration concert in their honor in 1991. They were also the first recipients of the University's Frances S. Summersell Award for service to education.

Gloria's dedication to music and the arts in Tuscaloosa has involved her in many organizations. She is chairperson for the Tuscaloosa Symphony, a member of the Tuscaloosa Fine Arts Council Board of Directors, and a member of the Society of the Fine Arts. She is a former board member of the Children's Hands on Museum and the Alabama Music Teachers Association executive board. She is also active with the Tuscaloosa Piano Teachers Forum, and the Tuscaloosa Music Teacher Association. She is a member of Mu Phi Epsilon, the national music sorority, and Pi Kappa Lambda, the national music honorary. Gloria has helped to organize and is on the board of the Orchestra League of Alabama. The state-wide League's purpose is to share musicians and ideas for better management and fund raising.

The manager of the Tuscaloosa Symphony (TSO) Pamela Penick, daughter-in-law of Amanda Penick, said that Gloria as chairperson of TSO, "has been the guiding star to light the way through some very difficult times." She has been chairperson since 1992. Her strong leadership led TSO through big changes. Their conductor Ransom Wilson left suddenly and the manager resigned. This happened just as Gloria was taking command. She found a new manager, set up a new staff and new office procedures. The search for a conductor took the whole 1992-'93 season with each TSO production conducted by a different conductor. Adrian Gnam was selected. During this time TSO grew from a part-time civic orchestra to a part-time professional orchestra.

"Gloria has such finesse and savvy that she is a great figurehead for our orchestra," Penick said. "She has been most generous with heavy contributions and hosting social functions at her home. She has been a guide and inspiration to me and to all. The musicians are comfortable with her because she is a respected musician. They know that she knows their feelings and needs as musicians.

"She has very much helped to put TSO on the map. She is an entrepreneur. Through her Foundation she has brought famous musicians here and often has had TSO perform with them. This has given so much exposure to TSO. She has underwritten many of TSO's guest artists including our first in the 95-'96 season, violinist Gil Shaham," Penick said.

Celeste Burnum, on the Foundation board and Vice-president of TSO, said, "From being a very gifted student, Gloria has become a leader of the music world. She uses her musical talent, leadership ability, and fund raising ability to make things happen. She is a real mover in this country and we are just fortunate to have her."

Fred Goossen, UA music professor and music critic for the *Tuscaloosa News* is on TSO's board. He said, "Gloria Moody has brought her powerful leadership ability to the TSO. Her leadership more than any other has put the orchestra on a good solid financial foundation. She got us through a rough transition when Wilson left. It's not just her leadership. It's her financial contributions and her wonderful contacts. She's able to bring high ranking soloists to town.

"She's simply an enthusiast, a trained musician. She's interested in the orchestra not as a civic duty, but as an enthusiastic musician. She's a serious pianist, very capable, still performing well. She has miraculously kept up. Most musicians don't if they don't have to. It's hard work. She brings a serious artist's interest which is unique. Very few professional musicians are chairperson of a symphony.

"The shift from a civic to a professional orchestra was a quantum leap. There were huge changes. She is a powerhouse for TSO and the state. Gloria has made a difference to Tuscaloosa and Alabama."

Written by Abigail M. Toffel

102

ALBERTA BROWN MURPHY

You Can Do Anything You Want,
If You Do It Well And Don't Harm Anyone.

Alberta Murphy steadfastly kept the above admonition from her grandmother Cowden and lived by it always. Everything she attempted she did thoroughly and well and with great enthusiasm. Furthermore, she exceeded her grandmother's counsel not to harm anyone. Rather, her work benefited many. If Alberta's name were to be mentioned today in any political or legal group in Alabama, at least one person would remark, "Many lives have been touched by that wonderful woman. It was my privilege to have known her." She was a woman well-known not only for her legal knowledge but for activism in the field of civil rights. Her beauty was also noted by many, including news reporters, and often the commentary embraced more than her physical attractiveness, but an inner luminosity as well.

For those of us who know Alberta, beginning her story with the little details of her birth may seem the height of redundancy. Anyone who has ever seen this tall, vital woman enter a room and coalesce the ongoing conversations into a purposeful discussion, knows good and well that Alberta Murphy was born. We only wonder that she had not emerged full grown from a cactus flower, complete with law degree and one of her trademark large hats. Nevertheless, some statistics are more or less mandatory.

In Harrisonville, Missouri, (the year shall be her secret) Alberta Murphy was born to Albert Brown and Bess Cowden Brown, the second of their two children. Christened Mary Elizabeth, her name was changed later to Alberta. At the time of her birth, her father and his brothers jointly owned and operated a large farm in Missouri. When Alberta was about three years old, the partnership was dissolved, the proceeds were divided, and the Albert Brown family moved to another farm outside San Benito in the southernmost tip of Texas not far from Brownsville. They were one of the first Anglo families in the area, and Alberta and her brother, George, who was five years older than she, had numerous Mexican playmates and grew up completely bilingual. Even now, so many years later, she can go into a Mexican restaurant and delight all the waiters as she gives her order in a perfect Mexican-Spanish accent.

Alberta was never destined for a humdrum life, even from the very beginning. One of her earliest recollections was the horseback ride she had with "Pancho" Villa, the Mexican revolutionary leader. As she was playing in the yard, Villa, accompanied by his Mexican troops rode up to the house and, apparently captivated by the sight of the pretty little Anglo child, leaned down from his horse, swooped her up with one hand, placed her in the saddle in front of him, and took her for a gallop down the road and back. "And I never saw him again," Alberta adds a little wistfully. She also recalls from the same period that Mexican soldiers stopped her father one day as he drove across his field in a farm wagon. They challenged him and fired their rifles at him, but were not very good shots and did no harm. Such annoyances stopped after General John Pershing and American troops sent to secure the border were encamped nearby, some of them in the Brown yard. She remembers Pershing s presence in the community being cause for considerable comment and excitement that was further enhanced by President Woodrow Wilson's visit to the area during that same period.

Shortly afterward, at the age of 32 years, Bess Cowden died suddenly, presumably from a heart attack. Alberta remembers the concern and tenderness with which her father held Bess in his arms. She also remembers the urgency in his voice as he told George to run as fast as he could (they had no telephone) to the clinic to get Grandma Cowden. Very early in Alberta's life, Grandma Cowden personally demonstrated the importance of aiding the less fortunate by establishing a small maternity clinic which provided sanitary delivery conditions and child care instruction to the women of the community. When it became quite evident that Albert would be unable to operate his farm and care for two young children, his mother-in-law took on that responsibility in addition to her clinic, and it was Grandma Cowden who became the role model and inspiration for the child who grew up to be a lawyer championing the civil rights of others.

Alberta's formal schooling began at a younger age than was usual for most children because she became, in effect, "responsible" for her brother's education. George was expected to ride one of the family burros to school each day, but the beast refused to move from its home territory without a companion of its own species by its side. Grandma solve the problem by suggesting that it would do Alberta no harm to go along with George. She lifted the little girl onto another *burritito*. From then on, the two children rode off on their contented donkeys to the one-room school where all eight grades were competently taught by Miss Alma Prentice. In spite of her youth, Alberta had no trouble keeping up with the school work and in due time was ready for high school with the rest of her class.

In 1902 Congress had passed the Reclamation Act by which the federal government became an active participant in the irrigation work of the arid Southwest, and the U.S. Reclamation Service assisted farmers financially and technically in constructing irrigation systems. Later the original Act was revised and greatly enlarged; and, in 1923, the Reclamation Service was succeeded by the Bureau of Reclamation. With the cooperation of the U.S. Army Corps of Engineers, the Bureau planned and implemented a comprehensive development of water resources available to the western states for their optimum utilization. To facilitate this work, the areas of the Southwest were divided into Irrigation Districts.

About the time Alberta was ready for high school in San Benito, her father was appointed assessor and tax commissioner for the local Irrigation District. The family moved into town obviating the necessity for any further burro transportation to advance Alberta s education. Another facet of Alberta's heritage is demonstrated by the fact that her father not only knew the name of every farmer in the district, he was noted for remembering each acreage and water allotment without having to consult his records. If a man met Albert Brown on the street and asked when he would be getting water, the commissioner told him right then and there the date and the number of gallons he could expect.

With a natural flair for the dramatic, Alberta surprised absolutely no one when, after graduation from high school, she expressed a fervent desire to go on the stage. Accordingly, and with full family approval, she went to New York City to "pound the pavements." After many months and hundreds of auditions, it became quite clear to her that, "Nobody was going to fire either Greta Garbo or Tallullah Bankhead just to give *me* a job." Her father urged her to put an end to such fruitless effort and to look for some real work as he did not want to "go broke" supporting her in New York. That she did, and very shortly found work in one of the government offices in Washington, DC.

Her work in Washington must certainly have given her contact with legal proceedings of some sort and possibly engendered an early interest in the law,. However, she made no active decision to pursue that career until the day when news reports went out in the press and on the radio telling the world that Bruno Hauptmann had finally been convicted and sentenced to death for the kidnap-murder of Charles and Anne Morrow Lindbergh's two-year-old son. Alberta's first thought on hearing the news was "How wonderful those men [the attorneys] must feel!" Here was a profession that empowered one to do something in the world. With George Washington University only a few blocks from where she lived, it was convenient to enroll in that law school. Aside from the tension and concern she felt during the preregistration tests, she had no problem being accepted even though female attorneys were a rarity in those days. She was one of two women in her class.

In that same class was a young man who attracted her attention with his brilliant and witty answers to the professor's questions. As time went on she found that he was not only clever and intelligent, but also extraordinarily courteous and thoughtful of others. In 1946, after both had been graduated from law school and were practicing attorneys, Jay W. Murphy and Alberta Brown were married in Virginia. By 1947, Jay, who was working as a research analyst for Civilian Foreign Intelligence, became dissatisfied with government work. He felt attracted to the academic world, and came to the University of Alabama as associate professor of law.

Alberta was in private practice at the time with the Washington law firm, Tucker, Todd, Donahue, Dillon, & Sellers who were handling the case of *Carolene Products vs. the United States* in an appeal of Carolene s conviction of violation of the "Filled Milk Act" which prevented, among other things concerning milk and milk products, the coloring of oleomargarine to make it look like butter. She won the company the right to color margin the yellow it is today instead of the unappetizing white it was. Because of the state and federal scope of this large and long-running case, Alberta was not able to leave Washington at the same time as Jay and did not join him in Tuscaloosa until some months later.

Soon after her arrival in Tuscaloosa, the Murphy home became a kind of salon where the university and political communities gathered to discuss local and national problems and to meet visiting academics, artists, and newsmen. Alberta was an avid reader far beyond academic necessity and occasionally chided or actually nagged her friends for not being able to comment on new books. Her neighbors remember her as a strikingly handsome woman given to exotic clothing and distinctive hats which, good Texan that she was, she ordered on a regular basis from Nieman-Marcus.

In May of 1948, their son Stanley Jay was born. When asked, some forty years later, what it was like growing up as Alberta Murphy's son, he replied without a seconds hesitation, "It was absolutely wonderful." Alberta not only had participated in all his school's activities and was known as a fantastic Cub Scout den mother. She had always found time somewhere in her schedule to give him personal attention and help at home. Asked if he had ever known his mother to be afraid of anything, Stanley's answer was not so immediate. After a moment s reflection, he said thoughtfully, "Fear is not a word associated with my mother." This characteristic became abundantly manifest after she entered into private law practice in 1953.

By the early 1950s, with civil rights demonstrations, sit-ins, and violence in cities across the United States, the quiet little city of Tuscaloosa entered a period of serious unrest. The Murphy home became a center for civil rights activism at the same time that it was a stabilizing and direction-finding force effective in keeping serious turmoil at a minimum. Both Alberta and Jay threw their legal expertise into civil rights causes taking unpopular employment discrimination and criminal cases. Jay's first labor arbitration case in Tuscaloosa was *Zeigler vs. Mallisham* in 1955. Joseph W. Mallisham, a black ALF-CIO organizer in the meat-packing industry was dismissed by Zeigler Packing Company ostensibly on grounds of insubordination. Whereas in actuality his only rebellious act was to support, as union leader, a white female employee's cause – an action deemed legally and socially unseemly. In another case, a young black man was arrested while driving down the street for the crime of "staring" at a white woman in his rear-view mirror. Alberta successfully defended him. She was totally dedicated to using her intellectual ability and legal training to benefit those who had neither the power nor the strength to protect themselves.

The Murphy's unstinting efforts in civil liberties activities, their support of enlightened political candidates, and their legal aid to persons affected by prejudicial laws earned them considerable disapproval throughout the entire state. Almost every evening, their meals and their sleep were interrupted by threatening telephone calls urging them to cease their activities and/or "get out of town." Nevertheless, they continued their efforts. Alberta worked for the Justice Department in the field of community relations with the difficult task of helping small Alabama towns adjust to racial equality.

By the early sixties, the old equilibrium between the races could no longer be maintained. Rosa Parks' refusal to sit in the back of the bus in Montgomery in 1955 and Martin Luther King s subsequent bus boycott and the later Freedom Riders had already challenged public conveyance seating all over the country. Autherine Lucey had registered for classes and later had been dismissed at the University of Alabama. Then in 1963, Governor George Wallace "stood in the schoolhouse door." That is, he blocked a door at Foster Auditorium in an unsuccessful attempt to prevent Vivian Malone and James Hood from registering for classes at the University. In Birmingham, Alabama a black church was bombed and civil rights demonstrators were being assaulted by attack dogs, fire hoses, and by club-wielding police.

During this tumultuous period, Alberta assumed the presidency of the League of Women Voters of Greater Tuscaloosa (LWV), and with Zelma Wyatt as Voters Service chair, voter registration became the impelling objective of the League.

At that time, all voter registration was done at the county courthouse, a forbidding place for prospective black voters who were often rudely treated and were seldom able to register to vote. In order to register, black applicants were required to read or recite passages of the Constitution of the United States and to answer a number of esoteric questions about American history and government. Alberta and other League members went to schools, stores, and homes in black communities throughout the county to encourage and instruct people how to register to vote. With the resurgence of Ku Klux Klan activity and its rumored existence within the police department, the project was not without hazard. Of course, Alberta, because of her long-time activity in civil rights causes and her total disregard for personal safety, was particularly vulnerable.

Fortunately, a second strong stabilizing influence existed in Tuscaloosa. Within the black community, a tightly organized and rigorously selected group of ex-military men— war veterans known as The Deacons – emerged for the purpose of neutralizing Klan efforts. They were highly respected and quickly served to temper and give perspective to black civil rights efforts. Some of the members acted on an advisory committee composed of five whites and five blacks that kept Mayor Snow Hinton apprised of impending difficulty. The Deacons also adopted the responsibility of secretly "protecting" white civil rights workers, among them Alberta Murphy. As Joseph Mallisham, labor leader, Deacon, and current City Council member expressed it, "When we saw the way she went all over the county any time of day or night to instruct voters without any regard for danger, we knew that woman needed some kind of protection." The Deacons had ways of knowing everything that went on, and they knew exactly when and where Alberta or other civil rights people would be working in the black communities. Unbeknownst to the white participants, the Deacons discreetly shadowed them, always alert for any dangerous situations that might develop.

On one particular night, Alberta returned home late from encouraging and coaching prospective voters out in the country as two Deacon cars shadowed her from a distance. Before long they noticed two suspicious cars pull onto the road, one in front of Alberta and the other behind. One proceeded to shine his bright lights into her rear-view mirror to blind her while the other drove slowly ahead of her to box her in. The Deacons foiled the play by getting their cars between Alberta and her annoyers who shortly gave up the contest and turned off at the next corner. Alberta was inconspicuously shadowed to her home in safety. Without the watchful eyes of the Deacons, there would certainly have been many more such incidents. Tuscaloosa was fortunate in having two such influences as the Murphys and the Deacons at work.

Alberta did not increase her popularity or decrease the element of danger surrounding her when, in some way never publicized, she secured a copy of the questions asked prospective black voters, copied it, distributed it widely, and rehearsed people on the answers. Mr. Mallisham said, "By hanging on to the voter registration project, she taught us the importance of voting and helped us gain the power of the vote."

At the polls, Alberta and other League members volunteered to help new voters who, at this point, were totally bewildered by the voting machines and the whole complicated process. Of course the poll officials ordered the League women out on the grounds that they were acting illegally, but the officials could not maintain their position very long in the face of Alberta's legal knowledge. She proved that such assistance was perfectly lawful as long as it was requested—as it was, numerous times.

Over the years, she continued her untiring advocacy for the powerless, the poor, and the disenfranchised. She worked for the Justice Department in the Federal Mediation and Conciliation Service. She was a member of the American Arbitration Association, handling many large employment discrimination cases for blacks. Her early interest in mental health and the treatment of the mentally ill resulted in her appointment by Appellate Court Judge Frank Johnson to serve on the Human Rights Committee at Bryce Hospital. In that capacity, she monitored the *Wyatt vs. Stickney* case which ultimately resulted in better housing and treatment for the mental patients.

In 1968 she went as a delegate with the desegregated challenge delegation – the National Democratic Party of Alabama—to the National Democratic Convention in Chicago. As if all this were not enough, Alberta also taught classes in political science at the University of Alabama. Her students were as fascinated by her personality as they were excited by her practical but thorough manner of teaching. One young political follower, a graduate student, tried to crash a party at the Murphy home pleading that she was the most *beautiful* woman in the world. His fervid declaration emphasized the adjective in a totally non-material sense. In teaching good government, by working for and showing concern for the underprivileged, Alberta exemplified a kind of nobility that moved many people besides her students.

It was her teaching activity, she maintains, that precipitated her into the political arena. "I thought if I was going to stand up in front of a class and lecture on political responsibility, I'd better practice it myself." And so, it was in 1972 and again in 1974, she ran for congress from the Seventh District of Alabama. She did not win, but she left her mark. Her name became synonymous with "liberal," though this was neither a compliment nor an advantage to her or her family. Quoting from *The Birmingham News* for August 21, 1975:

> Dr. David Mathews, who switched from the presidency of the University of Alabama to the [head of Health, Education, and Welfare] post earlier this month, was a non-partisan appointed [by President Ford] . . . The three GOP congressmen from Alabama registered no objection to his nomination, . . . they, like the two Democratic senators from Alabama, endorsed Mathews vigorously.
>
> But this attitude did not extent to one of the assistants. Mathews wanted . . . Stanley Murphy . . . And here began Mathews' first brush with Alabama party politics at the Washington end.
>
> The three Alabama GOP congressmen have nothing personal against Stan Murphy. In fact, they don't know him. But they do know that his mother is Mrs. Alberta Murphy of Tuscaloosa, who ran as a Democratic candidate for Congress in 1972 and again in 1974. Not only is Mrs. Murphy an active Democrat, but she is also a liberal who repeatedly charged that the incumbent she was trying to unseat . . . is so conservative that he might as well be a Republican.
>
> Maybe it was a verdict of political guilt by association, but the Alabama Republicans refused to clear Murphy for the position.

Stanley did, however, accept another position with HEW at a lesser salary which did not require Congressional approval.

Then, with her political career behind her, Alberta returned to private law practice. She worked a good bit of time with her son who had by his time come back home to Tuscaloosa. Although she continued to accept arbitration cases all over the country, she also maintained a local practice where it would be almost impossible to estimate the amount of legal advice she dispensed pro bono.

In December of 1992, Jay W. Murphy died leaving Alberta alone after almost 50 years of stimulating company, interesting conversation, and exciting work. Although she occasionally regrets and sometimes rebels against the enforced inactivity of her senior years, she recognizes without reservation the advantages of age. She appreciates the privilege of perspective, of being able to look back on a full life and gratifying career. This is the viewpoint of a woman who has accomplished much and is content. It is also the opinion of all who came in contact with her. There are many people whose lives are freer, richer, and more inspired than they would have been if Alberta Murphy had never come to Alabama. Alberta Murphy now lives at Pine Valley Senior Living Community in Tuscaloosa, Alabama.

written by Joyce Mahan

The foregoing brief account of Alberta Murphy's life is based on conversations with her, Stanley Jay Murphy, A. L. Vreeland, and Joseph W. Mallisham. Paul Pruitt, Tom Canterbury, and John Blackburn were also very gracious in answering questions and helping to establish certain names and dates.

SARAH CABOT PIERCE

Being Born With A Sense of Mission Has Shaped My Life.

To borrow an expression from the late Edward R. Murrow, "I must have been born with a sense of mission." In my childhood in Wetumpka, Alabama, I knew my family felt involved and responsible for many civic matters concerning our historic small town.

I recall when one of my maiden aunts was our church treasurer. She privately spoke very critically of the ladies in our church who gave large bridge parties, but who failed to pledge funds for the church. Also in for censure by my family were those who failed to contribute to such worthy causes as the Red Cross. We very much frowned on those who did not pay their bills, too. As a merchant, my father classed the "slow pay" folks right behind the "no pay."

I heard the story many times about how my grandfather stood on a soapbox outside the county jail and urged an angry mob to allow law and order to prevail instead of a lynching. Four black men had been accused of robbery and murder of several old people in their home. Grandpa had wired the governor in Montgomery to send help. Because of a flood on the river, the National Guard or militia had to detour around and through Millbrook to reach Wetumpka. They arrived too late, the lynching had taken place.

Although he was born in New England, Grandpa Cabot Lull spent his life in our small town. He served the town as mayor on several occasions and was chairman of the Elmore County Board of Education. He also was elected probate judge once when there was a reform mood in the air. So much for my indoctrination into the responsibilities of citizenship.

I graduated from The University of Alabama in 1932 and from the Pulitzer School of Journalism at Columbia University in 1933. In a brief career as a reporter I worked on papers in Dothan and Tuscaloosa.

Shortly after marrying Donald Pierce of Tuscaloosa, I was offered a fellowship at the University of Alabama provided I would take graduate work and would teach journalism. I did this for three years in Tuscaloosa. My husband's business caused us to move to the Montgomery area in the 1940s just prior to World War II.

During World War II, we lived in Atlanta. While I was doing publicity for the Atlanta Red Cross, I was very impressed with a unique organization I kept reading about in the *Atlanta Journal* and *Constitution* called the League of Women Voters. I decided it must be a select group of unusually intelligent women interested in good government. Every action they took was so obviously for the betterment of the city or county.

For example, they supported the extension of the city limits north into an affluent area. Prior to an election (I have forgotten whether for city or state) the League had a two-page spread in the *Journal* giving impartial information about the candidates. Right there on the page in black and white, one candidate was shown to have "served time," I believe, for bootlegging. Newspapers still publish Candidates Questionnaires today with the help of the League. They listed the candidate's education, jobs held, plans if elected, and stands on some issues.

I knew we would be returning to Alabama at the end of the War so I wrote to an intelligent, college classmate who lived in Montgomery. I described this splendid organization and suggested we ought to start one in Alabama. She replied that Alabama was "not ready" for that kind of organization. The League had been established in Alabama in 1920, but it had declined by the late twenties due to active political participation of a number of local Leagues. This type of politicking was contrary to the League's non-partisan policy. The State League disbanded in 1928. However, some of the local Leagues were active in the 1930s. The Birmingham League operated an employment service during the depression.

We moved back to Wetumpka where my husband, little girl, and I had an apartment. Shortly after returning to the state in 1947, I was invited to meet in Montgomery with a group of women interested in starting an Alabama League. My friend had evidently given my name to the organizer of the group. I attended a small gathering at the home of Mrs. Fred Couey who represented the National League of Women Voters, which was promoting an expansion into states that had no state Leagues. In the South, these were Alabama, North and South Carolina, Mississippi, and, I believe, Louisiana.

The time was evidently right because the war had brought women out of their homes and into all manner of jobs during the war. The war had caused women to feel more independent, more interested in the world and in careers. They were ripe for getting involved in public affairs. Mrs. Couey had come to Montgomery because her husband was connected with Maxwell Air Force Base. She had served on the state board of the Connecticut League and had been asked by the National League to undertake organization in Alabama. Within a year of our start, a group of five provisional Leagues were under way in Alabama: Montgomery, Wetumpka, Anniston, Florence, and Tuscaloosa.

We formed a state League committee by 1950 in preparation to establish a state League. The five provisional Leagues each chipped in ten dollars to help with expenses. That spring with the help of the fifty dollars, I attended the National League Council meeting in Washington, D.C. I had been chosen delegate because my sister lived in Washington and I would have a free place to stay. I traveled by day coach and was accompanied by my little girl for whom I had provided a big pillow and a large grocery bag of snacks for the overnight trip.

The highlight of that adventure was a League breakfast where the distinguished statesman Averell Harriman spoke. I sat with North and South Carolinians. At the large table to my left, I spied Texas Congressman Lyndon B. Johnson. As we arose to leave, I confronted him with a big smile and said I was from Wetumpka, Alabama, and that I knew Lady Bird who had visited her cousin in Wetumpka several times. He said, "Lady Bird is here," and, cupping his hand to his mouth, he called loud and clear, "Lady Bird!" and over she came. She cordially asked me about my plans, and I explained that I had a full schedule.

We held the first state convention of the new Alabama League in the spring of 1951 in Tuscaloosa. Our business sessions were held in Doster Hall on The University of Alabama campus. We were shepherded through proceedings by an attractive national board member from Oklahoma City. I was one among several who had no experience at presiding, but we all plunged in with a will and undertook our assignments.

Without opposition in our convention sessions, we chose to work for abolition of the state poll tax. This was a straight forward, uncomplicated issue that needed to be addressed by somebody. We especially felt it discouraged voting by women and poor blacks who were the chief victims of the law. World War II veterans were excused from the tax.

We plunged into the subject, preparing graphs, charts, and statistics to show the unfairness and the undemocratic results of the system. We used a newspaper clipping service at the end of our first year, discovering that all daily and as many weekly newspapers, were unanimously in favor of abolition of the poll tax. I believe one exception was the weekly *Greenville Advocate* of Greenville, Alabama.

We joined forces with American Association of University Women, Business and Professional Women, and, to a lesser extent, labor unions in promoting our cause with the state legislature. In 1954 under the leadership of Governor Gordon Persons, the poll tax was reduced from a possible thirty-six dollars to three dollars for a person to register to vote. After registration, one dollar and fifty cents was the annual tax. All poll tax was abolished by the courts in the 1960s.

The Montgomery League was the first in the state to get under way again. Wetumpka was next. Our town, seventeen miles north of Montgomery with a population of about five thousand, has some farming, a small amount of manufacturing and a good number of residents commuting daily to work in Montgomery - as my husband did. In those early days, I was an earnest member of the small Wetumpka League. With a membership varying from twenty-five to thirty-five in its short life, scarcely more than ten years, its accomplishments were impressive.

At the initial enthusiastic gathering of women at our community Center, Mrs. Couey described the League to us. A temporary chairman named a nominating committee for officers and we were under way. To my surprise, I was elected president.

To me, our most difficult task as a provisional League was not the requirement to do a "know your town" study, but rather to hold a fund drive. That meant soliciting money for an operation even before we had begun to operate. However, we hit upon a scheme to raise the money. We persuaded a highly regarded local artist, Kelly Fitzpatrick, who was famous in our region, to exhibit his paintings for a small fee.

Teachers in the local elementary school were so enthusiastic they marched their classes to the exhibit at the community center, a class at a time. Those children who wished paid a dime. We scored considerable success, not only in raising money, but for sponsoring a cultural event. Fund raisers were generally frowned upon by the League in those days. We were told they were much more time consuming than just using personal solicitations, which would also provide opportunities to explain our purpose and program.

Our Wetumpka League's first feat of audacity was to study and promote city planning. Wetumpka has a beautiful setting with high hills just back of the business district to the east, the picturesque Coosa River in the center, and the residential section on the opposite bank to the west. The town's motto is "The City of Natural Beauty." We invited the mayor and his council to lunch while we successfully laid out our proposal. The council not only passed the planning and zoning laws but made a League member chairman of the planning commission.

Another action of note by the Wetumpka League was our promotion of a law to abolish the office of Justice of the Peace, a situation that cried for reform. That was a controversial issue we quickly learned, but, shaking in our boots, we nevertheless stuck bravely to our cause. At the same time the Elmore County Bar Association took the lead and legislation was passed that would take the teeth out of the office by removing criminal cases from the office's jurisdiction.

Our bravest, most daring undertaking was to promote legislation to put Elmore County officials on a salary system, abolishing the fee system. We employed a gentle white haired gentleman, a retired auditor, formerly with the State Department of Public Accounts, to examine the books of the county officials. He was treated courteously at the courthouse when he began his examination of the county books, which included the probate judge, the tax assessor, the tax collector, and the sheriff.

Our study showed that the two great river dams in the county, Jordan on the Coosa and Martin on the Tallapoosa, brought in ad valorem taxes which, when added to the other income sources, provided a salary for the probate judge that was as great or greater than that of the governor. Other county officials also were handsomely compensated.

This issue was indeed so controversial that, although the local newspaper printed our booklet "Facts on Fees in Elmore County," they declined to say one word about it in the news. And it was big news indeed. Fortunately, the *Montgomery Advertiser* gave it good play. It took three statewide amendment elections to get the law changed even though Elmore County voters voted about six-to-one in favor each time.

Not long after that effort I moved to Montgomery to live. Another Wetumpka League leader moved away and a third died. With these and other setbacks, the little band of hearty souls who were left suffered from general exhaustion and retired the Wetumpka League.

In the next 20 years from 1950-1970, I devoted much of my time to state League activities. I was state president from 1952 to 1954 and for a partial term in 1967 to fill an unexpired term. I was elected to a second term from 1968 to 1970.

My colleagues from the local Leagues, as well as those on the state board, were really fun to work with even though we worked hard on serious and important issues of government. We never seemed to have any prima donnas, dictators, nor any members aspiring to the spotlight. We continued to be undaunted even when our successes were few.

The truth is, we were often ahead of public opinion in trying to promote change in the government. Governor George C. Wallace described our dilemma when he encountered a group of us at the Capitol. On learning who we were, he smiled and said, "You ladies don't think like the majority of people in Alabama."

Beginning in the 1950s and into the 60s, we tried diligently to persuade lawmakers to improve the state's election laws. We discovered that boards of registrars not only had little money allotted to clean up the poll lists, they did not even try. The Montgomery poll list, for example, contained names of Confederate veterans long dead. Boards had few supplies to do the job, very short periods to register voters, and asked unreasonable questions for applicants to answer, such as "Explain the meaning of the U.S. Constitution." Some registrars were practically illiterate. We spent years pushing legislation to meet those and many other deficiencies in the election laws.

We constantly supported efforts throughout those years to encourage citizens to vote. That alone created some hostility toward us. A continuing dream we also had in those years was replacement of our 1901 state constitution with an up-to-date one. That dream is still on hold although the state judicial system has undergone considerable improvement.

In the turbulent 1960s, we felt there was a distinct danger that public disfavor with integration was going to see inadequate funding provided for public schools. In the meanwhile, private schools were popping up everywhere. In a study we published, we tried to show how vital free public education was for all of our children. I spoke on this subject to the Sidney Lanier High School P.T.A. I pointed out the possible consequences of having a well-educated upper-class from private schools and a poorly educated lower-class from inadequate public schools. Alabama would become a sort of "banana republic." During those busy years I also served on the State League Board as Legislative and Voter's Service Chairman.

In 1969, the National League got a head start on celebrating the League's history in a book released that year, *50 Years of a Great Idea*. The 19th Amendment gave women the vote in 1920 and the League sprang that same year from the National American Suffrage Association whose members had worked so hard to get the vote. A celebration took place that spring in Washington, D.C., with a ceremony at the White House. Dr. Katherine Cater, a state board member, and I, as state president, flew to Washington (at our own expense) to represent the Alabama League at the event.

I quote some portions from my account in the *Alabama Voter* of May 1969:

"We were ushered into the East Room and sat on little gold chairs alongside League members, senators, congressmen, and cabinet members. President Nixon walked in to the lilting tune of 'Hail to the Chief' played by the Marine Band. Very graciously he told us that the League of Women Voters is perhaps the most influential political organization in the county and one which deserves the support of all the citizens.' He spoke of our nonpartisan activity, 'Always in the public interest.' Mrs. Bruce Benson, our national president, replied in good fashion, as did John W. Gardener, Chairman of the League s 50th Anniversary Sponsors Committee. Mrs. Benson presented the President with a copy of the "Great Idea" book. We then surged out of the East Room toward the ballroom at the other end of the lobby to have coffee and refreshments with the President and Mrs. Nixon and the other distinguished guests. We were also pleased to chat with Postmaster General Winton Blount of Montgomery who was present."

Other interests with which I have been involved included editing a national sorority magazine, the *Aglaia* of Phi Mu, from 1954 to 1960. In 1967 I joined a group of Montgomery historical preservationist and formed Landmarks Foundation. I am still a board member. I also became involved with the Montgomery Area Mental Health Authority and served as president in 1975.

Now that the League is celebrating its seventy-fifth birthday, I find that I am a source of history about "back when" in the League. And who is to argue with me – they weren't there.

written by Sarah Cabot Pierce

JUDGE ANNIE LOLA PRICE
1905 - 1972

The Wonderful Record That Other Woman Have Made In Alabama Was Most Helpful To Me.

Judge Annie Lola Price credited the successes of female lawyers for aiding her professional achievements. The first woman appointed a state judge in Alabama, Annie improved Alabama by making informed judicial decisions. A member of the League of Women Voters, she also contributed to her community, both locally and statewide, through her civic activities.

Born in Cullman, most probably in 1905 (she did not like to reveal her age), Annie was the daughter of Dr. William Henry and Lena Mae Culpepper Price. Her parents' families had been pioneers, settling in Cullman County when land first became available.

A local physician, Dr. Price provided well for his family both financially and culturally. Annie recalled that "He was a great believer in learning." Dr. Price devoted attention to his children, teaching them the "Three Rs" of "spelling, reading and arithmetic" and "the enjoyment of literature." She remembered, "When I was little he spent a great deal of time with me." Her father's tutoring influenced her ability to think critically and to make fair decisions. Annie excelled in her hometown's public schools, graduating from Cullman High School at age seventeen.

Lena Mae Culpepper Price died during the influenza epidemic that swept the country and Alabama in 1918. Her daughter, eager to further her education, traveled north to attend Athens College. At home, her widower father sold the large family home and rented rooms which were easier for him and the three remaining Price children to manage. Annie returned home on weekends to help with household chores, primarily cooking and cleaning.

When her father abruptly died in 1923, the orphaned Annie Price realized that her younger sisters, Orpha and Frances, and brother William needed her guidance and love. She resigned from Athens College and rented rooms in Cullman. Responsible both emotionally and financially for the children, she suddenly found herself in the role of surrogate mother. She arranged for the children's schooling to continue and quickly learned basic parenting skills. "A home knits the family together, and from the time my father died I always tried to keep the family together." Watching every penny, Annie also sought employment. "We had previously lived well, enjoying things we wanted and two family cars. My father always made a very good living."

Having taken a shorthand course in Birmingham, Annie applied for work in local offices. She took dictation in a laundry until she was offered a better position. Two Cullman lawyers, A. A. (Quill) Griffith and Joel B. Brown, hired her to be their secretary. In the men's law office, Annie performed routine tasks, such as filing and researching cases, and served as their stenographer in court.

Griffith and Brown recognized that their legal secretary was an intelligent woman and began suggesting that she utilize their books and cases to study law. "I did not study it too seriously at first," she explained. Annie initially believed that her studies would improve her stenography and would "enable me better to understand the work of the office." She soon became infatuated with the law.

"I never even gave a single thought to going into law practice," she remembered. "It never crossed my mind. Everyone in my family, for years back, had been doctors, not lawyers." Advising her as she read thick lawbooks and asked pertinent questions, Annie's mentors provided her a legal education rivaling that of a university's.

With such individualized attention and hands-on experiences with applications of Alabama law, Annie quickly absorbed reams of essential legal knowledge. She focused on legal precedents that were widely used and became aware of more unique cases that tested her ability to conduct legal research. Within a few years, she felt confident enough to attempt to pass the Alabama Bar examination.

Her aptitude enabled her to answer skillfully the questions posed by the State Board of Law Examiners in Montgomery. Only four women were in the group of thirty-one candidates. She answered the rigorous questions posed by university professors and sagacious attorneys. Annie was admitted to the bar in 1928 (less than one-half of the applicants passed). Annie was one of the last people in Alabama to accomplish this feat without graduating from law school. She also was one of Alabama's only female lawyers. Ironically, at that time, Alabama women were barred from jury duty and had few legal rights.

Working in Griffith's firm, Annie privately practiced law in her hometown. Sometimes she appeared in court alone, defending clients, and at other times she and Griffith used a team approach. Annie's first case posed an interesting dilemma. Her clients, two young boys, had confessed to a burglary. Despite their professed guilt, the tall, slender Annie professionally defended them and felt some success in her argument because the jury's verdict rendered the minimum sentence.

In 1935, Annie's mentor, Griffith, who had been named judge of the Eighth Judicial Circuit, appointed her as court reporter. Retaining her law practice on a part-time basis, Annie speedily recorded court transactions in shorthand. She traveled a four county circuit and reported thousands of cases. "This was very interesting because being an attorney I was able to grasp the points of law as they were presented," she told a reporter. "I also was able to help Judge Griffith 'run down' points of law during trials."

Her intimate contact with a multitude of cases enhanced her knowledge of state law. She learned a variety of legal strategies and became aware of how attorneys interacted with the judge. Also, some of the cases were sent to the Court of Appeals, and she had to read the superior court judges' opinions. These experiences would help her shape her own judicial philosophy and manner when she was named to the bench.

After a decade of carefully transcribing court testimony, Annie embarked on a new application of her legal knowledge. James E. Folsom, whom Annie had known in Cullman, was inaugurated governor in January, 1947. Among his appointments, he named hometown people to prominent administration positions, including Kenneth Griffith, the son of Judge Griffith, as legal adviser. Griffith asked Annie to be Folsom's assistant legal advisor, and she moved to Montgomery. She would live in the capitol city the remainder of her life.

Three years later, Folsom appointed Annie Price as the gubernatorial legal adviser when Griffith became Cullman's probate judge. She was the first Alabama woman to achieve that position. Geoffrey Birt of the *Alabama Journal* commented that Annie distanced herself from political conflict: "Throughout the time she was a member of the governor's staff, no one ever saw her affected by the storms which sometimes swept through the capitol." Her behind-the-scenes tasks including saving the Capitol's lunch-rooms from bankruptcy and making them economically self-sufficient. Within a year, she acquired a much more powerful role when she became the only woman judge in the state.

In January, 1951, just days before his term expired, Governor Folsom appointed Annie Price to Alabama's Court of Appeals, the "state's second highest tribunal," to fill the vacancy after Judge Charles R. Bricken died. She shunned notoriety and feared rejection by the other judges. She chose to take the oath of office in Secretary of State Mabel Amos's office, just hours after Folsom's announcement.

The first woman to sit on the state court of appeals, Annie was overwhelmed with criticism. "A lot of male heads wagged in wonder and apprehension." Newspaper editors, lawyers, and judges denounced Governor Folsom for selecting a woman whom they considered unqualified for "the most important appointment" Folsom made in office "from a judicial standpoint." Critics cited Annie's lack of a formal legal education and unfamiliarity with appellate courts as being possibly detrimental to the high court's standards. They feared that she would be unable to grasp "complex, subtle questions of law" and declared "Folsom has thrown Miss Price in over her head."

Bricken's death changed plans. Originally Annie was slated to resign her role as adviser to become assistant attorney general. She found herself in a highly publicized position. A *Montgomery Advertiser* editor made a pun of her name, "Miss Justice Anne Price." He noted that previously she had been "inconspicuous and uncontroversial." The paper reported "Our impression is that she was an *efficient, courteous* functionary who maintained an unspectacular but unbroken loyalty to the governor."

The *Montgomery Advertiser* printed an editorial stating that her appointment was "jarring to the legal profession" and frivolous. The Montgomery journalist argued that Annie had never tried a case and believed that her presence would add no prestige to the court. "No one could contend that on a pure basis of *experience* that Miss Price is qualified for her post." The journalists admitted that they were "genuinely sorry to have to say this of Miss Price, for she is . . . *a winsome and admirable person*." Urging Folsom to reconsider because "this court rules on the precious liberties and rights of Alabama citizens," the reporters stressed that "none but the most highly qualified may rightfully preside on this bench." They emphasized "her experience does not entitle her to this eminence."

The editorials concluded that Governor Folsom had appointed her only because she was a woman and from north Alabama, both politically empowering considerations. The essays also noted the inconsistencies in Alabama law that permitted a woman to serve as a superior court judge but banned her from jury duty. Ironically, Annie would be able to overrule male jury's decisions in her courtroom but would not be permitted to issue verdicts from the jury box.

Governor Folsom responded that Annie Price had exceptional qualifications for the position. "The public reaction to her appointment was good," he later recalled. "At that time when she was appointed, there were very few women on such courts in the United States. She never disappointed me in any way, and I did not ever put any pressure on her." Trial lawyers such as E.O. Boswell of Geneva, Alabama, wrote letters to the editor, protesting vituperative editorials. Boswell declared, "From my association with Miss Price in a legal way, I am convinced that if she receives from her associates on the bench the cooperation, which unquestionably she will, in my opinion she will add dignity and prestige to the court."

From the first, Judge Annie Price handled discriminatory situations that she encountered with aplomb. Mabel Amos humorously described how when Governor Gordon Person presented his opening address to the state legislature, specific arrangements had been made to seat the state's dignitaries. After the chief justice and supreme court had been seated, Judge Robert B. Carr led the court of appeals into the courtroom. Judges Annie L. Price and Robert B. Harwood followed the presiding judge but were stopped by the doorkeeper who mistakenly shouted, "Halt, you can't go in there. These places are reserved for the judges." Annie enjoyed telling amusing anecdotes, especially the story of how Judge Harwood convinced the man to let her be seated.

Receiving an annual salary of $9,000 (which was later raised by the legislature), Annie began her judicial service to the state of Alabama. Judges Carr and Harwood welcomed their quiet peer, who frequently consulted them about court protocol and legal questions. Although at first they might have worried about her legal background and ability to serve, they attempted to ease her transition onto the court. After her debut, however, they quickly became aware of her numerous fine qualities, most importantly her keen legal judgement and common sense.

Considering her as an asset not a burden to the court, Judges Carr and Harwood countered Annie's opponents. Newspapers continued to second-guess Folsom's appointment. Ruling fairly and justly from the bench, Judge Annie Price began to earn the confidence of and respect from some of her critics. Within six months of her appointment, the *Montgomery Advertiser* admitted that Judge Price had gained advocates because "our informal inquiries indicate that there is a surprising volume of support for her among some of the leading North Alabama lawyers."

During the year that Judge Annie Price filled the unexpired court term, she won accolades both from her peers and from the public. Running for election in 1952, She encountered three serious male contenders, many of them backed by powerful groups and the state bar. Judges Carr and Harwood were unopposed. The 1952 campaign was bitter, with one journalist suggesting that Judges Carr and Harwood should each take on one of Judge Price's opponents to make the campaign more chivalrous and fair.

The Honorable Annie Price, however, fought her own political battles well. She traveled to almost every Alabama county to speak, while still preparing for regular court sessions. She earned the most votes in the May 6 Democratic primary. Then she handily defeated Solicitor George C. Johnson of Athens in the June runoff by accruing over twice as many votes as he did.

The *Birmingham News* welcomed the "voter's choice" because it "marks a new step ahead on the progress of women to equal rights and opportunities with men in all respects." Although Alabama women had been elected secretary of state and state auditor, primarily administrative positions, officials considered Judge Price's election more important because she had been elected on the basis of her ability to render informed and fair decisions that would have direct impact on Alabamians.

"Price's victory was no fluke," the newspaper remarked, noting that female support "alone could not have brought victory. Male voters favored her in large numbers. She had the backing of many lawyers who knew her ability and fitness." Price's election also "marks the steady decline of the idea that women cannot possess the calmness, the dispassionateness, the objectivity desired on the bench. There are many good women judges in the country. Alabama has its first, and one of the first in the nation to serve on so high a court."

Judge Price was re-elected without opposition to three additional six-year court terms in 1958, 1964, and 1970. Her critics quickly silenced their comments and instead, Judge Price was lauded. The *Montgomery Advertiser*, in December 1954, labeled her "brilliant" and "gracious." "She is a credit to womanhood," the *Montgomery Examiner*, which selected Judge Price as "Woman of the Week" on May 3, 1951, praised. "By her able and dignified performance she has silenced those who doubted that a woman could do the job."

Judge Annie Lola Price devoted her life to serving Alabama's superior courts. On the state court of appeals, she focused on insuring that justice was delivered. She worked daily in her book-lined chambers in Montgomery's Judicial Building. Judge Brown, her former employer, had a nearby office as presiding justice of the state supreme court. Every Monday, she conferred with the other appellate judges about cases.

Wearing her black judicial robe into the courtroom as the clerk cried, "The Court of Appeals is now in session," Judge Price heard civil cases on Tuesday afternoons and criminal cases on Thursdays. She carefully listened to clerks read case lists and often asked lawyers to clarify points. Some cases were heard in a few minutes, while others argued by defense attorneys resulted in lengthy sessions.

She wore her reddish-brown curls in a conservative style. Annie dressed professionally, wearing appropriate dresses and dignified suits. She preferred not to wear hats. A friendly person, she delivered her verdicts in her soft, northern Alabama accent. She treated attorneys appearing before her graciously but displayed a stern demeanor to command respect if mistreated by counselors. Having experienced her own personal sorrows and hardships with her family, she tended to be a sympathetic judge..

A serious advocate, she devoted her days and often nights to researching the cases that she heard. Surrounded by paperwork, especially after her election campaign, she often left her office with "homework" to "get current." Believing that education never ceased, she immersed herself in lawbooks from the state law library, especially when the court was recessed from July to September. Judge Price studied the minute details of each case, relying on her past legal experiences in Cullman as well as new knowledge that she acquired from legal discussions with Judges Carr and Harwood. Her mind became an amazing data bank of legal information as she considered transcripts, briefs, and arguments.

"When I first saw how much work was involved in this job, I was scared." She was also concerned about male lawyers criticizing her work, but she "tried not to worry about it, and problems always seem to work themselves out. My co-workers in the court were very nice to me, and some came around and offered to help me in any way they could."

Enjoying research, reading, and conferring with colleagues, Annie labored over writing her opinions. "I try to keep my opinions brief and concise," she told a reporter. "This is difficult, since writing has always been hard for me." Handwriting drafts, she painstakingly revised her wording and carefully cited her legal sources and elaborated on her reasoning. A clerk then typed up the opinions, which usually were both understandable and fair, and released them every Tuesday. Her colleagues commented that her rulings were penned "in indelible ink." In fact, her written decisions were so infallible that the Alabama Supreme Court rarely reversed her opinions, convincing many people that Judge Price was fully capable of performing her job.

Having served the court well, Judge Price was named presiding judge of the Alabama Court of Appeals when Judge Harwood was appointed to the Alabama Supreme Court in 1962. Seven years later, when the Alabama Court of Criminal Appeals was established, Judge Annie L. Price and the members of the court of appeals automatically became members. She was designated that court's presiding judge, and her outstanding performance on the bench impressed legal authorities across the United States.

Judge Annie Price expressed her gratitude to Governor Folsom for starting her on the path to her amazing judicial career. Without his opening the door for her to prove that she could capably serve on Alabama's high courts, she admitted that other women might not have received similar professional opportunities. Annie attempted to improve women's lives not only by being a role model and by expanding options in the legal profession for women, but also by securing legal victories.

She especially focused on securing for Alabama women the right to serve on juries. Throughout her legal career, Judge Price vocally decried the bias against women jury members. Jean Herman, president of the Montgomery League of Women Voters in 1952, cited Judge Price when she complained, "It just doesn't make sense to say that women shouldn't serve on juries. The fact that Annie Lola Price can hold the office she does but can't be on a jury shows how utterly ridiculous it is."

U.S. District Attorney Ira DeMent called Annie a "thorough scholar in the law" and "an inspiration to women in the profession of law." Annie agreed that female lawyers encountered discrimination in their male-dominated field (approximately sixty Alabama women practiced law in the 1950s) but believed that such obstacles could be overcome. Annie urged women to pursue their professional goals. She said that anything was possible for them if they worked hard enough. Committing herself to civic and professional organizations, Annie often spoke to women's groups who admired her. She worked with Alabama women to improve working and social conditions.

She was elected president of the Alabama Women Lawyers Association in 1951 and in 1957. Judge Price demanded that female attorneys seek more equitable conditions in their profession and that they maintain freedoms in state government. She also promoted state legislation to improve working conditions in industry, especially for female laborers. Citing reports that Alabama ranked low in regulating working hours and wages for women, Annie sought protective laws. She encouraged women to vote for female political candidates because "a woman in the Legislature can focus attention on necessary reforms." Annie participated in the National Association of Women Lawyers.

Judge Annie Price was also dedicated to civic work conducted by the League of Women Voters, the Montgomery Business and Professional Women's Club (she had been president of that group), the Altrusa, the American Legion Auxiliary, the Order of Eastern Star (she was past worthy matron in Cullman), and the Zonta Club. Judge Price assisted the Alabama Women's Commission and the Alabama Ethics Commission and supported Girls' State with her leadership. Every Sunday she worshiped at Montgomery's First Baptist Church, devoting time to church activities throughout the week.

Living with her sister, Orpha Black, in a Felder Avenue duplex, Annie also kept a home in Cullman where she visited relatives. She had learned to fly airplanes at the Cullman School of Aviation, receiving her private pilot's license in 1943. She recalled, "I took my first flight ten years before I got my license. And on that first flight we were in the air only ten minutes when we had to crash land on a cotton patch." Annie accumulated more than two hundred hours in the air, flying her personal plane cross-country between her two homes. She joined the Ninety-Nines, a group of early female pilots formed by Amelia Earhart.

At her Montgomery home, Annie enjoyed reading, especially *the Reader's Digest* because its condensed form fit her busy schedule. She cooked with her sister, watched movies, and dined with friends in town, having little time to prepare for parties. She disliked shopping and used what little spare time she had for legal research, community activities, and her piano lessons.

In June 1972, Annie traveled to Florida for a brief vacation. She was suffering from cancer. She wanted to relax and enjoy the peace and quiet of the beach. Her trip was abruptly ended when she became deathly ill. Rushed to Montgomery's St. Margaret's Hospital, she died on Sunday, June 18, 1972, just before eight in the evening. The *Montgomery Advertiser* printed a front page announcement as well as an obituary.

After a funeral service at Montgomery's First Baptist Church, Annie's body was taken to her hometown. She was survived by the siblings that she had raised after their parents' deaths; her brother, William Carl Price of Detroit; her sisters, Orpha Black of Montgomery and Frances Williamson of Panama City Beach, Florida; and her nieces and nephews.

Judge Annie Lola Price was buried in Cullman's city cemetery. In addition to Judges Aubrey M. Cates Jr., Reneau P. Almon, John C. Tyson III, and John O. Harris from the Alabama Court of Civil Appeals, judges from Alabama's Supreme Court and former Governor James E. Folsom served as her honorary pallbearers. Other leading judges paid tribute to the woman who had made unique contributions to Alabama's legal system. The graves of her early legal mentors and life-long friends, Judge A. A. Griffith and Judge Joel B. Brown, are near her final resting place.

On October 3, 1972, the Alabama Court of Criminal Appeals held a memorial service in the Supreme Court chamber for Judge Annie Lola Price. Opening the court's fall term, numerous relatives, citizens, colleagues, and state luminaries reflected on Judge Price's legal career. Secretary of State Mabel Amos presided over the ceremony with other speakers including Folsom and Annie's pastor Dr. J. R. White. Attorney Nina Miglionico, a Birmingham City Council member, stated, "Women will remember most her quietness, her dignity; I never once heard her say an unkind thing."

Judge Harwood eulogized that, "Judge Price's gracious dignity and gentle ways, reinforced by a fine legal mind, sound judgment and common sense, cast a beneficent influence on the entire court." He recalled, "I cannot remember ever hearing Judge Price utter a complaint." He lauded her personal strength, noting that "certainly she never bowed to any physical ailment. Even though grievously afflicted in the latter months of her life, she kept conscientiously and cheerfully to her tasks to within a few days of her death. She was unswerving in her search for true justice, and her gallant courage was a hallmark of her life."

Harwood reflected on her gentle nature yet firm convictions, "Judge Price quietly assumed her responsibilities, and quietly she surrendered them. Her influence will long linger in these halls, and our memories of her will remain spring green."

When Judge Annie Lola Price was posthumously inducted into the Alabama Women's Hall of Fame, Mabel Amos spoke, remembering how her friend had retained a sense of humor to counter discrimination and had conducted her work honestly and fairly. A plaque commemorates Annie at Judson College, where the hall of fame's archives are located. Mildred Griffin Yelverton profiled Judge Price in her book, *They Also Served: Twenty-five Remarkable Alabama Women*. Her valuable essay is one of the few biographical resources available about Annie. *Alabama Journal* reporter, Geoffrey Birt, painted this contemporary portrait of Judge Price. "She is remembered as a quiet, pleasant woman, with pencil in hand, writing down brief memoranda or checking references, but always with time to pause for a laugh."

Loyal to her profession and compassionate toward her community, Judge Annie Lola Price, from stenographer to presiding judge, used her legal prowess to make Alabama a better place. Working for the people of Alabama, Judge Price, according to Judge Kenneth Griffith, "left a great legacy" because "she had those qualities which go to make up a gentle woman." Alabama Bar Association officer, Roland M. Nachman, summarized Annie Price's life, "She was not only a fine judge but a great lady in every sense of the word."

written by Elizabeth D. Schafer

PHYLLIS JEANNE EDWARDS REA
1921 - 1993
Begin Early And Never Let Your Efforts Lag.

Phyllis Rea's profound motto served her well during her terms as state president of the Alabama League of Women Voters (1972-1977, 1978-1979). Also editor of the Voter (1968-1972) and active in the Auburn League of Women Voters (but never president of her local League), Phyllis improved both her immediate community and communities statewide by emphasizing the necessity of informed citizenship.

Through her League work, Phyllis pursued court litigation and election law reform, and helped improve the state constitution. She advocated consumer protection and betterment of education and the environment. Within the League her leadership made the state league more effective because of her efforts to improve communications between the state board and local leagues. Accentuating state League service to local boards she and state officers visited these groups at least once a year.

Phyllis openly proclaimed her position as state League president to be the best job in the state. She described her tasks as challenging, rewarding, and unique. Phyllis constantly encouraged women to become more active in politics and urged them to run for election to public office.

Born on December 20, 1921, in Richmond, Indiana, Phyllis Jeanne Edwards was the daughter of Dr. David Morton Edwards and Elizabeth Way Edwards. Her father, a renowned Quaker educator, was the president of Earlham College located at Richmond. The Edwards family's Quaker ties traced back to England before William Penn came to America. Dr. Edwards, a scholar who had studied in the British Museum, had also been president of William Penn College in Iowa and executive secretary of the Society of Friends in America's Indiana Council on International Relations. Throughout her life Phyllis always lived in college towns.

Dr. Edwards moved to Wichita, Kansas in 1934 when he was named president of Friends University. Phyllis was popular in her Wichita high school, enjoying meeting people and making lots of friends. In August 1939, her father was killed in a tragic automobile accident and Phyllis never drove again. Enrolling as a freshman that fall, Phyllis concentrated on her education as she knew her father would wish. As a campus leader, Phyllis often shared classes and activities during her sophomore year with a young man named Robert Rea. They discovered they had many similar interests and began dating in 1941 and continued dating until her graduation the following year.

Phyllis attended graduate school at Boston University earning an M.A. in English literature. While a student she worked as a reporter for the Quincy newspaper. After graduation in 1943, she accepted the position as head of the journalism department at Westbrook Junior College in Portland, Maine.

During World War II her fiancé, Bob Rea, trained as a naval aviation cadet. Phyllis and he corresponded, sharing their trials and tribulations during these years. Much later, as her husband, he edited a collection of these letters, *Wings of Gold: An Account of Naval Aviation Training in World War II: The Correspondence of Aviation Cadet/Ensign Robert R. Rea*, which were published by the University of Alabama Press in 1987.

Phyllis accepted Bob's proposal during her Christmas vacation in 1944. On his commissioning leave, he traveled to Maine where he traversed snowdrifts to marry Phyllis on Valentine's Day 1945. They honeymooned in Boston then visited her brother Paul Edwards in New York. They sadly separated at Grand Central Station where she caught a train north to Maine and he headed south to Florida.

When she finished her duties at the college, Phyllis moved to be with Bob. World War II soldiers' orders changed frequently, and Phyllis disliked living out of her suitcase, having to pack, move, and unpack clothes that were wrinkled.

Released from duty in November 1945, Bob and Phyllis returned to Wichita where they lived with his parents for one year while he went to school and taught flying. He entered graduate school at Indiana University the next fall, finishing his Ph.D. in English history and accepting a position at the Alabama Polytechnic Institute in 1950 as assistant professor of history.

Phyllis immediately liked the small-town atmosphere of Auburn. The Rea's daughter, Pamela, had been born April 13, 1946, keeping Phyllis busy, but she participated in numerous community groups, serving as vice president of the Friends of the Library and president of the campus' Newcomers Club.

Urged by friends and her husband to attend League of Women Voters meetings, Phyllis joined in 1957, the year Auburn's League was formed. Phyllis energetically filled local league positions, submitting publicity to local newspapers as public relations chairman, and also chairing the membership, state constitution item, constitutional revision, foreign relations, and state organization committees as well as being on the board and first vice-president.

She remembered, "The early Auburn League program was all so new to me that I didn't function too exactly to begin with. I went to the meetings and was very interested but I wasn't too sure what was going on. I do remember the first time we started working on the survey, the Know Your Town survey, and how involved and interesting that was and how thoroughly we all got involved in it."

Phyllis' public relations work was especially strong because of her academic and work experiences. She prepared weekly newspaper articles. As publication chairman she edited the first <u>This Is Auburn</u> booklet, a city survey published in 1968. She also fielded questions for the newspaper column, "Know Your City Government," begun in 1969, researching and writing answers for local citizens.

In the 1960s and early 1970s the Auburn League pursued a variety of issues including evaluating welfare services and studying the city's financial structure, public schools, and planning. League members, including Phyllis, sought to improve the juvenile court and to help the poor obtain adequate housing. They attempted to find alternatives to the city job tax and hoped to reform legislation through constitutional improvements. Voter services, town meetings, membership drives, and candidate nights were important activities to better their community.

In the 1960s, Phyllis edited the <u>Auburn Voter</u> for several years before joining the State Board and in 1968 agreed to edit the state newsletter the *Alabama Voter*. This work familiarized her with the state League as well as local Leagues, enabling her to consider serving as state League president.

After she was elected state League president in April 1972 (Alabama League membership averaged 800 women), Phyllis admitted that the only reason she considered being state president was that "I felt that we had a need to have the state board concentrate on the local leagues and visit them and get out more to really talk to them and to explain to them what the state board was doing and did do for them. I think that occasionally there was some misunderstanding because the communication lines weren't that open."

One of Phyllis' first projects as state League president was the Survey of Possible Election Law Litigation (SPELL survey). SPELL brought cases to court and became the basis of election law reform bills that she wrote with Jane Katz and Olivia Harrison. This packet of seven bills were influenced by litigation in which Phyllis testified.

"The litigation problems with election law difficulties in Alabama began the night after I became president of the League in `72," she stated. "When I got home I received word that the students were going to descend en masse upon the board of registrars in Opelika the very next day and they were going to demand their rights and the privilege to register."

Phyllis called the national league's litigation office the next morning to secure its support. The national officers agreed that she could sponsor the students in court. The students hired buses to take them to the courthouse and, despite long lines, everyone was registered. Rea laughed, "So that one dissolved and I thought all our problems were over and I could relax."

Later that summer an ACLU lawyer called Phyllis and asked her to find witnesses to testify in a lawsuit against the Tuscaloosa County Board of Registrars. A faculty member and his wife were leaving the country through an exchange program and had been denied an absentee ballot. Usually registrars permitted individuals whose work required them to be out of the state on election day to receive such a ballot. Phyllis was aware of a similar problem which occurred with Auburn League member, Claire Huck, and her husband. All of the people familiar with the Hucks's case were out of town, so Phyllis had to testify in Federal District Court in Birmingham on August 25, 1972.

She considered the trial to be "fascinating" and stressed that "We thought we had a marvelous case," but one month later the ACLU lawyer called to say they had lost the case because the judge ruled that faculty teaching out of the country had a choice. He considered such activities to be a vacation. When this case was appealed to the Supreme Court, that body refused to hear it ruling that it was a state's rights issue.

In September Phyllis became involved in another Tuscaloosa case due to a national League stipulation that only the state president could be the plaintiff in a court case, not a local league. In this case Phyllis testified that she considered the county's board of registrars lack of Saturday registration to discriminate against employees and students. A third case in south Alabama in February 1974, addressed a black couple's lawsuit that election of board of education members at large was discriminatory because it did not insure equal representation.

Even though every case she testified in resulted in a loss, Phyllis remarked, "I always felt that while we never won anything in litigation, we gained a great deal of experience and nearly everything we were fighting for and losing did become law under the voting rights act. So it was not lost in the long run." She insisted that the legal failures did not hurt the League's image and eventually inspired legal reforms that removed obstacles to voters.

Phyllis recalled, "Everyone was in absolute terror at the time, and we all thought 'Oh, dear, they're going to think of the League of Women Voters as those terrible radicals,' but the fascinating thing was there was absolutely no publicity on any of it excepting in the Tuscaloosa paper" and that was sparse. "It was really almost disappointing. We'd expected to make some kind of impact because we certainly went through enough agony and soul-searching to do it in the first place, and I must say my favorite pastime is not necessarily testifying in federal court."

Participating in litigation cases had set the League on a different course. Work for directors mushroomed as more major issues and new problems were added to the program and co-chairman positions were created during Phyllis' tenure. League members encountered more bills to support or oppose and the need for more money to conduct educational work. With too few women to address each issue, Phyllis and League members sought novel ways to cope with the challenges they faced.

She told an *Opelika-Auburn News* reporter that "the president's role is very complicated," but admitted that despite all of its demands and pressures it was "stimulating – fun. I've enjoyed it tremendously." Describing her volunteer work as a full-time career, she estimated that she answered hundreds of letters to provide information to researchers, ranging from schoolchildren to professors to government officials.

Averaging twenty pieces of League mail daily, Phyllis kept office hours and hired a temporary secretary to help with the overwhelming paperwork. Jotting information in a daily log to keep track "So I know who I wrote, when and what I said," Phyllis maintained the voluminous League records in file cabinets in her home. She called and contacted local leagues on a regular basis and wrote articles and speeches to be published and presented throughout Alabama.

In particular, Phyllis supported the League's nonpartisan political work. "We're interested in forming a concerned citizenry. We look at both sides of an issue. We're not trying to influence anybody. We support issues but we never support candidates or political parties."

Phyllis eagerly accepted every "call to action" from the national or state chapter to lobby the legislature. Noting that the state League usually had good relations with the national organization, Phyllis commented that sometimes the state and local Leagues disagreed on an issue. "The whole League principle is that we act on a consensus of opinion," she emphasized. Phyllis recommended telling local leagues that "It is not necessary that you study every single thing that comes up; it's ideal but if you find there is no interest in a particular problem in your community and your members are becoming bored and disinterested because of emphasis upon something they don't feel is important, you would do better to let that one sit on a back burner and concentrate on something that they are concerned about." She stated that sometimes the public criticized the League for not fixing broken stoplights or enforcing leash laws because many citizens "haven't the faintest idea" League work is on statewide issues.

In order to curry good relationships between state and local boards, Phyllis either traveled by bus or with fellow Auburn League member Nancy Lair who drove her around the state. Phyllis visited every local League at least once a year, realizing that she saw parts of Alabama that she probably would never have been aware of without the League. She also traveled to areas to speak at organizational meetings and charter chapters. Her trademark glasses, friendly smile, and slight frame clad in short-sleeved tunics, pantsuits, and jackets became familiar to politically interested Alabamians.

Soon after the presidential gavel was turned over to Phyllis, she was encouraged to lead a state fund drive. She remembered, "We started out with full enthusiasm and some years it has worked better than others. The trouble is that it's difficult to raise money across the state because it takes woman power and you run into the fact that in Alabama most of the industry is, of course, concentrated in Birmingham." These areas, Phyllis discovered, were more likely to donate funds, which raised another concern. "We have had to work very constantly trying to find an equitable way for the state to raise money and share with the local Leagues."

She recalled the League's fiftieth anniversary, "Oh, that was a very exciting time." For the Auburn League, Phyllis wrote a skit, "The Life and Times of the

League of Women Voters," in which costumed members—one woman wore a dashing raccoon coat—reenacted historic moments of the League. Phyllis' production then went statewide. A few years later Mary Swenson Miller interviewed Phyllis for her master's thesis, "Lobbyist for the People: The League of Women Voters of Alabama, 1920-1975."

Phyllis also supported the League's Legislative *Voting Record*, compiled by Jane Katz. "I think that has done more to inform legislators from the far-lying counties that don't have a league or have little contact with it because the legislative voting record reports on every county, on every legislator, on his action of a selected group of bills that we feel have a broad spectrum of interest."

By publicizing legislators' voting records in an objective non-judgmental manner, Phyllis trusted that the League would "help citizens to evaluate the performance of their legislators and also to understand better the legislative process." She also felt such reports would woo legislators to be congenial to the League: "There isn't a man alive who doesn't like to see his name in print, particularly if he's political, and doesn't check things to see if he's been quoted properly."

Phyllis professed that the League's campaign educational materials, including candidate's questionnaire, voter guide, PBS interviews with major candidates, and pre-runoff interviews were valuable in informing voters. She was proud that election day reporting of local returns by League members for ABC-TV, enabled the network to predict races. "Each year they say the League is the most dependable and accurate group."

She credited the League's sponsorship of the presidential debates as boosting public respect for their work. "I saw people with their mouths open saying `I just didn't understand, I didn't realize that the League was recognized other places. We thought you were nice but....' They were astonished," Phyllis remarked. "I think it has done more to bring the League name before the public and to raise people's opinions of us than anything else that ever happened."

She noted that "the people who are the most attracted to the League are often people who have just come to the state or have just become interested in political affairs and there is a rapid turnover especially in places like Huntsville" where people employed in space and military positions are frequently transferred. Many of these League members moved from northern states and wanted to understand southern politics.

In 1973 Phyllis participated in a citizens conference to implement a statewide campaign to gain approval of the Judicial Article of the constitution. As county women's coordinator, she exuberantly talked of the successes, "Let me tell you, it was an exciting experience. Knowing that you were a part of the action—that your particular little cog was an essential part of the campaign machine was immensely gratifying."

She confided, "I didn't even mind traveling by bus to Montgomery, Birmingham and Huntsville to appear on talk shows. I was selling a product that I believed in. And the satisfaction that came to all of us on the day following the election when we knew we had won was indescribable. We knew we had been effective and we knew that without the efforts of each of us, it couldn't have happened. We felt that we were a part of history."

Although federally funded programs required access for citizens, Phyllis criticized that this "sounds great and democratic and fair, but the catch lies in finding innovative and successful ways of obtaining public feedback. This is where the challenge lies—both to the public and to the governmental agency involved." She complained that the major problem was an inexperienced and uneducated citizenry who trusted professional politicians and special interest group representatives to make their decisions, not realizing that those people were often self-serving and interested in profit not the welfare of the general public.

Proudest of her work with publications, especially the legislative voting reports, a poll watchers booklet, Facts and Issues about environmental management practices in Alabama, and Get Ready to Vote in Alabama, Phyllis stressed, "This kind of thing is a service to the public because it's unbiased, impartial information. We have no axe to grind—all we're for is better government."

The League sought ratification of the Equal Rights Amendment. She sent the League booklet, In Pursuit of Equal Rights: Women in the Seventies, to state legislators in Montgomery, asking for their support. She noted the League's anniversary on February 14, stating, "On this occasion we remind you that the commitment and determination which overcame insurmountable odds to win the right to vote a half century ago is now directed toward ensuring women equal opportunity under the law. We feel that passage of the Equal Rights Amendment is essential for the full potential of all citizens, men and women, to be realized." She hoped the League's publication "should help you to dispel the needless fears which have been used to oppose ratification."

In her efforts to convince the Alabama legislature to ratify the Equal Rights Amendment, Phyllis wrote Governor George Wallace asking that February 15, 1976, be proclaimed Susan B. Anthony Day. She told Wallace, "The League of Women Voters feels particular kinship with this great woman inasmuch as our organization was founded February 15, 1920, to help educate women on their newly-won right to vote. Had it not been for the hard work of Susan B. Anthony and other courageous women we might still be struggling for the right to vote today." She also had August 26, 1976, declared Women's Equality Day, urging Alabamians to "wrap-up ratification of the Equal Rights Amendment."

At this time she also mounted a letter writing campaign through state newspapers demanding a new state constitution, stating the over-amended, obsolete document was "too silly for words" and needed to be revised. At the annual Auburn League meeting, she noted the state constitution had not been rewritten since 1901 and it was "filled with detail, burdened with obsolete material, lengthened by unnecessary, sometimes even frivolous, provisions, made rigid by numerous restrictions and amended and amended and amended."

Demanding that the state debt be limited, that committee chairmen be more accountable, and that the speaker of the house be selected by secret ballot for "protection from political coercion," Phyllis also wanted home rule because "At present, citizens and county officials must go to their legislators to get help when they want something done locally. And then they remember where the help came from at election time."

In February, 1977, she also attacked tax reform proposals in the state legislature as being "patchwork and piecemeal." She stated that the League "has felt for many years that Alabama needs a general overhaul of its basic tax structure in order to achieve a more equitable system. Sound tax reform, however, must include a realistic evaluation of revenue needs at all levels of government, anticipated loss and gain of revenues, and a careful consideration of the effects of tax changes on taxpayers."

In addition to monitoring the state government and presiding at state conventions throughout the state, Phyllis represented the Alabama League at national conventions, hearing such inspiring women as Ruth Bader Ginsburg speak. She participated in a League bicentennial forum in New Orleans with other southern League presidents, congressmen, lawyers, and journalists to discuss if the Constitution would be applicable to twentieth century problems and issues.

She accepted her final presidential term only because the woman elected president moved and "No one else wanted to take it in midstream so just before the yearly meeting I became president again." By late 1970s socioeconomic conditions for women had changed and the League's focus on women's rights had metamorphosed into seeking equal opportunities for all Americans.

Primarily concerned with effective citizen participation in politics, Phyllis underscored the League's purpose. "The League is not just another social group. We are a group of women and men with a serious purpose—which is to encourage people to take an active interest in government on all levels—local, state and national—and to demonstrate that the informed citizen can influence what happens in government and how."

At a June, 1979 seminar at Auburn University, Phyllis told participants, "It boils down to this: You can't afford to sit back and just let things happen. You need to be involved and informed but even more than that—you need to know how to take action and to be politically effective." She stressed, "When a person has made the decision to discover how and where he can invest his time in a very real effort to make himself count in the matter of who is elected and what legislation and laws are passed, it is a major step forward."

She outlined how people can be politically involved. "There are three important ways immediately apparent: he can vote; he can go into a political party and work as a volunteer in that party's activities; he can join an independent, nonpartisan organization which concerns itself with governmental issues in order to study such issue and work for those measures which interest him."

Of voting, Phyllis insisted, "There is more to this basic right of citizenship than simply pulling a lever or making marks on a paper ballot. We have learned the hard way that by only a few votes—sometimes even one vote—the outcome of an election can be determined." Phyllis lamented, "even more devastating .... is voter apathy .... the hundreds of people who simply don't vote at all because they are convinced that it doesn't matter." She warned, "It is very chilling, and even frightening, to realize how easily—through the 'open door of voter-apathy,' an unscrupulous gang can get in and take over." She stressed that political parties were important. "I see political parties as the link between the individual and government officials."

In order to become an effective citizen, Phyllis said, "There are opportunities every day, if you are looking for them," such as public hearings, city council, library board, county commission, planning and zoning meetings. "Just by your attendance you serve a double purpose—you learn and you put our public servants on notice that you are watching them (or supporting them)." Phyllis urged individuals to encourage voter registration and voting.

She advocated research. "If you want to know more about members of the legislature or your congressional delegation—clip from the newspapers, read the articles telling how they voted on different issues. Better yet, go talk to them, ask their opinions, listen, and then tell them how you feel about the issues. If you can't see them personally, write to them, keep a carbon, and when they reply, check to see whether they have answered your questions."

Despite discouragement and isolation she recommended, "Acting alone is better than doing nothing at all but ten voices are more effective and one hundred or five hundred people speaking on the same theme has an impact." Of citizen grassroots campaigns, she commented, "Group action has great value in itself, for important as winning any specific political campaign may be, the most valuable element in it, is the stimulation of the participant's sense of personal involvement and the feeling of responsibility for his government. In fact, I believe this is the essential ingredient of democracy."

She advised citizens to respect people who disagree with their opinions and refuse to be convinced to switch allegiances, "where there is a form of government that is inefficient and unresponsive to the people, there are sure to be people who benefit, directly or indirectly by maintaining that form of government. These people will not accept a change without a determined battle. They usually have plenty of money to finance their campaigns, and they are by no means always scrupulous about presenting the facts."

"Nothing will give you greater satisfaction than to be a part of a living proof that the democratic process is still valid—that all political power is still vested in people like you and me, that we can change things. Being involved in an activity like this, a community-wide effort, brings alive the realization of your responsibility for your government in a way that nothing else can. Everyone involved in the project will have benefitted, they will have learned more about the town, its problems and its needs. They will have become better citizens just from the fact of having been involved."

Outside League circles, Governor George Wallace appointed Phyllis to the Statewide Health Coordination Council to review state actions regarding public health and the National Committee to Save Our Public Libraries where funding was a major problem. Phyllis noted, "There's always so many demands on the taxpayer's money that the libraries often get short changed. But libraries are vital to us and our children."

After she retired as state president, Phyllis continued to be active in the Auburn League "because I've got the habit." After six years of presidential duties that "fills your days and nights" she was ready to turn the reins of leadership to new women, insisting that, "In any organization, it's important to have a change in leadership. It's time for someone else's views to be shown."

Freed of state League responsibilities Phyllis enjoyed tending her garden, cooking, and entertaining her numerous friends at parties she hosted in her home. She visited her daughter and son-in-law, Pamela Rea Machemer and Paul Aubrey, who teach mathematics and British history at a Pennsylvanian Quaker boarding school. Phyllis adored her grandchildren, Robert and Kate, and saw her sister Lois Fudge, a pianist, when possible. She and Bob enjoyed their retirement years, traveling and writing.

Suffering from disabling arthritis, which her mother had also endured, Phyllis' health declined. Phyllis Rea died on Friday, May 28, 1993, of cancer. She died just two years shy of her golden wedding anniversary. Choosing to live her final months in her home, she was cared for by nurses from Hospice of Lee County who fondly recall her delightful sense of humor that remained until the end. Phyllis acted so cheerful despite being a terminal patient that many of her friends said that with her upbeat attitude it was difficult to tell that Phyllis was dying. Shortly before her death she carefully dispensed her scrapbooks and files, insuring that they would be saved for researchers interested in the League and Alabama politics. The *Opelika-Auburn News* printed an obituary noting her loss was devastating to family and to the community. They also noted Phyllis' numerous contributions to the League.

The Auburn League of Women Voters annually bestows the Phyllis Rea Award to recognize a person in the community "who has demonstrated in time and energy that she/he embodies the principles of the League of Women Voters; that is, to be an informed and active participant in our representative government." Leah Rawls Atkins, a close friend of the Rea family, established the award in 1993 to honor Phyllis' community contributions, stating "For many years I have observed the commitment and hard work that Phyllis devoted to the League. She has inspired many young women to commit their own time to League projects and I feel it is most fitting that in the years to come her inspiration will live to hearten future generations." Phyllis' friend and dedicated League member, Olivia Harrison, was the first person to receive the award.

Phyllis said that "one of the things that is the hardest to teach people, but that anyone who really cares about the League and really believes what we believe has to realize, is that all change is gradual. That when you leap in without knowing the background, without knowing how you arrived at your own position, you can get yourself in hot water." She stressed that members carefully study issues and know both sides "to confront the argument." She maintained such high standards not only in her thirty plus years of League work but in her own life. Phyllis was proud of her work and the League's accomplishments, summarizing "We've done some things that I think are very worthwhile."

written by Elizabeth D. Schafer

CLARA LULL ROBISON

Help Elect The Best People For The Office
And Oppose The Ones Who Are Not.

A lthough she never held public office, this is the story of a small town Alabama woman from Wetumpka, Alabama, who, all of her life, took politics personally and seriously. She was imbued with the notion that she had a responsibility to help elect the best people for office and to oppose the ones who were not. She was my mother, Clara Lull Robison. Prior to elections she quietly campaigned up and down our street, often taking along a sack of peas to shell to show it was just a neighborly visit.

Mother's brother served as mayor of Wetumpka. Her father was mayor several times and served as probate judge of Elmore County in the 1890s. Wetumpka is seventeen miles north of the state capital, Montgomery, on the beautiful Coosa River.

As a small child I became aware, just after World War I, that Mother was outraged at Old Senator "Cotton" Tom Heflin (he of the string tie and large black hat) because he vociferously opposed "the pure, white Southern lady" voting. I visualized him as a monster with horns.

As an example of her personal involvement in the community, I recall some years ago that the merchants in the cities around the state began the custom, in the hot summer months, of closing a half day each week, usually Wednesday afternoons, to give their employees time off. When this happened in nearby Montgomery, Mother urged my father, a merchant, to take the lead in this. But he assured her the locals would never agree. So she persuaded a friend to accompany her in visiting all the businesses with a petition to sign agreeing to the half holiday, and they succeeded.

I recall another municipal problem—at least Mother thought it was. We had dusty streets in the summer and muddy ones in the winter. Mother felt compelled to do something about it. Oh, how I hated to be sent out to "water" the street in front of our house with a garden hose. The sun was brutal. But Montgomery-to-Birmingham traffic created quite a lot of dust on our street. Again, against my father's best advice, she found friends living on each of four main residential streets to accompany her to get the residents to sign a petition to have the streets paved. Impressed with the list of petitioners, the City Council agreed to pave the streets.

For many years of her life, Mother was a slightly rotund little lady with a sweet, gentle face and blue eyes. Her curly brown, graying hair was worn in a knot on the back of her head. A mother of four, her looks belied her actions. Once while she was standing at the curb in front of my father's store, two men were in earnest political conversation, one a candidate for what we now call district attorney. He was waving his arms and was making many promises if elected. His back was to Mother while his listener faced her. She opposed his candidacy. After listening to his speech, she caught the eye of the other fellow and gave him a big wink. Whereupon he broke into loud laughter. The candidate swirled around to see the cause and found a motherly-looking lady gazing innocently in another direction.

After Mother was elderly she was distressed one summer to see the city park looking neglected with weeds. It was situated on a lovely, picturesque bend above the Coosa River that flows through the center of Wetumpka. I lived next door. She called on me to get up early one morning and to drive her and her yardman to the park to cut the weeds. She continued to improved her town and participated in many activities for the benefit of all.

During World War II a large, tall, wooden pen was built in the center of downtown Wetumpka to collect donations of all manner of metal products for the war effort. On the top of the pile was mother's five-gallon, Wear Ever, aluminum jelly-making and fruit-cake mixing pot. I felt like averting my eyes every time I passed. It hurt me so to see that grand old pot go to war.

Her last good deed, I believe, was to send me in her place to petition the businesses of the town to close a full day every week. This was during World War II when the public had more money than things to buy. It was believed that cutting a day of business each week would benefit the economy and would encourage the public to spend more on war bonds. I traveled her same route with a friend and we accomplished our goal.

An amateur politician, Mother was an independent politically and always voted for the person rather than the party. She declared to the end that she had never failed to cast her ballot in any election. She joined the League of Women Voters in 1947 when it was organized in Wetumpka.

written by Sarah Cabot Robison Pierce

Hazel Brannon Smith
1914-1994

Even If I Was Just One White Person, I Was A Beacon Of Hope To Thousands Of People. They Looked On Me As A Symbol Of Hope ... Who Stood Up For What Was Right.

Hazel Brannon Smith, a courageous editor, was the first female editor to receive the Pulitzer Prize. She spent a half century as a newspaper crusader fighting racism and other social ills. Smith was born on February 4, 1914, in Gadsden, Alabama. At the age of 16 she graduated from Gadsden High School. Because she was too young for college, she began working at the now defunct Gadsden *Etowah Observer.* Beginning with personal items, she soon was reporting front-page news and selling advertising.

After resigning from her job, she entered the University of Alabama where she majored in journalism and earned the high honor of managing editor of the *Crimson White* student paper. She once told the acting president of the University of Alabama that she was determined to be her own boss. "I told him," she said later in life, "I don't plan to take dictation when I finish college, I plan to give it. I've been liberated all my life."

Soon after her graduation in 1935, the Delta Zeta sorority beauty queen left Alabama for Holmes County, Mississippi. After borrowing $3,000, Smith bought a failing weekly, the Durant *News*, and within four years she had paid off the debt on it. In 1943 she bought the *Advertiser*, Mississippi's second oldest newspaper, in nearby Lexington, the county seat of Holmes County. She would own the paper in the farming town on the fringe of the Delta for 42 years. In the mid-1950s, she acquired two small weeklies, the Banner County *Outlook* in Flora and the *Northside Reporter* in Jackson.

Enjoying her role as a country editor, she became known for her broad brimmed Hattie Carnegie hats, flamboyant clothes, and her Cadillac convertible. Elected twice as a delegate to the Democratic National Convention, she became an old-fashioned states rights Dixiecrat—no hint of the civil rights activist she was later to become. She was noticeable though. Famed reporter Damon Runyon in 1940 described her as the "prettiest delegate" at the convention.

Her outspoken nature soon became evident through her editorials and her regular column, "Through Hazel's Eyes." Throughout the 1940s and early 1950s, she appealed to an end to open gambling and liquor sales, illegal practices that were sanctioned by the local sheriff. She once wrote, "There are some sheriffs in office in Mississippi who have lied to every man, woman, and child in their counties, but they have no more remorse than an egg-sucking dog."

In 1946, she was found in contempt of court after interviewing the widow of a black man who had been whipped to death. Two years later she accused a local jury of leniency for acquitting a defendant of gambling and bootlegging charges.

While on an ocean cruise, she met her future husband, Walter B. Smith, the ship's purser. She brought her Northern-born "Smitty" home to Lexington. They settled down in a house on a hill in the woods and drew up plans for their Southern-manor dream house.

On July 4, 1954, though, their lives changed forever. That day Smith – a traditional Southern belle, an ultraconservative Dixiecrat – underwent a marked evolution of conscience. When Holmes County sheriff Richard F. Byrd shot a young black man in the back on a public street, she became incensed. William Minor, a Mississippi journalist, said 40 years later at Smith's funeral that this incident was what changed her, "She was not a racist but she was not aware or highly sensitive to this issue of racism or injustice until that moment."

In a front-page editorial, Smith blasted the sheriff for the unprovoked shooting of the black man for allegedly "whooping" too loudly. She accused the sheriff of "violating every concept of justice, decency, and right" and said that he was "not fit to hold office." The sheriff sued her for libel, and a local, all-white jury awarded him $10,000. Although the Mississippi Supreme Court reversed the decision the next year, ruling that Smith's editorials had simply related the facts of the case, public opinion among the whites of the county was unforgiving.

One of the few white Southern editors to speak out against the white extremists of the era, Smith soon found herself taking on the White Citizens' Council, an anti-integration group, who made her its prime target with advertising boycotts against her paper.

The Council had been organized after the U.S. Supreme Court outlawed school segregation in 1954. Its purpose was to subvert the law by using economic and social pressure to maintain segregation. Smith had refused to support the organization that was particularly strong in Holmes County. The second poorest county in Mississippi, Holmes County had been a seat of rabid racism since slave revolts were brutally put down there before the Civil War. In the 1950s, some of the most outlandish racist statements uttered in the state legislature came from a pair of Holmes County delegates.

In one of the longest boycotts in newspaper history lasting nearly 17 years, the *Advertiser* lost all its business except for the power company, the phone company, and a few public-service ads. "The community pushed her, they radicalized her because they didn't leave her any place else to go—though she was never really a radical," Minor said of Smith.

Her columns in the 1950s were hardly liberal. She defended Joe McCarthy and once warned that a vote for Adlai Stevenson was "a vote for integration." She didn't advocate integration. Speaking about the Supreme Court decision in 1954 to integrate the public schools, she said, "No, I wasn't for it and I wasn't against it. I recognized that forced segregation creates an inherently unequal situation."

What Hazel Brannon Smith advocated was, simply, human rights for blacks. The more the white community attacked her, the more staunch she became. She persevered. She survived with sympathy and money from the North where she became fairly well known as a lonely brave woman taking on Jim Crow.

"She was a brave and crusty woman," said University of Mississippi history professor David Sansing. "She had to be brave to do that in Holmes County."

"She was one of those people who wasn't afraid of being hurt," civil rights leader Aaron Henry once said of her, "and people were being hurt. We all knew people who were killed."

Dr. Ed Mullins, dean of the University of Alabama School of Communications, said that when he was a student at the university in the 1950s, Smith was already talked about as a role model. "Professors Charles Scarritt and John Luskin held her up as an example of a high standard in journalism."

Over the years harassment continued against her. Her home was vandalized. Her newspaper office was set on fire. Her husband lost his job as administrator of a county hospital (although he later found another job, it was a lesser one). "I'm sure that if she had been a man, that they would have lynched her," said Minor. In 1958 the White Citizens Council launched their own paper, *The Holmes County Herald*. The paper was subsidized by well-to-do Council supporters.

Smith was entertaining friends in her home on Halloween night 1960 when the sound of exploding firecrackers brought her outside to see an eight-foot cross burning in her front yard. As teenagers retreated into nearby woods, Smith took a picture of the blazing cross and removed the license plate from the Chevrolet station wagon the young people had left behind. Smith later found that the automobile was licensed to Pat Barrett, the local prosecuting attorney, whose son Smith suspected of taking part in the cross-burning. In an editorial she wrote, "The cross was burned on my lawn this time. Next time, it could be yours."

Two months after the cross-burning, the *Clarion-Ledger* ran an article accusing Smith of meeting with black leaders. Two representatives of the state Sovereignty Commission, the Mississippi state agency organized to fight integration, had signed an affidavit saying they had seen Smith's car outside the *Free-Press*, Jackson's black newspaper. They claimed that Smith met with several black leaders, including Medgar Evers, secretary of the state NAACP. Senator T. M. Williams of Lexington made a speech concerning the affidavit on the Senate floor. He charged she was a shrewd and scheming woman who was trying to dictate the policies of Holmes County. Smith said in her paper that she was simply dropping off copies of the Free-Press in Jackson under her contract to print the paper.

The Sovereignty Commission used state funds to finance the Citizens' Council. In January 1961, she first criticized the Commission for approving up to $5,000 a month for the Council. By March she was calling for the abolishment of the Commission. She said that Mississippians' freedom was being threatened by the agency's tactics, which represented "our own home grown variety of fascism, Mississippi-born and nurtured."

As the 1960s began, Smith continued to defend blacks against unfair treatment. She was still not an integrationist. In July 1960, after she had won an award from the University of Southern Mississippi for her courage, she denounced the *Herald* for saying she had won the award for supporting integration. Smith believed that blacks and whites preferred to live separately, but that desegregation did not have to bring turmoil because both races wanted to live in peace. In the mid-1950s she had said she believed equalization of school funding was the best way to preserve segregation and avoid litigation.

In May 1963, Smith criticized the local sheriff for arresting Hartman Turnbow, a black man whose home had been firebombed. Smith interviewed Turnbow, who had recently attempted to register to vote, and concluded that it was ludicrous for the sheriff to accuse him of firebombing his own home.

In covering the firebombing incident, ignored by the Council's newspaper, Smith wrote news stories and also expressed her moral outrage in editorials. Proclaiming that a "lying editor" is "no good," she also commented editorially on her role in a suit brought by the U.S. Justice Department against the Holmes County sheriff for civil rights violations. Smith testified during the case that she had heard the sheriff say, "I do not intend that any Negro will vote while I am sheriff." Defending herself in the face of accusations from the White Citizens' Council newspaper that she had lied, Smith said, "Every one of us should be willing to stand up and be counted for what is right."

The next month, after the unprovoked killing of Alfred Brown, a black mental patient shot in the back one block from her newspaper office, Smith interviewed dozens of black residents to determine the facts. The killing occurred just four days before the murder of Medgar Evers, a civil rights leader, in Jackson. The law would not give her any information. The Council newspaper ignored the story. When Smith published an account critical of the police, two policemen filed a $100,000 libel suit against her, but later dropped it.

The week after the assassination of President John F. Kennedy, Smith wrote an editorial charging the South with abdicating its leadership to bigots and extremists who had created the atmosphere in which Kennedy was slain. "First Lincoln, Now Kennedy. The South Kills Another President," read the editorial's headline.

In 1964, Smith appeared on a biracial panel with civil rights leaders in Washington, D.C., to discuss the disappearance of three civil rights workers in Neshoba County. "You don't have to have a sheet to belong to the Klan," she said. "It's as much a state of mind as anything else." Soon after her comments during that "Freedom Summer," one of her papers, the Jackson *Northside Reporter* was fire-bombed.

With the Voting Rights Act, blacks gradually began to win pieces of the political structure in a county which was 71% black. State Rep. Robert Clark in 1967 became the first black elected to the Mississippi legislature since Reconstruction. Clark was an early supporter of Smith and rallied blacks to boycott white merchants who had boycotted the *Advertiser*.

Ironically, Clark and the black leadership broke with Smith. Clark complained that Smith never realized that blacks no longer needed whites to speak for them. "Hazel was a great help to blacks for a long time, but as they came into their own in Holmes County, they developed their own leadership. It was another era, and they didn't need her. It wasn't really rejection, but she didn't understand."

She struggled on with her newspaper which was now the second, lesser publication in Holmes County. She sold some land holdings and borrowed money to keep going. Although Smith had to mortgage her property and built up a debt of $80,000 and traded her Cadillac for a Nash Rambler, she never gave up her dream to build her mansion. She unwisely used every penny she could muster to erect her dream house Hazelwood and to furnish its 14 rooms. It was a brick-columned house on a wooded hill at the western edge of town, a Greek Revival house modeled after *Gone with the Wind's* "Tara."

In November 1982 her 66-year-old husband, who was then administrator of the Holmes County School system, was cleaning the gutters of their home when he fell from the ladder and died. Rose Tate, her longtime housekeeper, said Smith seemed to deteriorate after his death. Her memory began to fail as her financial troubles escalated.

The last issue of the *Advertiser* was printed on September 19, 1985. The next year the bank foreclosed, took her newspaper, repossessed her home, and hauled away her furniture.

"The truth put her out of business. That's exactly right. The truth," said J. S. Travis, a black man with a shoe shop just off the old town square in Lexington, next to the plain, concrete-faced building that once housed the *Advertiser*. Almost $250,000 in debt, the ill and disoriented crusader left Mississippi to go back home to Gadsden to live with her sister Bonnie Geer.

Three years later she moved to the Royal Care Nursing Home in Cleveland, Tennessee, to be near her niece. When she died on May 14, 1994 at the age of 80, few residents in southeast Tennessee knew that a giant in the civil rights movement had lived among them.

Although Smith had paid a large price for speaking out against racial injustice, she did receive much national acclaim. In 1952 she was the recipient of the National Headliners award from Theta Sigma Phi, the highest honor given to a female journalist. She received the 1960 Elijah Lovejoy Award for Courage in Journalism and the 1963 Golden Quill Editorial Award from the International Conference of Weekly Newspaper Editors. In 1964 she was named Woman of Conscience by the National Council of Women of the U.S.

Smith was a charter member of the Mississippi Press Women and served as its president from 1956-58. In 1971 she was named the first Woman of Achievement by the Press Women. Also in 1972 she was selected by the National Federation of Press Women as its Woman of Achievement. On June 20, 1987, she was inducted into the Mississippi Press Association s Hall of Fame.

Her highest honor, though, was the 1964 Pulitzer Prize for Editorial Writing given for her previous year's work. The Pulitzer committee in presenting the award stated it was given to her for her "steadfast adherence to her editorial duty in the face of great pressure and opposition."

After receiving her Pulitzer, Smith described what she saw as her role as an editor: "All we have done here is try to meet honestly the issues as they arose. We did not ask for, nor run from this fight with the White Citizens' Council. But we have given it all we have, nearly 10 years of our lives, loss of financial security and a big mortgage. We would do the same thing over again...My interest has been to print the truth and protect and defend the freedom of all Mississippians. It will continue."

Ironically, as her remaining possessions were cleared from her house when she prepared to move back to Alabama, an old certificate was found amid the piles of newspaper and clutter in the den where she had written most of those tenacious "Through Hazel's Eyes" columns. It was the 1964 Pulitzer Prize.

In 1984 reporter Cathy Trost noted in a *Wall Street Journal* article that the famed editor "fantasizes that a movie will be made about her, and she will get money for her life story." That fantasy never came true for Smith, a victim of Alzheimer's disease. By the time the April 1994 movie, *A Passion for Justice: The Life Story of Hazel Brannon Smith*, starring Jane Seymour was televised, Smith was near death. She never knew that her fight against intolerance and bigotry finally was told and that thousands of viewers did at last catch a glimpse of her noble career.

At her funeral, Mississippi syndicated columnist Bill Minor delivered a fitting eulogy to a bold journalist who had taken a strong stance against racism during the most turbulent times in Mississippi. "At a time when there were very few voices speaking up for racial justice and showing courage in the face of organized bigotry, she was a lone voice and that took great courage."

written by C. Joanne Sloan

DORAH HEYMAN STERNE
1896-1994
Work For Community Improvement
and Have Friends Of All Ages.

Dorah Heyman was born on October 29, 1896 in Atlanta. No doubt her parents, Minna Simon and Arthur Heyman, had high expectations for their first child and only daughter. Their expectations were met and surpassed. Dorah Heyman Sterne was an outstanding community leader, a loving wife and mother, a devoted relative and a loyal friend.

From the time she came to Birmingham in the 1920s as the bride of Mervyn Hayden Sterne, Dorah was involved in the League of Women Voters, American Association of University Women, the National Council of Jewish Women, the Girl Scouts of America and many other organizations. Named to commissions on education and prison reform, she worked to improve people's lives all over Alabama. Dorah was also on the Jefferson County Commission on Economic Opportunity.

Dorah's father, Arthur Heyman, was a lawyer in Atlanta, Georgia. He was born near Albany, Georgia. Her mother, Minna Simon, was from New Orleans. Dorah had three younger brothers. Two are deceased – Charles was a businessman in Rome, Georgia, and Herman was a lawyer in Atlanta. Her brother, Joseph, is a retired business consultant and lives in Atlanta.

Dorah graduated from high school in Atlanta in 1919. Then she earned a B.A. degree from Smith College in Massachusetts with Phi Beta Kappa honors. As an alumna of Smith College, Dorah Sterne was awarded a Smith College Medal in 1985 for her active involvement in civic organizations in Birmingham and throughout the state. From the late 1920s until the early 1970s, her husband, Mervyn Hayden Stern, was a Birmingham business man and a civic force. He died in 1974 from a stroke. She lived at 2437 Tyler Road in Birmingham from the 1950s until her death. Their daughter, Dorah Heyman Stern Rosen, was born in 1933. She was an active volunteer and very involved in city politics until she retired. Dorah's grandson, Allan Rosen, said at her memorial service that what he had learned from Nana was "to work for community improvement and to have friends of all ages."

She also believed strongly in family ties. Dorah was very close to her parents and her brothers. Friends and family were very important to her and she was also close to her brother's children and their extended family. She had life long friendships, spanning decades, with Dr. Abraham "Russ" Russakoff and his widow, Irene. Another important friendship was between the Sterns and Bernadine and Charles Zukoski, a former mayor of Mountainbrook. Granddaughter, Dorah Rosen, said, "Nana really cared for the Ruskoff children and the children of many other friends. She had warm relationships with many people decades younger than herself. Those who were visiting from outside Birmingham usually made a special point to visit her."

Though she had many concerns and obligations, Dorah remained close to her family in Georgia. Her brother, Joseph Heyman, still lives in Atlanta, where Herman's widow, Josephine Heyman, also lives. Her daughter, Dorah Lawrence Rosen, and granddaughter, Dorah Lee Rosen, live in Birmingham. Dorah's grandson, Allan Hayden Rosen, granddaughter-in-law and great-grandson, Michael Rosen, live in Carrboro, NC. Her grandson, Neil Rosen, and great-grandson, Jacob Isadore Rosen, live in Washington, DC. Dorah was also close to the Sterne clan and her many relations through marriage. No matter how busy she was, Dorah never forgot her friends or colleagues. Her reputation as a gracious hostess was widespread and well-deserved.

Dorah was perhaps most proud of her work in the 1940s on the Osborne Report which recommended many of the same changes mandated by Judge Pointer. She focused on education – school systems, child care, and traditional culture. Dorah was also proud of the many Girl Scout projects she worked on, especially for the establishment of a summer camp for African-American Girl Scouts. Her niece, Jane Katz, was influenced by Dorah's work with the League. Jane was State LWV Legislative chairperson and LWV lobbyist from 1964 to 1986.

The Sterns established a scholarship at Birmingham Southern College which is reserved for students who live outside the South. They were one of the founders of the Museum's Art Education Council. The Sterns also worked to improve the city libraries.

Although her granddaughter, Dorah Rosen, says Dorah was not religious, she believed strongly in her Jewish heritage. She was a member and served on the board of Temple Emanu-El in Birmingham.

Dorah Stern served on state committees concerned with raising educational standards for schools and colleges and with instituting prison reform as well as on the Jefferson County Commission on Economic Opportunity. She was a regional leader of Girl Scouts of America and served on the boards of the Birmingham chapters of many organizations, including the American Association of University Women, the League of Women Voters, and the National Council of Jewish Women. She received many awards and citations. The last honor during her lifetime was a Community Award from the Women s Studies Department at the University of Alabama in Birmingham.

Dorah Heyman Sterne was 97 when she died on April 9, 1994. Margie McDermott, president of the League of Women Voters of Greater Birmingham, wrote this article for the LWV's newsletter *The Voter* to commemorate Dora's life.

We celebrate the memory and mourn our loss of our dear friend, Dorah Sterne. Mrs. Sterne was a special friend to the Birmingham League. In 1973, she almost single-handed saved the Birmingham League from being disbanded by the National League Board. She sent out a very successful appeal for contributions to 1,000 people which put our League on a sound financial base.

During the years 1973-74 we officially became the League of Women Voters of Greater Birmingham. On May 22, 1977, we celebrated our 25th anniversary with a Silver Tea held in the Bowron Room in the Birmingham Public Library. We presented Birmingham League Memorabilia to library archivist, Dr. Marvin Whiting. Mrs. Sterne was Honorary Chairwoman. Mrs. Sterne reminisced about the League's failures and successes in its early days here.

It was at this tea that Mrs. Sterne discussed with Gaynelle Tatum and Judy Hand the idea of our League obtaining an office. (A permanent League office had been needed for many years.) Mrs. Sterne offered to donate the money to pay the rent. She did this until her failing health prevented it in the last couple of years (from 1977-1992). The office was established at the Commerce Center where it remains today.

Dora was the only Life Member of the League of Women Voters in Alabama. She was a League member for 50 years. She was a special friend to us and we shall miss her.

written by Abigail M. Toffel

Photo courtesy of NASA

KATHRYN RYAN CORDELL THORNTON, PH.D.
1952 -

I Figured I Would Take The Hardest Road And Any Other Choices Would Be Easier.

A stronaut Dr. Kathryn Thornton explains how she selected her career as a nuclear physicist. "And that philosophy has served me fairly well." She was the first female Alabamian in space, the first Alabamian to walk in space, and the second American woman to walk in space. Kathryn has flown on three shuttle flights, including the spectacular Hubble Space Telescope repair mission. She has logged 593 hours in space and holds the record for spacewalking by female astronauts. Kathryn is also the first American woman to make two spacewalks. A devoted mother, she encourages children to pursue careers in science and engineering and to make the world, and the universe, a better place to live.

Born on August 17, 1952, in Montgomery, Alabama, Kathryn was one of six children. Her parents, William Carten and Elsie Elizabeth Ryan Cordell, owned and operated Cordell's Drive-In restaurant where the children worked during summers. Coming of age during the Space Race, Kathryn was aware of such watershed events as Sputnik's orbit and Alan Shepard's fifteen minutes above the earth. "I didn't know when I was a child that I wanted to be an astronaut because there weren't any women astronauts."

As a child, the brown-haired, green-eyed Kathy played "moon landing" with her

145

siblings. "When I was a kid we got a tape recorder for Christmas and walkie talkies. We used to go as far away as we could go on the walkie talkie and record it on the tape recorder and it sounded just like the Apollo missions which were going on at the time. We pretended like we were on the moon." As a ten-year-old, she convinced her three brothers and two sisters to be mission control on top of a Montgomery hill while she skateboarded downhill with her walkie talkie to the "moon." When she "landed," she radioed to her siblings, reporting lunar conditions that she encountered. Kathy Thornton loved school, especially science and mathematics, which many people did not consider appropriate for girls to study at that time. A physics teacher at Sidney Lanier High School encouraged her to focus on that subject. "My dad thought I should do something useful. He didn't classify physics as useful." Labeling herself a nerd—"All the girls in physics class were"—she earned straight A's and graduated in 1970. Her parents told her to select an in-state college, and "Auburn was the place for me. I couldn't have made a better choice, even though I didn't know it at the time."

Kathryn admits that in college "I didn't know what I wanted to do when I grew up." She decided to face the toughest challenges that she could find. She found intellectual soul mates in the physics department. Enjoying the puzzles that physics presented, Kathryn recollects "I tried math and then chemistry, but when I found out you had to pay for what you broke, I changed my mind." She also jokes that she doesn't like to wash test tubes.

"I remember having a good time. It was friendly, unpretentious, and very open and warm. Not every place is like that." One prank that she enjoyed involved wearing white lab coats and carrying Geiger counters and then scaring "the football players, who were sunbathing on the top of a building, into thinking there had been a radiation leak at the campus reactor."

Kathryn excelled in her studies. Her classes were taught mostly by male professors and attended primarily by male students. Her professors remember her as a shy student who quickly mastered concepts. She agrees, "I'm pretty quiet. I don't usually talk much to people. I don't know. I usually just stay in the receiving mode." In college, her studies came before clubs and social activities. She refused an invitation to a fraternity sweetheart rush party because it interfered with her chemistry lab.

She especially credits the physics department head, Dr. Howard Carr, for insuring that Auburn physics graduates received a balance of technical and theoretical education. The intensive hands-on training in Auburn engineering and physics laboratories, building and repairing equipment, prepared her well. It gave her an edge over other astronaut candidates who had more classroom experiences than real-life applications. She also taught physical science labs for Dr. Charlotte Ward, gaining new perspectives on how the world functions. Kathryn received her B.S. in applied physics on June 6, 1974.

She continued her education because "I still didn't know enough. I always wanted to learn." Earning a graduate fellowship to the University of Virginia, Kathryn finished a M.S. in physics in May 1977 and a Ph.D. two years later. Her dissertation, "High Energy Proton Production in Medium Energy Nuclear Reactions," resulted from nuclear physics research programs that she had participated in at the Oak Ridge National Laboratory, Brookhaven National Laboratory, the Indiana University Cyclotron Facility, and the Space Radiation Effects Laboratory. Kathryn conducted statistical analyses of heavy-ion nuclear reactions and light-ion production by bombarding various nuclei with high-energy ion beams. Her scholarship qualified her for election to honoraries including Sigma Xi, Sigma Pi Sigma, and Phi Kappa Phi and organizations such as the American Physical Society and the American Association for the Advancement of Science.

In 1979, Kathryn Thornton earned a prestigious NATO postdoctoral fellowship to continue her research at the Max Planck Institute for Nuclear Physics in Heidelberg, West Germany. She returned to America in 1980 and accepted a physics position at the Army Foreign Science and Technology Center in Charlottesville, Virginia.

Several years later she saw an announcement that the National Aeronautics and Space Administration (NASA) was looking for a new class of astronaut candidates. She met the qualifications, and filled out an application. It was a "chance in a million" to fulfill NASA's high standards. She believed that becoming an astronaut would be the best way to utilize her scientific training and technical ability.

Kathryn endured interviews and medical examinations. On May 23, 1984, NASA announced the names of seventeen astronauts selected from 4,934 applicants to be members of its Group 10 of candidates. Dr. Kathryn C. Thornton was listed. She responded to congratulatory phone calls, "It's pretty incredible, I never expected it."

She was excited about her new professional adventure. Kathryn moved to Houston, Texas, trading in her quiet life as a physicist for the very public role as an astronaut. "It's an experience that not many people in our generation are going to have," she told reporters. "It's one I want to have." She married her student adviser, Stephen T. Thornton, after she completed her Ph.D. in 1979, becoming stepmother to his two sons, Kenneth and Michael. Her husband decided to remain in Charlottesville where he was a professor of physics and director of the University of Virginia's Institute of Nuclear and Particle Physics. Kathryn took their two-year-old daughter, Carol Elizabeth (born on March 16, 1982) to Houston.

"The first couple of years of having a new baby were real hard" and "there were times when I was pretty sure I'd reached my limit." Kathryn said that the sacrifices the couple have made are worthwhile. "You just cope. You do what you have to do. We see each other when we can. So far, it's worked out, but it's not the way I want to spend the rest of my life." She emphasizes that she would have regretted not becoming an astronaut. She says she would have always wondered what could have been.

She credits her husband for enabling her to pursue her dreams. "I don't think I could have survived as long, if my husband wasn't as supportive as he is. He gets down about every three or four weeks for long weekends" and they talk daily on the telephone. Stephen Thornton lauds his wife, "Kathy is very talented. In my opinion, she's never been challenged in life. She's very bright."

Kathryn's children are a big part of her life, too. Daughters Laura Lee (born on December 2, 1985) and Susan Annette (November 20, 1990) were both delivered during Kathryn's training program and in between missions. She described her dual life to *Washington Post* reporter, Kathy Sawyer, who published "The Astronaut's Two Orbits: Kathryn Thornton, Shuttling Between Her Roles as Mom and Space Pioneer," on February 8, 1994. Kathryn told Sawyer that her children "don't think it's any big deal" that their mother is an astronaut. "It's the way things have always been as far as they're concerned. Their friends' mommies and daddies are astronauts and they don't think it's anything special."

When she first arrived at Johnson Space Center in 1984, Kathryn began a training and evaluation course. Finishing in July 1985, she qualified as a mission specialist assigned to a future space shuttle crew. She explains, "Becoming a part of the NASA space shuttle program has started a new career for me. A mission specialist does practically everything in the program except actually pilot the shuttle." Her advanced training involved science and engineering classes and hours practicing on flight simulators, where she studied jets and spacecraft.

Kathryn endured survival training and served on the escape test crew at the Kennedy Space Center in Florida. She simulated emergency rescues of flight crews and workers on the launch pad to make escape procedures safer. Assigned to the Astronaut Office's Mission Development Branch, she aided in the development of payloads for future missions. Kathryn verified flight computer software in the Shuttle Avionics Integration Laboratory (SAIL)—where she almost gave birth to daughter Laura—and was a member of the Vehicle Integration Test Team (VITT), supporting the STS-26 mission at Kennedy. She has also been a capsule communicator (CAP-COM) at Johnson for several shuttle missions.

NASA announced on November 30, 1988, that Kathryn's first spaceflight would be on STS-33. Training intensified, and as a civilian mission specialist, Kathryn boarded the shuttle Discovery and was launched into orbit on the night of November 22, 1989. "Liftoff felt like someone gently pushing me from behind. I thought it would be much worse than it really was. I had expected to be almost shaken apart." The change of gravity felt incredible. At first it "felt like an elephant sitting on my chest." Then zero gravity occurred and "I just said, `Oh Wow,' as my feet floated up in the air." Other than her excitement about being in space, she adjusted well.

Transporting a classified military payload, Kathryn and her crew mates deployed a spy satellite created by the National Security Agency to detect signals from Soviet military installations. She also supervised experiments for the Star Wars missile defense system and military projects and space medical projects with mission specialist Dr. Story Musgrave. The astronauts took a holiday break, and Kathryn ate Thanksgiving turkey with all of the fixings sealed in vacuum-tight pouches and cans.

She also observed the Earth, amazed at seeing entire continents in one glance. Kathryn admits that she gained a greater appreciation for nature as a result of her unique viewing range. "It's really just one big world," she contemplates. "Maybe all the people out there are neighbors. I spent a lot of time looking out the window thinking about things like that." She also senses the perpetual nature of our planet. Kathryn said that ecologists would like the astronauts "to say the Earth is so fragile, that we're going to destroy it," but "I can't say that. We are very limited in the temperature we can live in and the chemistry we can live in. We can destroy us. We can't destroy this

Earth. We're the ones to worry about, not the just the planet."

Welcomed by an orange and blue sunset, Kathryn landed on November 27 at Edwards Air Force Base. She had orbited the earth seventy-nine times and accrued 120 hours, 6 minutes and 46 seconds in space. She had to keep quiet about the details of her Department of Defense mission. Kathryn returned to her Houston home before dawn, shed her flight suit covered with NASA insignia, kicked off her steel-toed combat boots, and fell asleep exhausted. After days of floating in zero gravity, her body felt extremely heavy.

After a brief maternity leave, she entered training for her second flight. One month after her daughter Susan was born, NASA had announced that Kathryn was assigned to STS-49. Launched on the shuttle Endeavour's maiden flight on May 7, 1992, Kathryn performed a variety of tasks during the seven day mission. With the shuttle crew, she retrieved, repaired, and redeployed the Intelsat VI, a commercial international telecommunications satellite. Mission Control enjoyed teasing the astronauts like waking them up to Boxcar Willie wailing "I Wake Up Every Morning With a Smile on My Face."

Preparing for the assembly of the space station Freedom, Kathryn tested space station construction techniques. She also explored Extravehicular Activity (EVA) rescue procedures to capture untethered astronauts drifting in space. She was startled when an alarm on her spacesuit signaled her to secure herself in an airlock and hook up to a cooling umbilical cord to resolve a temperature problem.

Her EVA of 7-hours and 45-minutes exceeded the combined total of the two previous woman spacewalkers, American Kathryn Sullivan and Soviet Svetlana Savistkaya. She reflects on her spacewalking experiences, watching her home planet from 365 miles away as the shuttle orbited at 17,550 miles per hour. "You exit head first and looking up," she says, then "after the first `Wow!' you become comfortable."

Returning to earth, Kathryn prepared for an even greater challenge. The billion-plus dollar Hubble Space Telescope, the largest astronomical observatory launched into orbit by a previous shuttle mission, transmitted blurred images. NASA decided that a group of astronauts, including Kathryn, would be assigned to restore its focusing capabilities. For ten months, Kathryn practiced fixing the telescope by working over four hundred hours in the neutral buoyancy water tank, which mimicked zero gravity conditions, at Huntsville's Marshall Space Flight Center.

Kathryn blasted into space on Endeavour on the night of December 2, 1993, which was also her daughter Laura's 8th birthday. The youngster jokingly commented, "I want to sue the government and NASA. They wouldn't let me see my mother." Kathryn was the sole woman on the Hubble service and repair crew. She wore a bulky EVA spacesuit that would weigh four hundred pounds on earth. Kathryn skillfully managed the bulky garment as she maneuvered her svelte frame—at 5'4" she weighs a mere 115 pounds, most of it muscle. "I never thought I would be regarded as big enough or strong enough" to walk in the EVA suit, she admits. She explains how she accomplishes her goals despite such obstacles, "It's about 90 percent attitude."

As she exited the shuttle's cargo bay for her EVA, she remembers, "I just thought, `Please, let me do it right.'" During the repair mission to capture and replace the telescope's solar power wings, in which she was joined by teammates, Kathryn balanced a damaged forty-foot long, four hundred pound solar panel over her head for ten minutes until it was time to release it into space. Journalists compared her to a female Atlas.

Perched in deep space on the end of the shuttle's robotic mechanical arm, Kathryn steadied the solar array, trying to prevent damage to the telescope and the shuttle. "There was nothing to it." As she waited, Kathryn says, "I was looking at a few dings in the solar cells where they had taken hits over the years." During the "eye surgery," the astronauts also installed corrective lenses in a phone-booth sized device known as the Corrective Optics Space Telescope Axial Replacement (COSTAR). Kathryn's technical expertise, acquired from her hands-on collegiate training, enabled her to quickly and resourcefully fix unexpected problems on the spot. This prevented NASA from having to allocate funds for additional shuttle missions to repair the telescope.

During her EVAs, Kathryn established new space walk records, totaling 21 hours of EVA. The Hubble Space Telescope was successfully repaired. She landed on the evening of December 13 at the Kennedy Space Center. The Hubble crew, having traveled 4,433,772 miles in 163 orbits, earned much acclaim. They skillfully clarified the telescope's view of the cosmos (it revealed marvelous images of the Shoemaker-Levy 9 comet colliding into Jupiter in July 1994) and extended the time of its usefulness. Kathryn and her colleagues also boosted public support for NASA and continued space exploration. With the STS-61 crew, she toured Europe, visited President Bill Clinton at the White House, and appeared on the popular television sitcom, "Home Improvement."

Happy to return home, she focused on her family. "I tell my daughters that they need to go to college and have a marketable trade or career because the chances are overwhelming that they will end up having to help support their family. I want what they do with their life to be their choice, so what I push on them at every opportunity is to get the educational background. Then they will have the opportunity to choose to do whatever they like."

An excellent role model, Kathryn is especially interested in talking to school children. She hopes to excite kids about technology. "To keep our nation in the forefront technologically, we must keep producing a new crop of scientists and engineers. The scientists and engineers of the next century are in kindergarten now, and we must start preparing them and encouraging them immediately. We need to make science fun for them—show them that science is a fascinating, hands-on learning experience and not a boring exercise of learning by rote."

Telling youngsters about her outer space adventures, she describes careers in science and urges children not to be afraid of challenges or risks. She says she is always dreaming of future space travel and concludes her talks by saying that she hopes that the first person who will step on Mars is in the room.

Kathryn also returns to her hometown and alma maters. She was honored in October 1992, at Auburn University's celebration of the centennial of women's admission to the University. Two years later she was a featured speaker at a twenty-fifth anniversary moon landing conference at Auburn. She has also donated sentimental collegiate items, such as pictures of Auburn's first female graduates and an Auburn license plate emblazoned with STS-33, that she carried into space with her.

"I can't imagine," she said in her soft Alabama accent, "that any other job that would hold my interest would be that much easier. I'd still have all the problems that having three kids causes, just day-to-day life. But I can't imagine any job that would be more fun" than being an astronaut. She is devoted to her children and worries about strains on them. She considers their best interests first. "Leaving home each time is the hardest thing of all. It's tough on families. After you've done that, strapping on a rocket is no big deal."

Stephen Thornton escorts his daughters to each launch and landing, then takes care of them while their mother is in outer space. During the mission, the Thorntons talk by video phone and write letters transmitted electronically to their five-bedroom brick home. Pendants of their mother's mission patch hang from necklaces that Kathryn gave her daughters.

More comfortable in jeans and tennis shoes than a spacesuit, Kathryn accompanies her daughters to the normal activities that she enjoyed as a child: playing softball, camping with Girl Scouts, competing on the swim team, and attending church. She also likes to scuba dive and ski. Kathryn has been known to bake cookies at two a.m. in order to meet the demands of being a mother.

She admits that it is impossible to "ever do anything completely" and tries "to skim what's really important off the top and let the rest go." Kathryn argues, "Women can't have it all—we can have a little bit all of the time, or all of it a little bit of the time, but we never have it all, all of the time. If you think about the changes in our society, particularly as far as women are concerned in the last one hundred years, it's mind boggling.

"Now women are heads of household in half the homes in the United States. Most mothers of young children just thirty years ago were not outside of the home earning a salary. Today they are about required to do that," because "without the contribution of women, about sixty percent of the households in America would be below the poverty level."

Kathryn said that common sense is necessary to balance the responsibilities that she faces. Children need constant attention, and space flight training can add up to twelve-hour days. "I take one flight at a time. Every time I get ready, I say this will be my last one. The pressure to get ready is really difficult." Before a mission, she is quarantined one week from her family to prevent exposure to contagious diseases. And after her return, she is expected to make public appearances throughout the country.

In order to succeed as an astronaut, "You have to be self-directed, a self-starter. You get a job to do and you just go off and do it." She comments that being an astronaut is a lot like becoming a parent, "Generally, you don't get step-by-step direction on how to do something. Most importantly you have to enjoy learning, because that's what you'll continue to do through our whole career here." The "training is never over. You stay in what we call the pilot pool, meaning you continue in the simulators to maintain proficiency until you get assigned to a flight. We also have technical jobs in the office." When she's not training for a specific mission, Kathryn specializes in communicating with shuttles in flight. "I spend most of my time supporting other astronauts who are in space." Although she's been an astronaut for eleven years, she only spent a few days in space. The communication task "is the next best thing to being there. You're part of the team. You probably know more about the mission than the crew. But they do have a better view."

"We're trained to do a lot of the generic type things, such as satellite launches and space walking. That's just a basis. When you get assigned to a mission, that determines specifically what you do. You may use some of that training or you may not. But at least you have a starting point." The best part about being an astronaut is that her job is always changing. "As soon as you learn something, you move on to something else. There's nothing routine about it. It's a lot of fun."

Currently an active astronaut, Kathryn's fourth mission is scheduled for September 1995. She will be the payload commander of the second United States Microgravity Laboratory mission (USML-2), a sixteen-day trip, designated as STS-73. She will monitor experiments in fluid physics, biotechnology, and combustion and materials sciences. "I would like to go to Mars. I want to look around, explore, see what's there." This probably will not happen, because "We need to get a space station up to start with. I think that needs our support at this time. And then, perhaps we can move on from there to a lunar colony—developing an outpost on the moon." Kathryn stresses that space science must be advanced with new methods and technology. "We need to learn to sustain ourselves in space. We aren't going to be able to carry everything we need to go to Mars. For long durations of space flight we need to learn about reusing air and water and things like that, which we're going to learn on the space station. The time you don't want to learn that is halfway to Mars."

She is proud of the ideas and advances in technology resulting from the space program and their impact on society. "That knowledge finds its way into all of our lives, into our economy and products and things" to improve our quality of life. Kathryn believes that universities and government agencies should cooperate as fully as possible to expedite NASA's proposed objectives by generating and following through with space-oriented research.

A team player, Kathryn Thornton promotes NASA, not herself. She is labeled as "serious," "fun," and "spunky" by friends and crew mates. K.T., as the astronauts call her, wishes journalists would focus on NASA's achievements not her personal glory. Astronaut John Blaha told the *Washington Post* that Kathryn is "not pushy. She doesn't need to be out front. But if she is pushed out front, she performs like Joe Montana."

Kathryn Thornton is one of a growing troupe of female astronauts who are thriving in what once was a male-dominated agency. Even though she considers being an astronaut as just a "regular job," her intellectual talents and Alabama "down-to-earth" manner have enriched the global community. Whether in orbit or on land, "Every day is different and it's an exciting feeling to learn something new. I've always enjoyed that and I'm still enjoying that."

written by Elizabeth D. Schafer

CHARLOTTE BERKLEY REED WARD, PH.D.
1929 -

At Home Nobody Ever Told Me There Was Anything I Couldn't Do Because I Was A Girl.

D
r. Charlotte Ward is an Auburn University physics professor who has made outstanding contributions in bettering her community. She has served three terms as president of the Auburn League of Women Voters. Charlotte won the 1995 Academic Freedom Award presented by the Auburn University Chapter of the American Association of University Professors. She has devoted her life to higher education and the study of science and technology. She has embraced her own philosophy.

Educated as a chemist during the 1940s and 1950s when few women entered that field, Ward, who is fond of mystery novels, especially the Cat Who series penned by Lillian Jackson Braun, puns about her professional achievements, "I made a career about being the woman who was first."

A self-defined "professional wild-eyed liberal" who is well respected on a traditionally conservative campus, Ward explains that she would not pursue work that she did not enjoy: "I only do things for fun." Known for her entertaining sense of humor, Charlotte is also held in high esteem by her colleagues, friends, and students for being extremely fair and non-judgmental in her relations with other people.

A woman of many interests, Ward can usually be found in the thick of community activities. With her long hair pulled back into a ponytail at the nape of her neck, she is as comfortable in sweat suits to explore the outdoors as she is in an elegant scarf-draped dress and jacket to lecture in the classroom.

Born in Lexington, Kentucky, on February 19, 1929, the daughter of Henrietta Ilhardt and William Ritter Reed, Charlotte had an unusual childhood. She is proud of her genealogy. Her father's family were Scotch-Irish, "the usual stock of the South," who moved from Virginia to Kentucky after the American Revolution. Her mother's people were English Catholics who immigrated to Maryland with Lord Calvert.

One great, great-grandfather became a pressman for the Louisville Courier Journal, working for its famous editor Henry Watterson. "I always say grandma thought that civilization stopped at the Louisville city limits, everywhere else was just the backwoods." Charlotte said. Another grandfather was the son of German immigrants who settled in Cincinnati. A commercial photographer, he moved to Kentucky, near Lexington, where her mother grew up.

Charlotte's father met her mother when she was a home economics student at the University of Kentucky. He was working near campus. Ward's maternal grandfather had done well financially selling real estate and gave both of his daughters rings as college graduation presents. He also promised the girls trips to Europe if they did not marry for two years after graduation, but according to Ward, "Neither one of them got to Europe."

Charlotte's parents were married about five years before she was born. Her mother died several months later. There were no antibiotics or sulfa and "It wasn't unusual for women to die of infections after childbirth and that's what happened to my mother." Her father, a traveling salesman, "did not particularly want his daughter to be raised Catholic. He gave me to his great aunts who had helped to raise him" after his own father had abandoned his mother.

Infant Charlotte moved to her father's hometown, Mount Sterling, Kentucky, where three great aunts and a great uncle, all unmarried, devotedly raised her. Charlotte's paternal grandmother's siblings "took care of everything. They took care of their parents until they died. They gathered up all the family strays, of which I was one." Not one for wallowing in self pity, Charlotte asserts, "they were my family so I always felt kind of sorry for kids who just had ordinary parents because I had four older, doting adults catering to my every whim. It's a wonder I ever even learned to walk. I was spoiled rotten."

Her great aunts were influential in molding Charlotte's perception of womanhood. "These three women were very strong people. They didn't depend on their brother or any other males. They were the strong members of the household. Aunt Bess, who was the oldest of the sisters, tried desperately to bring me up to be a southern lady and she felt she was not successful." In tribute to her great aunts, Charlotte named her two daughters Bess and Emma Rae.

Her Uncle B (James William Wilkerson) was a "remarkable influence" on Charlotte. The oldest of her caregivers, he was devoted to her education. Together they took walks, and "He told me about nature, baseball and politics—what else does a girl need to know, anyway?" She credits her uncle for initiating her love of science. They observed birds, identified trees and flowers, and located constellations together.

Charlotte enjoyed collecting specimens including shells or leaves. "I was just born in the wrong century. I should have been a nineteenth century naturalist." She also ties her political interest to her uncle, whom she claims "was a true son of his yellow dog democrat father. He was fascinated by politics which was dinner table conversation at our house." Her family had deep Democratic roots. "It was the general feeling among my relatives that the Democratic Party was the best and they would vote for a yellow dog if he ran on the Democratic ticket."

Charlotte frequently visited her father, stepmother, and brother. In addition to her immediate family, Charlotte's primary mentor during childhood was Anise Hunt, an "umpteenth cousin." Hunt had been elected circuit clerk of Montgomery County, Kentucky, in her early 20s, serving until her death in her 70s. She started both Boy and Girl Scout troops in Mount Sterling, taught Sunday School, and assisted with the Baptist Young People's Union. Anise was well known for her generous nature such as providing funds for people who wanted to attend college.

She gave Charlotte one of her first jobs, selling driver's licenses at the courthouse. This work opened Charlotte's eyes to the inequities in society. She helped illiterate people sign their forms: "They'd touch the pen as I signed their name to make it legal." Her social conscience was alerted when a black man told her his name and it was the same as her great-grandfather's. This made her confront the fact that her people had once owned slaves. Anise was "my ideal" and made her aware that she should "give something back" to her community.

During her senior year she discovered chemistry. "I always said I might have been a physicist from the beginning, except, by skipping a grade in high school, I missed physics. She started college at age sixteen, attending her mother's alma mater (her youngest son would later graduate from Kentucky in political science and economics, making three generations of UK graduates). At college, Charlotte encountered what she terms "alphabetical discrimination." This form of discrimination often results in students from P to Z lacking sufficient courses on their schedules or being forced to take the very worst electives or professors.

"I decided that I was not going to major in something that I could not do well in when I could make an A in chemistry without working. So I became a chemist, and never regretted it." Kentucky's industrial chemistry program had a wonderful reputation. During World War II the program compressed a five year curriculum into four years in order to get men out to service positions. I was the "only girl who lasted the course." One other girl took chemistry classes but she went to medical school.

Charlotte encountered other discrimination, too. "Nobody at home ever told me that there was anything I couldn't do, but then there was my department head. He was a great teacher. I model my entire teaching career on him. He was a truly fine teacher but he did not think that women should be in the sciences." Nervous because of his attitudes toward women scientists, "I'd screw up my courage, grit my teeth and go into his office to get my schedule approved each quarter and listen to his little homily on had I considered being a technical secretary or chemical librarian because there weren't jobs for women in chemistry. So I'd listen politely and go right on with what I aimed to do all along." She finished her B.S. in 1949 and decided to go to graduate school but she did not ask the department chairman for a reference. Several other professors were "happy to write" recommendations for her.

Charlotte decided to go to Purdue because it paid the highest rate for graduate assistants. Borrowing enough money from the bank to live on until her first paycheck (which she paid back before her first summer break), Charlotte "knocked the top off of" Purdue's entrance test. The inorganic chemistry professor who monitored the tests "waylaid me in the hall" and asked to be her adviser. Charlotte, however, completed her master's with another man who focused on general chemistry and rarely supervised graduate students. He and his wife were childless and "adopted" her.

Charlotte married soon after she finished her M.S. in 1951. She had met her husband, Curt Ward, at Kentucky where he was a graduate student taking her undergraduate physical chemistry class. He had joined the navy the day after his seventeenth birthday and attended officer training courses. When the war ended the following year he used the G.I. Bill to attend several colleges. They met again at Purdue where Curt was working on a Ph.D. He asked her out to a performance on campus and they were married the next fall. "We agreed we wouldn't have a baby the first year we were married and due to the fact Em was two weeks late we didn't."

Armed with an M.S. in chemistry Charlotte briefly considered obtaining a Ph.D. in physics. She had completed her first course in quantum mechanics at Purdue and was intrigued by the work. Charlotte had several friends who were working on physics Ph.D.s but they seemed to be "taking forever to finish" because they were building scientific equipment such as cyclotrons from scratch. Charlotte decided, "I'd better stay a chemist and get out." She compromised by minoring in physics and exploring research in overlapping areas.

After daughter Emma joined the Ward family, Charlotte attended and taught classes during the day. Curt conducted his laboratory research at night. She ran his errands for him, checking out chemicals and equipment from the chemistry supply closet, while he watched the baby. They saw each other at breakfast and supper. Charlotte boasts, "Em was a good baby," stating that she only cried once, the night Charlotte was anxiously studying for a complicated math test. "I had this squalling infant in one arm and a vector analysis book in the other, not making much headway with either of them."

Charlotte chose a new advisor to direct her dissertation research, but admits that perhaps she should have remained with her master's advisor who later won the Nobel Prize. "He's the only Nobel Prize winner who knows me by my first name."

Seeking a career as a physical chemist she was taught by a gifted student named Leo, who was a good synthetic chemist. Charlotte and Leo successfully produced a compound that Purdue professors had been trying to make for years. Dismayed that "even fumble-fingers Ward could do it," the faculty decided that the compound was not unique enough to patent and did not consider useful applications for it. In later decades as concern for the environment, especially the deteriorating ozone, increased, Charlotte states, "It turns out that the compound that Leo and I made does not have any chlorine in it. It might have been possible to use it as a refrigerant without having it harm the ozone."

At Purdue there were no women on the chemistry faculty and few female students, especially in Charlotte's specialty, physical chemistry. She encountered discriminatory attitudes, most vexing from her major professor. "He really did think a married woman's place was in the home, especially if she had children. And so once Em came, he didn't really see why I was insistent on going on finishing the degree." Charlotte grew frustrated as "He just didn't see why it mattered whether I got it or not. He was very helpful, pushing Curt right on through, telling him to get out and get a job."

Curt finished the next year and was employed by Union Carbide in Buffalo, New York. Charlotte lacked at least one semester of research and needed several months to write up her laboratory work. Charlotte grew frustrated, "And here I am with the dissertation in limbo. A year passed . . . ." She finally passed her final oral examination five weeks before her son was born and received her diploma in the mail the week after they came home from the hospital. Charlotte was inducted into Sigma Delta Epsilon, the women's science honorary, as well as Phi Beta Kappa and Sigma Xi. She was not invited to join the chemistry honoraries because women were excluded.

Fortunately her husband did not embrace the discriminatory attitudes that Purdue's faculty did and encouraged her to persevere. Charlotte praises him, "I think my husband hung the moon." When she was pregnant with their first daughter, "I quit every night and Curt made me go back every morning. I asked him why and he said he knew I wouldn't be fit to live with otherwise. And he was absolutely right. If I hadn't had that kind of support and help and encouragement from him, I never would have made it because I certainly wasn't getting it from anyone else." She wistfully whispers, "he took his whole vacation" to take care of toddlers "so I could go and get the thing finished." Charlotte credits her marriage for her personal happiness, admitting that she both admires and loves her husband. "I would say he is perfect, but I wouldn't want his head to swell."

After spending three years in New York, Charlotte and Curt decided they both wanted to teach. Curt had acquired the industrial experience necessary to join a chemistry faculty (colleges favored such a background because most students were employed by industry). He began to read help wanted ads. One day he asked, "'Where's API?' And I, a native of the southeastern conference, said 'that's Auburn.'" Interviewing on a deceivingly warm February day in 1957 when the campus was decorated with enchanting daffodils and tulips, Curt eagerly accepted a position for the next fall.

At Auburn Charlotte was an early pioneer in teaching elementary science for children on educational television. The Ford Foundation had designated Alabama and South Carolina as the two neediest states in the country and provided funds to the Alabama Educational Television Network for instructional television programming for schools. In addition to taping lectures in the studio, Charlotte wrote resource guides for elementary science teachers. Emphasizing earth science, Charlotte hoped to enrich instruction with experimental demonstrations not available in the classroom. She suggested library resources for extra activities and discussed current topics and discoveries in science.

Public television still occasionally runs tapes of Charlotte's shows (she taught via television until 1972). She humorously tells, "It was funny one time I was at a League workshop in Birmingham, several years ago. This woman said `I know why I know you! My children watch you right after Captain Kangaroo!'"

At Auburn Dr. Howard Carr, head of the physics department, told Charlotte that he had been impressed with her television work and that he wanted her to teach a general curriculum physics course. She agreed to be an associate professor in physics in 1961, explaining with her stock answer, "I'd do anything to get out of housework." Thus began her thirty-three year career in Auburn's physics department. Charlotte became a member of the American Association of Physics Teachers.

Charlotte and Howard were keenly interested in improving science education. Charlotte laments, "Auburn was offering nothing really intended to prepare young women who were going into elementary education to teach science. There was a course called Science for Secondary Teachers in the School of Education intended to be taught by returning coaches who were going to up their salary by getting a degree in educational administration and becoming principals. And it was a truly crummy course."

A new elementary education professor expressed interest in improving the class. "All Dr. Carr and I needed was a little encouragement and a source of customers. So he turned me loose to design a course in physical science for elementary education" and "for the next twenty-five years then my major responsibility was that course." Word spread around campus about the interesting woman who had a flair for making science make sense, and "As it turned out this became the science course of choice for various liberal arts curricula and/or business majors."

Charlotte welcomed students on the first day of class by writing "Science" on the blackboard and asking them what it meant. She found some informed students but mostly ambivalent and unmotivated pupils who considered science dull, incomprehensible, and remote from their lives. She told them that "however divergent our points of view, we all live in the same world," and that a basic understanding of science was necessary to make educated decisions about how to manage the world's resources.

She wrote a textbook for the course, *This Blue Planet: Introduction to Physical Science*, which presented students a conglomeration of essential scientific principles, illustrations, questions, and reading suggestions about all aspects of physical science. Written to be user friendly, Charlotte's book emphasized the people who have explored science and tried to help students think about how science could be applied to real world situations to assure quality of life.

She told her students that she wanted science to be exciting and fascinating to them so that they would become scientifically literate. She warned readers of dwindling resources. She urged them to become educated, more aware, and concerned to understand the natural laws of their environment in order to make "personal, societal, and political decisions." Charlotte underscored that science enabled comforts and conveniences, increased life expectancy and permitted more freedom and control.

She said that science and technology had been received with both positive and negative attitudes. Many non-scientists feared science as being too complicated, resulting in "widespread scientific illiteracy among the highly educated humanists as well as among the undereducated Philistines." She stressed that her students must shed their ignorance and understand how the world worked in order to "live harmoniously with one's environment."

She said that such illiteracy was intolerable because society depended on technology and needed scientific solutions to solve numerous problems. Charlotte hoped that her students—she estimates that more than five thousand students have passed through her classroom—"will eventually teach a much broader segment of the population in the elementary and secondary schools. They may also be influential in correcting scientific illiteracy on a much larger scale." She wished that these students would incorporate science into their lives and "be alive, aware, thinking, understanding, and acting to improve their environment, within and without, all their lives."

Charlotte, with the help of a graduate student, compiled a lab manual, *Physical Science*. She wanted to familiarize future teachers with the scientific approach so that they would thoroughly understand scientific processes such as observing, measuring, hypothesizing, and interpreting data. Aware of limited school budgets, she specifically devised the experiments to be simple and to require few resources. Charlotte professed, "The highest compliment a laboratory instructor in such a course can receive is `that was fun! I really understood it.'" Her lab instructors included then-physics student astronaut Kathy Thornton.

Charlotte loved teaching because "I enjoy seeing light bulbs going off over peoples' heads when they finally understand something." Motivated by her students, she penned two additional textbooks: *The World of Physical Science* and *Physical Science: A Humanities Approach*. In her office she maintained a lending library of scientific biographies and non-fiction as well as fiction with scientific themes. She tried to encourage students to read and realize education is a life-long process. Her advice regarding science was, "All I can really say is, give it your best shot. You might even like it and find it makes your world a more interesting place to live."

Charlotte will proudly tell you that she also initiated and team taught Auburn's Human Odyssey class, an interdisciplinary science and humanities course (previously known as the Ascent of Man based on Jacob Bronowski's work) and is currently writing the textbook for it. She also has taught a continuing education science class, "Saturday Critters," for 4th-6th graders, emphasizing "hands-on" experiences with science for the youngsters.

She believes that the educational system has flaws and that many students are unaware of their ignorance. "Certainly, most of the products of Alabama schools that I taught over thirty years at Auburn University needed to have learned a lot more before they got to my classes: how to read with understanding, use mathematics and logic to solve problems they hadn't seen before, to think critically and to take responsibility for their own learning." She is especially distressed that students do not think originally and "are looking for security rather than independence of thought."

Declaring herself "an ardent feminist" who supports equal rights, Charlotte joined the League of Women Voters in 1960 when her friend Anne Amacher encouraged her to attend a meeting. Charlotte admits, "I try not to belong where I can't be useful or active." Serving as president of the local league from 1963-1965, 1968-1969, and 1987-1989, she is modest about her leadership. She also currently serves on the board of directors. Charlotte has prepared and edited the Auburn Voter since 1991, keeping the lines of communication open between Auburn and state League members. She enjoys her position as Voter editor because she has a fondness for writing about topics in addition to her scientific articles, books, and chemical abstracts. As a member of the Women's Literary Society at the University of Kentucky, she published poetry in their magazine. Charlotte was a member of the faculty committee that established Auburn University's literary magazine, *The Circle*, and is especially proud of her series about Auburn's world famous fisheries department that appeared in that journal. She has also written well-informed letters to the editor. Angered by the proliferation of articles about how horrible working mothers were, Charlotte put pen to paper. "I remember one, `A Working Mother's Prayer' which, in my interpretation, said, `Lord, forgive me for working and neglecting my children.' This really got to me," she says. "To let out my frustrations, I wrote a very lengthy letter to the editor who then published it as an article."

As a member of Auburn's Planning Commission and Committee of `76, she has written in support of natural resources and schools, especially retaining programs in music, arts, and foreign languages, arguing that citizens should "choose the hard answers that will have the farthest-reaching positive results. Choose to support the schools, whatever else must wait. Children do not wait to grow up." She has also written about gender issues, mentioning that Jesus considered women to be equal human beings "as capable of self-determination as men," and citizenship, stressing that "supporting the candidate of our choice and telling our elected officials what we think are part of every citizen's duty."

Charlotte ran for Auburn's city council in 1980. Surprised that she won, she confides, "I just threw my name in the hat to see what would happen." Her husband joked how every four years he wanted to "throw the rascals out" and that he hoped she would not become one of the rascals. Charlotte considers her political tenure to be "a learning experience" because "there are no easy answers or solutions that please everybody." She most disliked being misinterpreted by the media and the lack of sufficient funds which could have eliminated many municipal problems. Charlotte resents "repression of human rights, lying in the pursuit of power, wilful ignorance and attempts to force a single point of view on everyone."

In 1976 Charlotte became the first woman elected faculty senate president at Auburn University. Former Auburn religion professor, Dr. John Kuykendall, described her service: "She was very democratic; she let every person say what he wanted to say and she was most open and willing to take criticism." Charlotte is also proud of her participation on the national council and executive committee of the American Association of University Professors, as well as being president of the state conference (1989-1991). With several other professors, she recently helped in the review process to have Auburn removed from that organization's censure list.

When she first moved to Auburn, Charlotte helped establish Lakeview Baptist Church as part of a missions committee that led an adult Bible class. She has taught

Sunday School since she was fifteen years old and was named a deacon at Auburn's First Baptist Church, the second woman to achieve that honor. Fellow deacon Walter Porter describes Charlotte as "a capable person who executes her responsibilities very thoroughly, yet who is not 'hung up' about being an oppressed woman. She does what she can where she is."

Being the leader of Junior Girl Scout Troop Sixty-four not only was Charlotte's favorite civic activity, but also the one that she considers the most significant and satisfactory. As a girl she enjoyed Scouts until there were no leaders. Charlotte wanted to make sure that "no other little girl would have to quit scouting. That's why I made my 'noble vow' to become a Girl Scout leader." When daughter Emma became a Brownie, Charlotte signed up as troop leader.

"I have been a ten-year-old at heart for thirty-seven years now because I think ten is the nicest age," she smiles. "At age ten you want to try new things and explore the world." With her troop (of which this essay's author was a fortunate member), Charlotte camped, hiked, told stories, burnt her share of marshmallows, hosted parties, bobbed for apples, and enjoyed watching her girls mature. For a bicentennial pageant, she wrote skits, emphasizing women's history. Her scouts remember their troop leader as being fun and fair, believing that everyone was important and should have a chance to try new things.

Charlotte continues helping current troop leaders, especially with projects involving weaving. She is gifted at needlework (she often knitted or embroidered Girl Scout badges during city council meetings) and has pieced quilts at the Lee County Historical Society's autumn fair and syrup soppin'. She sews her clothing, once claiming that the only store-bought dress she owned was her Girl Scout uniform.

One of the things Charlotte is best known for is her bicycle. She and Curt have never owned a car because "We never really needed one." She reasons, "You can get along without most things and we generally do." They wear goose-down clothing and wool in winter. Charlotte deals easily with rain, "we have this wonderful polymer coating called skin that gets dry with the swipe of a towel."

Her children accepted an automobile-free life, although now that they're grown, most own at least one car. She is proud of her four children (son Matthew was born after the Wards moved to Auburn). Charlotte raised her children to be independent, organizing her household with a Girl Scout Caper Chart where everyone had specific duties and responsibility. She encouraged her children to love science, giving them peanut butter jars to scoop up creek water and watch frog eggs hatch into tadpoles. Daughter Bess earned a Ph.D. in oceanography and is listed on the same page in *American Men and Women of Science* as her parents.

Charlotte retired from Auburn during the summer of 1994. She is looking forward to traveling more, visiting her grandchildren, and reading at home with her two cats. Reflecting on her contributions to society she said, "I wanted to provide some science literacy where it wasn't before. I think perhaps that's one of the most useful things I did." With a confident smile she concludes, "So I like to think maybe I made a little difference in the world."

written by Elizabeth D. Schafer

Photo courtesy of the Tuscaloosa News

ZELPHA STOREY WELLS

What I'm Doing, I'm Doing For God. Helping People Who Need Help And Giving Them Experiences That They Would Miss Otherwise. This Helps Them Learn To Live Together. It's Not Something You Can Put On A Sign.

Like any mother, Zelpha Wells wants only the best for her children. But Zelpha's motherly love extends past her own household. Once deemed "the Mother Theresa of jazz in Tuscaloosa" by an admirer, pianist Zelpha Storey Wells has spent more than 20 years giving nearly 10,000 Tuscaloosa children the gift of music.

On her own time and often a limited if not non-existent budget, Zelpha enriches the cultural life of Tuscaloosa's economically deprived children with free piano lessons. The free lessons are through Zelpha's Cultural Development Corporation, the organization she founded. Her life-long mission has been to show children that, if they can accomplish learning to play the piano, they can accomplish anything. Using music as her medium, Zelpha believes each child can learn good conduct; self-esteem; and respect for authority, peers and themselves.

"Those are the first, basic values the children learn, and then the piano and applied arts are in there second," the soft-spoken pianist says. "This is a character development program. They are not as much aware of what I am trying to do as I am. These are the kids who are left out of most things. Learning to play gives them self-esteem and confidence."

The Tuscaloosa native maintains that a child's socioeconomic status shouldn't bar him or her from experiencing the arts. Because of that belief she devoted her talents to insuring that low-income children get the cultural exposure they might not otherwise have. Zelpha's concept comes from her own background, which is steeped in the arts.

Her parents were Edmond Storey, a barber and sexton at the First Presbyterian Church in downtown Tuscaloosa, and Malinda Storey, a county school teacher. They enrolled their only daughter in piano lessons when she was five. From that point on her love for music never faltered. During Zelpha's sophomore year of high school, she met the person who would determine her future.

With a cousin in tow, Zelpha would accompany her father to the church on Saturdays and dust while he worked. In each of the empty Sunday school rooms sat a piano and she remembers going room to room tickling the ivories of every one. One Saturday an eavesdropper overheard the teen-age Zelpha's nimble fingers gliding over the keys.

"I turned around and there was this woman standing in the doorway, and she said, I enjoyed listening to you. Would you like to play the organ?'" For three years Zelpha took lessons each week from Priscilla Keeler, then the First Presbyterian organist and an organ teacher at the University of Alabama. Keeler not only tutored Zelpha free of charge but also bought her books and supplies.

"Subconsciously, that was what caused me to do what I do now. She really inspired me and that made me want to do something for the ones who can't afford to pay and would miss the experience otherwise."

Zelpha and Keeler lost touch after Zelpha graduated from high school, but were reunited recently. "I had a card forwarded to me from Alberta Elementary School a little over a year ago," she recalls. "I cried because it was from Priscilla Keeler. I just couldn't believe it. I immediately sent her a note off and included articles about the program (ZCDC). I told her that she's the person who's responsible for what I'm doing." Zelpha promised her mentor, now 80 and living in a Nashville nursing home, that they "wouldn't lose touch this time."

Her own age is a well-guarded secret - "It's just not important." Zelpha has performed and taught music for nearly 40 years. A graduate of Talladega College, with a bachelor of arts degree in piano/music education and a minor in organ, she studied at Columbia University, Fisk University, Peabody College and Vanderbilt University. In recognition of her performance and support of Jazz, she was inducted into the Alabama Jazz Hall of Fame in 1986.

She has accompanied respected musicians such as former Talladega classmate Vera Little, now a member of the West Germany Opera Co., and opera singer Julie Merrill. For more than thirty years she has also played Jazz in night clubs and special occasions - alone or with her trio. The Zelpha Wells Trio has included many of Alabama's best Jazz musicians - like John Bishop, Tippy Armstrong, and Jerome Hopkins. Now she plays with these excellent musicians: Joe Boyer, Roy Yarborough and Don Davis.

Zepha taught in public schools for 22 years. Her economically deprived students pleaded with her to give them piano lessons. She tried teaching impromptu classes at school during the 10-minute break between classes, but before she and a student could find middle C, the bell clanged and ended her lesson abruptly. She was frustrated when she recognized a need for a free or subsidized music program that she couldn't satisfy with her full-time teaching job. Zepha left the school system in 1973.

Even though a single parent with daughters Arngenel and Carmalita just toddlers, Zelpha took a sojourn from Tuscaloosa in 1973 to organize a boys' choral group at the Olatunji Center in New York City. However, she worried about her daughters safety and returned to Alabama. "I had to put my daughters' needs first," Zelpha said. Both Arngenel and Carmalita are now University of Alabama graduates and partners in Zelpha's music corporation.

Coming home, Zelpha was unemployed for a year-and-a-half, then secured a clerical job to generate a small income. But her dream of a free music program persisted. After she convinced her boss to give her the last work day hour to teach piano lessons, Zelpha started her classes in the Crescent East Housing Project with 15 students. She was so in demand that, in 1976, she incorporated her dream into Zelpha's Cultural Development Corporation (ZCDC).

"It's for those people who cannot afford to pay for lessons," she explains. "For years I kept thinking, 'How I could do this?' I knew I'd lose my retirement if I left the school system and I knew I couldn't half afford to do that. Well, I said, I've got to do this, there's a need. I just prayed over it."

A year after ZCDC's formation Zelpha took her classes to seventeen different city and county schools, giving free thirty-minute lessons to more than five hundred students, ninety-five percent of whom were either on the free- or reduced-lunch program. For students who cannot attend classes during the school year, Zelpha and her pupils gather in the basement of the music building at Stillman College for three-hour classes twice a week during the summer.

"It helped with integration then," Zelpha remembers. "It's not a black or white program. They'd have to do duets together and I'd tell them, We're going to have to do this as a family.'"

One of Zelpha's first graduates went on to receive a full college music scholarship and other students perform in area churches. ZCDC board member Monica Curry said she sees evidences of Zelpha's teaching ability —on the keyboard and in character development — in her own 12-year-old daughter, Adrienne Bailey, who has received private lessons from Zelpha for three years. "Adrienne picked it up in no time at all with Zelpha. She's a great role model for kids and they respect her. For those kids who have missed out on so much, attention-wise, she gives them a want to be able to succeed."

The twelve-month music program with the public schools and Stillman earns Zelpha just about seven hundred and eighty-five dollars monthly after taxes. Out of that she pays ZCDC utilities, supplies and gas to and from the public schools. Spare cash, if any, goes toward the pianist's personal expenses. She also receives a sum from the drug abuse prevention program, but says she earmarks that money for needs other than her own. "I can't take the money and use it for salary when we need other things. I just say, 'Well, I'll manage somehow.'"

Over the years many people have helped. On her insistence Zelpha's long time friend, Joe Namath, spoke to over five hundred children who were taken by bus to hear him. "I told him that I wanted these children to believe that they could do anything, but that they would listen better if he would say it. He always wants to know how we are doing. He tells me that we should be getting help from an agency so we don't depend on individuals. And we've tried, but money's hard to find."

Jack Marshall, owner of Kentucky Fried Chicken restaurants, is vice president of the ZCDC Board. For one successful fund raiser he loaned his Cadillac, originally owned by Elvis Presley, for display at the mall. The ZCDC charged admission to see it or to be photographed beside it. Security was donated by Riverchase Security. Dr. Nora Price, former Director of Instruction for the city schools, sent letters to all city school principals to introduce the free music program when it began. Mr. and Mrs. Frank Moody, Coach Paul "Bear" Bryant and Mr. Jimmy Hinton gave the money to get the program started. Musician, Ludovic Goubet, owner of the Chukker Bar, has sponsored a musical benefit for ZCDC.

Many others have helped: Jack Kapphan of Indian Hills Country Club; Father Ray Dunmeyer and Sister Mary Ann Warner, both of St Francis Catholic Church (Zelpha's church.); the Reverend and Mrs W.D. Billups of St Paul Baptist Church; Lou Sullivan and Felicia Coleman have helped with fund raising; Mr. Jack Warner, head of Gulf States Paper; Dr. Lamar Joslin; Ruth Fields; and Malinda Prude is the secretary. Hugh Devereaux owner of Alabama Protection provides free security for the building; West Gate Music store has donated music books.

Ruth Ellington, Duke Ellington's widow, is a good friend of Zelpha's and has encouraged her very much. She often invites Zelpha and daughters to visit her in New York City. Zelpha is also encouraged by two presidents of higher education. President of Stillman College, Dr. Cordell Winn, provides ZCDC with space to hold classes in the music department. President of the University of Alabama, Dr. Roger Sayers, offers free meeting space on campus.

In a 1994 letter of support, Dr. Sayers said, " I have been privileged to know Zelpha for many years and am convinced that her educational center will reward us with children who are a source of pride to the community and to the state. Her goal is not just the teaching of music but also the encouragement, even insistence, on the everyday practice of citizenship. In this day and age of troubled children, it is not just necessary, but essential that persons with her talent and goals should receive support to carry out this visionary project. The long-range implications for all of us are too important to ignore."

Coach Paul "Bear" Bryant wrote a letter of support in 1982. He said, "The enrichment this project has brought to its many participants is invaluable and the many personal sacrifices that have been made in order to continue this endeavor should not go unnoticed. A source of permanent funding is needed to insure the growth and expansion of this most worthwhile effort."

Zelpha's struggle to spark an artistic fire in children's minds motivated one young

Tuscaloosa boy, Joey Neggers, then 8, to give her half of a $100 gift he earned for scoring all A's one school year. "She's got a little bit of star dust in her," says Joseph Neggers, a professor of mathematics at the University of Alabama and Joey's father, of his long-time friend. "There's something in her that exceeds the normal. The kind of work she does for kids gets them off the streets and means that they won't be out dealing drugs. Anything the community can do for her is dirt-cheap compared to what she has done. We've got her at a bargain."

For her dedication to Tuscaloosa and the state, former Gov. Guy Hunt appointed her to the Alabama Commission on Aging. She received the 1993 Governors Arts Award which recognizes those making significant contributions to their communities' arts. In 1990 Alabama magazine cited Zelpha as an Alabama hero for her volunteers efforts to improve the cultural life of Tuscaloosa's children.

Twenty years ago Zelpha realized her dream of offering free piano programs. Now she is waiting to open ZCDC's home base in Tuscaloosa. In 1988 Charlotte and Moses Swaim of Tuscaloosa gave Zelpha a small home that they were trying to sell to house ZCDC classes, recitals and other art programs.

"He said, 'Zelpha, what do you want it for?' I told him and he said 'I'll give it to you. I believe in you and I believe in what you're doing.,'" Zelpha recalls.

Moses Swaim died in November 1994, just weeks short of the final restoration and seeing Zelpha's dream so close to a reality. But Mrs. Swaim remembers her late husband's dedication to the ZCDC dream. "We thought that what she was doing was wonderful—giving free piano lessons to kids who might not have that opportunity. She really impressed us with her record."

ZCDC moved the home from the Swaim property and restored it at its current location. Now the house sits squarely on Paul W. Bryant Drive, ready for young pianists to pound out melodies. Community schools and businesses and devoted patrons donated furniture, supplies and construction help to ready the center.

The center is fully stocked with music books. A washer and dryer are hooked up for students to wash clothes after school, and the kitchen is stacked with clothes for needy children. But a lack of operating funds to pay certified music teachers keeps the doors closed and students out.

``I don't have any help with teaching, that's my problem. That's what's holding me back. Our teachers are going to have to have a degree. I don't want this to be a second-rate program."

Initially Zelpha planned to settle in the house this spring, but was forced to postpone the music center's opening. She needs grant money and a permanent sponsor. Now her hope is that, like in the past, God will see that ZCDC's needs are met. But Zelpha believes when the money does comes that it will set the center's character development programs in motion for generations of children to come.

"This building can never be anything but what it is. It can't be mortgaged and we can't make any loans on it. This is not just for my lifetime, this is forever."

written by Suzanne Henson

MAUDE ROSIE LEE WHATLEY
1894 - 1989
Take Care Of Yourself And Do The Right Thing

According to the dictionary, a trailblazer is one who blazes a trail, a leader in any field, a pioneer. Maude Rosie Lee Whatley certainly qualifies as a trailblazer. She broke new trails for the children and adults of her west Tuscaloosa area who needed a better road to education and health care. In education she worked as teacher and principal for over fifty years. In health care she succeeded in getting a medical clinic built in this less affluent side of the city. The clinic was named in her honor. Her steps led her over new ground for black women. As one of the greatest advocates for her community, she paved the way for many to overcome poverty, health problems, and ignorance.

Born in Tuscaloosa in 1894, she was the fourth of eleven children born to Lucy Winn and Samuel L. Whatley. She was reared by a paternal aunt, Mrs. Annie Whatley Sewell. The families lived next door to each other. From childhood, her talents, skills, precociousness, and task orientation were observed and nurtured by her surrogate mother and her biological parents. She was loved and admired by her sisters and brothers. Her father was one of the first black shoemakers in Tuscaloosa and one of the first volunteer firemen.

Dr. Eddie B. Thomas remembers meeting Maude Whatley when he was about eight years old. "She was looking for someone to help at her house. My mother said it was okay and so she hired my brother and me. I was impressed with her from that first day.

She looked for the best in everyone and she made sure you lived up to your potential."
Today Dr. Thomas is Assistant Superintendent of Schools in Tuscaloosa and says
that Maude Whatley made him who he is. She was a "giant - miles ahead of her time,"
according to Thomas, who was one of her favorite journeymen.

"From our first meeting, I knew she had quality, dignity, self-respect and knowledge. She was a role-model for me and I wanted to learn from her. Ms. Whatley kept me
on the cutting edge - she passed her wisdom on to all of her followers." Thomas later
became a teacher at Central where Ms. Whatley served as principal. "Ms. Whatley was
a lean woman, about 5'5", with a monumental face and unusual energy," says Thomas.

She was educated at local schools, graduating from what was then Central High
School. Maude Whatley was the first black in the Tuscaloosa City School System to
receive an A.A. teaching certificate. She earned this professional degree from Columbia
University in New York City, N.Y. Before that, she completed Junior College at Tuskegee
and then earned her bachelor's and master's degrees from Wayne State University in
Detroit. Throughout her life she continued her education by attending summer education workshops at outstanding universities all across the country.

Dr. Thomas said that her education did not come easy. Because of segregation in
Alabama, Ms. Whatley had to go out of state. She paid her way and earned her degree.
He said, "She attended the best schools she could at that time."

Dr. Thomas smiled as he told the story of Ms. Whatley and a graduate school
incident which shows her strong dedication to excellence in education. One of her
professors stood up to lecture and began by saying, "I'm sure you all have did what
you was suppose to do..." She said, "Can you believe that? Well, I went right away to
withdraw from that class, and enroll in another one."

Thomas explained, "Her family didn't have a whole lot of money, but had a whole
lot of initiative." It was a solid, structured family that expected much of her. Her sisters and brothers were also successful in many types of work. One was a physician,
another a social worker, and one a business woman. She grew up in a segregated society. As a youth, Maude lived and worked with a white family for several years.

Maude spent more than fifty years as teacher and principal with the Tuscaloosa
City School System. Her obituary read, "To these assignments, she gave her full measure of devotion, working tirelessly as an instructor, disciplinarian and administrator
so that her students and professional colleagues might obtain the highest educational
standards." She was praised for her, "intellectual alertness, her organizational acu-
men, her leadership ability, and her great pride in not only her performance, but of
those for whom she bore a responsibility." She was also noted for "her industrious-
ness, and her indomitable courage that served her well" in all she did. She was proud
when her students excelled in academic or professional pursuits.

Dr. Thomas said, "When she became principal, Ms. Whatley's primary interest was
developing teachers." He said that he remembers the day she came into his classroom to
observe him. She entered into the classroom discussion and soon took over the teaching. Thomas says that he was not offended by her action, although later she apologized
for "interrupting" his teaching. He feels that every teacher in her school knew she was
an exceptional role model and they learned from her. She felt the teaching profession was
her "calling." She took her work seriously. She was always aware of the fact that hundreds
were counting on her, as she paved the way for a better quality of life in Tuscaloosa.

On the day Dr. Thomas received his doctorate from the University of Alabama,"Ms. Whatley was there—she was like a mother to me—along with many of my family members. She was quite proud of my achievement and told my mother that she had made me an educator. I was one of her favorites. My mother quickly reminded her that SHE birthed me."

Yet the Trailblazer never had favorites among her "children" as she called her students. She felt all children were important. She worked to make sure that none of her students went hungry or were without shoes and medical attention. Thomas says, "Ms. Whatley was <u>unequivocally</u> interested in the whole child. She taught citizenship as well as academics." She was dedicated to community development, evident by the strong parent-teacher association at Central.

John L. and Nellie Mae King, retired teachers still living in Tuscaloosa, remember Maude Whatley. Both had known her as a teacher and as principal. They, too, saw this remarkable woman as a role model - one of a kind.

Mr. King was one of Maude's students. He went to Alabama State to train as a teacher and came back to Tuscaloosa where he got his first job at Central School, the only school for blacks in Tuscaloosa at that time. "I went to Ms. Whatley, then serving as principal, and she gave me my first job."

Mr. King said he has always felt that Maude Whatley was a born leader. She had proven that through her career as teacher and principal. Later in life he saw her leadership skills in action as she chaired a committee charged with starting a health clinic for the west side of Tuscaloosa. Other members of the committee included her minister and several church members. "We all knew that if anyone could get the job done, she could. She was not a quitter," King said. "Many blacks were not receiving adequate health care and the committee set out to change that situation."

Whenever the committee became discouraged, Maude would tell them ways to get the job done. She felt the work was important for the whole community and that working together they could get the job done. "She wouldn't let us quit," he explained. "I remember Ms. Whatley as a woman with unusual energy. She worked many long, hard hours to see the path open for health care for all Tuscaloosans."

Mr. King said that there were no funds for the project. They all gave out of their own pockets at times. Ms. Whatley was their example. She continued making sacrifices, spending her own money to see that "her children" were cared for in the "best possible way. She gave a lot and she got a lot, " said Mr. King. Maude was able to find funding and support to see the Clinic established in 1977. The first clinic was housed in the Salvation Army building and provided free services one weekend a month.

Today the Center, named The Maude L. Whatley Health Center, is a primary health care center, offering a whole range of services not just preventive assistance including dental care, health promotion, health education and disease prevention. It is a fully staffed, non-profit, community owned organization. The Whatley Center has expanded to three ambulatory facilities that serve not only the poor, but offer affordable heath care to all. Although the service is not free, charges are set by the ability to pay and no one is turned away.

Mr. King says Maude never quit, even when the Clinic became an unpopular idea because some people didn't want it. The new building was to be as large as the County Health Department and many thought it would take away from the Departments business.

"Ms. Whatley kept working for the cause, in spite of the fact that many thought it would take patients away from the existing health care facilities across town. It was not competitive. It was more helpful and it served more patients." And it was needed, Mr. King explained.

Nella May King, remembers that Maude was always very interested in her students. "I, too, was a student of Ms. Whatley's. She took a special interest in me. My mother died when I was very young and she was specially concerned about my welfare."

Maude hired Mrs. King for her first job in teaching. She said that when Maude served as principal, Maude had the same special concern for every individuals that she showed for her.

"She would go somewhere every summer to continue her education. Blacks had to go away to get further education because of segregation in Tuscaloosa. She would come back to Tuscaloosa and share her new ideas with her teachers. She was always trying to improve herself and others. She felt her school was the best and she got the community to feel the same way."

"I remember her strong feelings about discipline. Ms. Whatley said, If you can't discipline, you can't teach.'" Mrs. King explained that Ms. Whatley was a "strict disciplinarian." I don't remember her ever using a strap or spanking any of the children. They just knew she meant what she said. They respected her."

Dr. Roland Ficken, Dean of the University of Alabama's College of Community Health Sciences had more praises for Ms. Whatley. "She had this marvelous talent for bringing people together. Maude was a very talented person with a fine education. She was a remarkable person - a child of former slaves. She was highly regarded in the community. Everyone knew who she was. They held total respect for her," he said.

"She would give us 'marching orders.' She was a strong disciplinarian. She was never afraid to be firm, even with adults. This attitude probably attributed to the fact that it took only a year for the community to decide that it was a good thing to establish a health care facility for the west side of Tuscaloosa. Others had tried to start one, but could not move forward with the project. Her dream was to provide that segment of the community with the same health care rest of the community had," Dr. Ficken explained.

"The community knew her well. She maintained an amazing knowledge of Tuscaloosa. Her mind was great "right up to the end of her life. She was as sharp as she could be.

"I think some of the most memorable times of that era was when those involved gathered at her home to brainstorm. She had such good ideas and had such great enthusiasm. And you always felt energized after being with her." Dr. Ficken said.

Ila Glynn, a Music Specialist from Montgomery, moved to Tuscaloosa with her husband and met Maude Whatley when she went to ask for a job teaching music. "She was a very striking woman, full of information. She was someone I wanted to get to know better." Mrs. Glynn says a full-time job was not available but she did do substitute teaching for Maude.

The friendship continued as the ladies traveled together on numerous occasions as members of the black organization, The Lucy Shepherd Art Club. They went to National and Southeastern meetings of the organization which had as its motto, "Lifting As We Climb." A teacher, Sadye Wright, and a doctor's wife, Marie McKenzie, traveled with them. "The conventions often included as many as 400 people and were mainly concerned with giving scholarships to young people. The youth gave orations and the winners got scholarships." The club is still active and at the dedication of the Maude L. Whatley Health Center, the Club gave a portrait of Ms. Whatley which hangs there today.

Mrs. Glynn and Ms. Whatley were included in the six black women, who applied for membership to the Tuscaloosa League of Women Voters (LWV). They admired the League's work and ideals and wanted to organize a chapter of their own. Instead of organizing another League, the six women accepted the invitation to join and integrate the existing one. Ms. Whatley joined the League in 1949 and remained active until she died. She worked hard for the organization during her lifetime.

According to Mrs. Glynn the city had no kindergartens for black children at that time. As a member of the LWV, Maude Whatley, Mrs. Glynn, and others set about to change this situation. "We all worked together. Ms. Whatley was a big help. She was able to talk with legislators, and write effective letters. She was well-known in the state as well as the city by that time in her life. We talked to everyone and did what was necessary to see the laws changed," Mrs. Glynn said.

About Maude tackling yet another task Mrs. Glyn said,"You never heard her complain. If you started to talk negative, she would tell you what you could do. She never said ugly things about people or criticized anyone. She was an unusual person. Her aunt reared her for several years and taught her many of these ideals."

Mrs. Glynn said she always found time to do what needed to be done. You never heard her talking about "not having time for this or that. She would just work until the job was complete. Many times she worked late at night finishing her school work as principal since she had no secretary."

Maude did take time out to have fun. She helped organize the Amity Study Club in Tuscaloosa which met Saturdays to play cards. She enjoyed the Club a lot. It is still active.

Maude served her church, the First African Baptist Church, all her life. She was a Sunday school teacher and superintendent of Sunday school for seventeen years. She was a member of the finance committee and was the first female trustee. She was avid in her study of the Bible and lived the commandment, "Thou shalt love thy neighbor as thy self."

When she retired, Ms. Whatley continued to work as a volunteer. She worked with the "Right to Read" program, a volunteer program where she taught adults to read and write. She also continued her private volunteer tutoring.

Although she never married, her "children" numbered in the thousands and her "family" included hundreds of friends. She received many awards and testimonials in recognition of her work. She humbly viewed her contributions as privileges and as blessings from God.

Dr. Eddie Thomas tells about his last days with Ms. Whatley. Three weeks before she died they called him to visit her at the hospital. The nurse said she wasn't eating right. When he saw her he reminded her of what she always told him about taking care of himself and about doing the right thing. She laughed and replied, "Okay, let's try it."

From her hospital bed Ms. Whatley bid Dr. Thomas to continue blazing trails. She said, "Eddie, be a role model for the children. Do what you can to help the children!"

written by Hazel Bruchey

ZECOZY AUSBORN WILLIAMS
1918 -

Make Up Your Mind What You Want To Do, What You Want To Be, And What Your Goals In Life Are. Then Say To Yourself, If I'm Going To Make It, I Have To Recognize My Bad Habits And That The Bad Are My Bad Habits. I Will Have To Break Them And Live The Life That People Can Read About And Improve Their Lives By My Accomplishments.

These words represent not only Zecozy Ausborn Williams' advice to young people, but the philosophy by which this remarkable woman has lived. Hers has been a life of hard work, self-discipline, and vision. She set worthy and difficult-to-achieve goals for herself and then accomplished them even when the task required decades to complete. Her faith in God served as a sustaining force in the effort.

Zecozy was born March 5, 1918, in Hope Hull, Alabama, to Annie Lee and William Ausborn. Her parents, like many other Blacks living in rural Alabama, were sharecroppers who faced difficult times. Segregated and poverty stricken Alabama offered her parents and her generation very little economically or politically.

Her Grandmother Molly was originally married to Anderson Flynn. One night

172

while playing cards, her grandfather bet his wife and daughter and lost. When the winner of the bet came to collect his winnings, her grandmother refused to go. She gathered up her belongings and her daughter and escaped. Luckily for the family, she later met and married Ned Jones. Some of Zecozy's fondest childhood memories are of Ned Jones whom she describes as a sweet man. A trapper and fisherman by trade, he would take her with him as he hunted and fished. His catches would be used for food and the animal skins dried and prepared for sale. Zecozy spent a great deal of time with him after her father died and her grandparents took the family in. Zecozy's mother eventually remarried. Between the two marriages her mother had eight children, losing two of the older children during their early childhood.

The public Negro elementary school for the Hope Hull area was the Tankersley School. Zecozy attended it through the sixth grade. Tankersley School had principal, J. W. "Jake" Williams, and two teachers. The building was made up of a kitchen and four classrooms and was heated by a pot belly stove. The students in each classroom would take turns going into the forest to collect firewood to heat the building. During especially cold times the parents might take up a collection to buy coal for the fire.

Zecozy's walk to school was relatively short, only three to four miles. Others had much farther to go. Their white counterparts rode school buses.

After graduating from the sixth grade, Zecozy ended her schooling. Then, on January 20, 1938, at the age of nineteen, she married twenty-five year old Essie Cue Williams. The couple met through her elementary school principal who was her husband's uncle. Essie Williams had also left school after the sixth grade.

The Williams family moved from Hope Hull and began sharecropping in an area of Montgomery County along the border of Lowndes County. They traded at the local grocery store run by Jeff and Ida Hall, paying their bills in chickens and eggs. Hall also bought eggs from them and encouraged them to sell their products in Montgomery. Soon Zecozy and Essie were buying eggs from other farmers and from Hall. They bought them for ten cents a dozen. Zecozy would then board the bus for Montgomery, where she sold the eggs for fifteen cents a dozen. Soon she added vegetables and chickens to her stock in trade.

During this period Zecozy also worked in Montgomery nursing new mothers and their babies. When the new mother and child came home from the hospital, she would help out for six to eight weeks.

In 1950 the Williams family moved to Montgomery. With them came their daughter Betty Jean and a niece, Juanita, whom they raised. Essie Williams went to work at the Coca Cola plant, and Zecozy did day work. Her day work clients included Dr. R. R. Ellison, head of Huntingdon College; Pauline and Stanhope Elmore; and Mrs. J. R. Corbit. She worked for the Elmores for more than sixteen years.

Shortly after moving to Montgomery, Zecozy began attending Carver High School at night. After coming home from class, she would go to bed when her family did. She would get up at 1:00 a.m. to study for an hour or two and then return to bed. She would then get up in time to have breakfast ready for her husband, who left for work at 6:30 a.m.

Kate Durr Elmore often helped her with her studies. She still remembers an assignment to write a report on a corporate stock issue. She did not know anything about stocks. Mrs. Elmore showed her how to read a newspaper stock market report and completed much of the background information Zecozy lacked. They studied Coca Cola, since Essie Williams worked for Coke, and Mr. Elmore headed the Montgomery Coke plant. In 1968, Zecozy Williams finally received her high school diploma.

While working and attending night school, Zecozy also was active in the community, beginning with voter education and voter registration campaigns. It started just after her move to Montgomery when Zecozy went to Bertha Smith's beauty shop to have her hair done. Mrs. Smith asked if she was registered to vote. Zecozy said she was not registered (less than five percent of adult blacks in Alabama were registered, compared to about twenty percent for the South as a whole), so Mrs. Smith invited her to Brenda's Bar-B-Que Place at Washington Park. There people met every evening as part of a program organized by Rufus A. Lewis. The program was designed to give people information on how to complete the voter registration forms.

After Zecozy registered she joined the education effort. She helped people understand what the process would be like and what information the forms would require. She also escorted potential registrants to the county courthouse.

In the 1950s and 1960s, the voter registration forms were four pages long, and the registrars changed the forms frequently. Registrants were also quizzed to determine how well they could read and write and whether they understood sections of the U.S. and Alabama Constitutions. They also had to list not only their current address, and current employer and the employer's address but also all addresses for themselves and all their employers for the previous five years. Whether questions were adequately answered was left to the discretion of the registrars.

Few black applications were judged acceptable, and registrars would discard the forms, telling the registrant, "You didn't pass." Zecozy retrieved the applications from the trash can to document what was being asked and how the grading was done. This information proved useful when, in the 1960s, she wrote to President Lyndon B. Johnson requesting that federal registrars be sent to Montgomery County. The information she provided became part of a package that led to federal intervention.

The Montgomery County Coordinating Committee for Registration and Voting in which Zecozy was active sought "to promote registration and voter education as to political responsibility through informed and active participation of citizens in government." In addition to teaching people how to register, the committee placed signs in black-run businesses that said: "Don't Talk Politics in Here! Unless . . . You Are A REGISTERED VOTER." In other words, do not complain about the government and what it is doing to you unless you have done something (that is, registered) to help yourself and to change things. The committee also distributed flyers providing the primary and general election registration deadlines and voting dates.

Upon the invitation of Mrs. A. W. West, Zecozy also joined the Coalition of 100 Black Women, another voter registration organization. Zecozy has also been an active member of the National Association for the Advancement of Colored People (NAACP), the Urban League, Alabama Arise, and the Order of the Eastern Star.

In the 1960s Zecozy worked with E. D. Nixon in helping to create the National

Democratic Party of Alabama. The NDPA was founded to challenge the whites-only policies of the Alabama Democratic Party and to give black candidates access to the ballot. NDPA challenges to the delegate selection process were taken before the National Democratic Party Convention of 1968. Zecozy Williams served as a NDCP delegate to that convention. She also worked in the presidential election campaigns of John F. Kennedy, Lyndon B. Johnson, and Jimmy Carter.

In 1966, Zecozy began work with Montgomery Community Action. She was still attending high school at night, but after the death of Mr. Elmore, she was needed less often and had time available. John and Bernice King had started a pilot program for Head Start at the Day Street Church. The program expanded and moved to the Metropolitan Church at Jeff Davis and Holt. Federal rules required that the Head Start program involve whites. The Kings asked Zecozy to help them find white women who were willing to help. Zecozy contacted several, and Mrs. Jack White agreed. Mrs. White later recruited another white woman.

Zecozy helped to raise money to renovate and clean up the building where the Head Start program first began. It then moved to St. Jude's School. She was hired as an assistant cook. Zecozy rose from assistant cook, to cook, to head cook.

Once she received her high school diploma, Zecozy Williams dreamed about getting a college education. About 1974, she learned that Dr. Frankie Ellis had, through Head Start, received twelve teacher training slots for the five counties in the Montgomery area. Ten of the slots were to be filled by Community Action in Montgomery. The recipients would be sent to Tuskegee Institute to work on bachelor degrees in early childhood education.

Zecozy told the nutritionist for whom she worked that she wanted to fill one of those slots. Her boss told her the schooling was not for her. So she went to the program director, who also rejected her request. That night Zecozy went home and cried, but her faith told her that God would work out what was right for her. She kept telling herself, "The Lord will work things out for the right time, place and person."

The slots for Montgomery were filled, but each time a person was offered the last available slot, he or she rejected it. Zecozy continued to pray. Finally, with just a few days left before the deadline for filling all positions, the phone call came. She was going to college!

College meant working with Head Start by day and attending classes largely at night. During the first year of school, she and her fellow students met at a central location and were picked up by a bus for the ride from Montgomery to Tuskegee. At first they were in class from 1:00-4:00 p.m. two days a week. Later their class time expanded to 1:00-8:00 p.m. Her supervisor gave her permission to attend classes during part of the work day. Then, in the second year, she got a new supervisor.

The new supervisor refused her permission to attend school. Zecozy then called someone higher in the organization and explained the problem. The next day her supervisor okayed the time off.

By the last year of the four year teacher training program, half of the twelve students had dropped out. The bus could not be justified for just six students, so they used part of their stipends to pool money for gas and car pooled to Tuskegee. During her last semester, Zecozy drove alone.

After facing one obstacle after another and meeting each one head on, Zecozy Williams received her Bachelor of Science Degree in Early Childhood Education on May 14, 1978. She was sixty years old.

Zecozy was motivated to complete her education (first high school and then college) by an occurrence at church shortly after her arrival in Montgomery in 1950. The deacon announced that the Sunday school teacher was going to be absent that day and a volunteer was needed to teach the class. The deacon looked to one woman in the congregation, a school teacher, who replied, "Don't ask me to teach Sunday School. Don't ask me. I'm a school teacher. I can teach school, but don't ask me to teach Sunday School." It bothered Zecozy that the teacher was willing to teach only in one area. In her own case, she realized that while she had Bible knowledge, she did not have an education. Zecozy wanted both. And, she wanted to be able to say she could and would teach both Sunday school and public school..

Once she received her degree, Zecozy began work at Head Start as an assistant teacher. From there she was promoted to teacher, then to head teacher, and finally became director of the Head Start center until her retirement in the early 1990s.

Zecozy Williams is retired, but she has not stopped working or volunteering in the community. She works part-time for Virginia Durr, who in 1966 encouraged her to join the Montgomery League of Women Voters and paid her initial application fee. Her volunteer activities include working with the New Providence Missionary Baptist Church, district church activities, and the Montgomery League of Women Voters. She has been elected to the LWV Board for 1995-96.

She is also helping to found the Montgomery Chapter of the National Political Congress of Black Women. The organization works in many areas reminiscent of the early voter education campaigns of which she was a part. It mentors African-American women and encourages their participation in political activities, including voting, and trains them to understand and operate in the political arena.

Zecozy's activities have brought her many awards, commendations, and certificates of achievement. These have come from the Montgomery Improvement Association, Governor George C. Wallace, President Lyndon B. Johnson, Head Start, New Providence Missionary Baptist Church, and other political, community and religious groups. Zecozy Williams set her goals and accomplished what she set out to do with her life. She has set a wonderful example for others to follow.

written by Anne Permaloff, Ph.D.

Kathryn Tucker Windham
1918 -

Enjoy The Filling And Throw The Crust Away.

Alabama's premier storyteller, Kathryn Tucker Windham, shares her father's words of wisdom that she has followed all her life. Undoubtedly, those words formed a guide for her as she collected ghost stories, historical tales, and recipes to document her native state's heritage in stories, books, and plays. She has made Alabama a better place through her civic contributions and used her sense of humor to inform and entertain.

The youngest daughter of James Wilson Tucker and Helen Gaines Tabb Tucker was born into a storytelling family. Every night after dinner, these storytellers congregated in their rocking chairs on the front porch to enjoy the night breeze and share their tales. Here, smelling the sweet fragrance of honeysuckle, wisteria, and her father's pipe, Kathryn heard tales of Alabama's "heroes and villains" and developed a love for her state and its oral traditions. Here, too, she heard stories about her family.

Her maternal grandmother Harriett Newel Underwood Tabb, who died two years before Kathryn's birth, had attended Marion Female Seminary and was a gifted harpist and painter. She married Edward Tabb and they moved to Texas. There he joined the Confederate militia and, while he was away, she ran their plantation. After the Yankees burned their cotton, the couple returned to Alabama where she taught school and encouraged her children to be creative and independent.

Kathryn's paternal grandfather, James Lee Tucker, was a circuit-riding Baptist preacher who, according to local lore, had once prayed a tornado away. He was a Confederate soldier who was captured and imprisoned on Ship Island. He walked home to his farm after his release in 1865. He married Catherine Stafford, and Kathryn's father was born the next year.

A member of the town council, James Wilson Tucker founded the Thomasville, Alabama Banking Company in 1895 and became president of the Farmers Bank and Trust Company in 1907. His third wife, Helen Tabb, was Kathryn's mother. She was the younger sister of James Windham's second wife, Annie. He had several children from his first two wives.

Helen Gaines Tabb attended Tuskegee's Alabama Conference Female Institute (Huntingdon's predecessor), graduating with highest honors. James Tucker, her brother-in-law, paid her tuition and encouraged her to become a schoolteacher. Nicknamed Heddie by the Tucker children, Helen quit teaching to marry James Tucker a year after his wife (her sister) died from childbirth complications.

When Helen became pregnant, James worried about her health. Remembering his wife's death, he decided to take her to Selma's hospital where physicians would supervise her delivery. In May 1918, Helen Tabb Tucker rode the train for the sixty-five mile trip and roomed in the hospital for almost one month. Kathryn was born the night her step-sister Annalee graduated from high school.

On June 2, 1918, Kathryn Tucker Windham was born. She grew up in a home filled with love and books. Kathryn enjoyed an almost magical childhood in Thomasville, Alabama. Her southwest Alabama hometown offered Kathryn reassuring rhythms of security and freedom, fueling future small-town childhood reminiscences. She knew everyone in town and enjoyed neighborly friendships. Happiness and laughter abounded. Gardens provided flowers for weddings and funerals. She spent many hours on her family's ivy-draped, screened-in porch, sewing and shelling beans with her mother and playing with friends. She skated and biked on the porch and cut paper dolls from pattern books and magazines. In the yard she caught lightning bugs and katydids and swatted at mosquitoes. She climbed oak trees and wore school dresses sewed by Miss Lillie Harrison.

The Tucker front porch faced the lumberyard, where oxen loaded pine logs skinned of bark onto flatcars headed to Mobile ports. Young Kathryn walked into town for ice cream cones and picture shows and heard tales of how her cousin, Earl, was once locked in a bank vault to prevent him from dueling with a political opponent. She dreaded piano lessons and rejoiced when a fire destroyed that despised instrument. One of Kathryn's mentors was her Aunt Bet, the town's postmistress. She was the first woman to register to vote in Clarke County and proudly voted for Democratic candidates every chance she could. She was famous locally for baking and decorating elaborate wedding cakes.

Sickly as a child, Kathryn occasionally was hospitalized. When she was able-bodied, she helped plow in the garden, watched kudzu (unwisely given by the extension agent) grow a foot a day over the coal pile, and fed the chickens, a chore frequently assigned by her elders to protect her from hearing gossip. She wooed her first love, Lyles Carter Walker, the town's tree-sitting champion. Kathryn worshiped her brother Wood, who was mentioned in Ripley's "Believe It or Not" for his semi-professional baseball playing talents. She counted train cars, wondering where they had come from and where they were going. Traveling to circuses with her father, she watched the Wallendas walk a high wire and laughed at vaudeville troupes.

Books were a vital component of her family home. They were shelved in glass-fronted cases. Thomasville had no public library, but Kathryn was entertained by her home library. She played the "Authors" card game and cherished a bookshelf that her father bought at the hardware store (it currently houses her rabbit collection). Her father read Bible stories to her and shared wisdom and advice, urging her to enjoy life. The Tucker's cook, Thurza, influenced Kathryn, expanding her storytelling horizons by sharing moral tales from the African-American community. All of these early experiences gave timbre to Kathryn Tucker Windham's narrative voice.

From childhood Kathryn knew that she wanted to be a newspaper reporter. In junior high she wrote her first newspaper copy, reviewing movies for the weekly *Thomasville Times* edited by her cousin, Earl Tucker. She also set headlines, selecting metal type from wooden type cases; made notices for rallies, funerals, and revivals; and operated the foot-powered press. She learned journalism techniques from discussions with Earl and his crew about the quality of articles in other Alabama papers.

Shortly before the stock market fell, James Tucker resigned his position at the bank to open an insurance agency. Kathryn continued to write movie reviews during the Depression. Her older siblings had all attended college to become doctors and teachers, with the exception of one brother who became the family's only millionaire by selling veneer. Her mother decided to enroll at Montevallo to renew her teaching certificate. Employed by a federal program, she taught adults to read using her husband's insurance office for a classroom. She also assisted him with his work by handling insurance claims and forms as his health failed.

In 1930 Kathryn acquired her first camera. The Kodak company donated box cameras to all children born in 1918, and she spent her afternoons taking pictures of everything that she encountered. She enjoyed school, especially extracurricular activities such as playing the snare drum with the band in Mobile's Mardi Gras parade. Teenaged Kathryn led cheers for the Thomasville High School football team and served as class president. She graduated in 1935 and earned scholarships to Huntingdon College, a Methodist liberal arts school in Montgomery. She worked in the biology-zoology laboratory for extra funds. Her English professor, Dr. Rhoda Ellison, encouraged her to write about her small-town memories. With friend Frances Lanier she wrote a column, "The Newshounds," for the campus newspaper, *The Huntress.* She once shocked the crowd at a press conference when she asked Governor Graves if, like other great men, he slept with one foot uncovered.

Kathryn's father died after her freshman year, and Helen Tucker managed the business. In 1939, Kathryn earned an A.B. from Huntingdon with an English major and a history minor. She applied for work at the *Montgomery Advertiser,* where she had dreamed of working since girlhood. The city editor, Hartwell Hatton, informed her that although she wrote well, he was not interested in hiring women reporters. Having never encountered gender discrimination before, she had not expected to be unfairly rejected. She returned to Thomasville to help her mother in the insurance agency and work as a stringer for the *Montgomery Advertiser, Birmingham News, Mobile Press-Register,* and her cousin Earl's paper. She wrote a variety of stories, hoping to be hired at a daily newspaper.

World War II enabled Kathryn to achieve her professional goal. When Allen Rankin, the *Alabama Journal's* feature writer and police reporter, joined the U.S. Army Air Corps, the newspaper sought a replacement. Familiar with Kathryn's work, city editor Meriwether Lewis Sharpley hired her in March 1941. The *Alabama Journal* (the *Montgomery Advertiser's* afternoon newspaper) offered her $15 per week with no overtime or bonuses, which was less than men in similar positions were paid.

Kathryn carefully listened to Sharpley instruct her to keep carbons so that she could compare her drafts with their published versions in order to learn her mistakes. Trying to intimidate her to work hard, he warned her not to return to work if her stories did not appear on the front page.

Rankin escorted her to the police station to introduce her to the officers, most of whom resented women reporters. Kathryn started each morning by visiting the police station and court to acquire reports. The policemen complicated her work by hiding or faking reports and teasing her when she made mistakes. She finally won their respect when she guarded the bodies of two drowned girls while policemen contacted relatives.

Filing her stories in the newspaper offices at the corner of Dexter Avenue and Lawrence Street, Kathryn learned to rewrite stories from the Associated Press wire with a Montgomery angle. As deadlines neared, she frantically typed while Sharpley paced behind her, tearing copy from her typewriter and criticizing her journalistic style.

Sharpley assigned his cub reporter to cover all the strange people with unusual stories, dubbing her the paper's "odd-egg editor." Kathryn wrote about large vegetables, albino squirrels, fruit shaped like people, and eggs with Japanese messages and maps etched on their shells. She interviewed an African prince and wrote about a Boy Scout who walked from Venezuela to Washington, D.C. to give President Franklin D. Roosevelt a flower. The AP wire picked this story up, and a New York newspaper called her for additional information. This was the first time someone outside Alabama was interested in Kathryn's work.

To earn extra money Kathryn wrote movie reviews for radio station WSFA and public relations pieces for the business page. She chronicled World War II Montgomery, from war bonds on the home front to servicemen at the battlefront. Her first photograph was published soon after the attack on Pearl Harbor when her editor wanted to prove how easy it would be to poison Montgomery's water supply. She also made her first professional enemies. Imitating New York columnist O.O. McIntyre, Kathryn decided never to take notes and wrote her columns from memory often reporting information, such as delays in the scrap drive, that officials had not meant for publication. Brigadier General George E. Stratemeyer banned her from Maxwell Army Air Base when she quoted him saying that the best men were used as instructors not in combat. Having befriended the 4th Aviation Squadron, a group of black troops, Kathryn managed to sneak on base to cover military stories.

During the war years, she also wrote about juvenile delinquency, trying to convince young girls who frequented the air base to go home. Assignments frequently took her to Julia Tutwiler Prison where she got along so well with the prisoners that she was offered a job as warden. As a Capitol reporter, she met with Governor Frank M. Dixon and covered Governor Chauncey Sparks's inaugural. She also interviewed Montgomery's last surviving former slave and Confederate soldiers.

In the summer of 1942, Kathryn left Montgomery to work for the U.S. Treasury Department in Birmingham. Hired to write publicity to sell war bonds statewide, Kathryn had impressed the state officer with her articles in the Alabama Journal about war bonds. He offered her a larger salary, and even though she hated to leave her friends and work in Montgomery, she accepted.

An inquisitive reporter, Kathryn had a knack for finding stories that somehow never got printed in the male-dominated newsroom. Indignant at discrimination that she encountered, the strong-willed Kathryn worked harder to earn respect from her colleagues and readers. This determination helped her as Alabama's promoter of war bonds.

Buying a car and traveling across the state to meet editors and radio station managers, Kathryn spent the night in every Alabama county. Carrying a 75 watt light bulb, because most hotel rooms she stayed in were too poorly illuminated for reading, Kathryn arranged and publicized rallies, located speakers (preferably wounded military men), and scheduled bands. She photographed county leaders and filed the same story in every location, inserting different names in the appropriate spaces.

Her remarkable war bond work was valuable for her future projects, collecting ghosts stories and historical legends, because she made contacts in every county. She learned a lot about Alabama's history and folkways and also discovered how to get along with a variety of personalties. Because of her work, Alabama was the only state where every county met every war bond drive's quota. Despite her successes, Kathryn missed newspaper work.

In 1944, Vincent Townsend, the city editor of *The Birmingham News*, Alabama's largest newspaper, hired Kathryn. She traveled the state looking for feature stories, including Alabama's first oil field and German war prisoners harvesting peanuts in the wiregrass southeast Alabama counties. Kathryn also covered the courthouse beat. Sharing an apartment at 2854 Fairway Drive with several other newspaper women, including college pal Frances Lanier, Kathryn often was awakened in the middle of the night to interview celebrities at the airport.

Driving Townsend to work, to conserve rationed gas, she listened to his stories about Birmingham. He assigned her real estate and aviation news, and Kathryn wrote a weekly column called "Ration Diary." She reported news from the Office of Price Administration about valid ration stamps, giving each report a human interest angle. In 1945 Kathryn became the paper's venereal disease editor, writing about the compulsory state blood test. She prepared war bond stories and compiled features about Birmingham servicemen and the tour of the Iwo Jima flag to Birmingham.

Taking time off, Kathryn traveled to New York to consult magazine editors about her articles. Having advised *Time* magazine about Birmingham residents, she toured that periodical's offices. Kathryn returned to find the *Birmingham News* closed. The International Typographical Union was on strike for five weeks. She sold her essay, "Alabama Wars on VD," to *Liberty* magazine, whose editor she had met in New York, and used the $400 she earned to buy her mother a desk.

The newspaper strike finally ended, and Kathryn and Cornelia Lively wrote a front page story in the first issue, on August 16, 1945, about Birmingham's celebration of the war's end. Kathryn alerted her readers that although the gas ration was over (she wrote about the elation of filling her gas tank), they should still conserve meat, butter, sugar, tires, and shoes. Now that she had fuel to travel outside the Birmingham area, Kathryn pursued feature stories around the state, including covering Governor Sparks's hunting trip.

Her car was stuck in mud and she walked miles through mud to get that story.

As veterans returned to their jobs at the newspaper, Kathryn began to hear about Amasa Benjamin Windham, a former newspaper reporter for the *Birmingham Age-Herald*. Working late one October night, she looked up from her work to see a man attired in a spiffy white Navy dress uniform exiting the elevator. A group clustered around him, celebrating his return. Kathryn continued typing until she was interrupted by Windham's appearance at her desk. He asked her to have dinner with him. Uninterested because she had heard too many stories about him, she refused.

She ignored him for three weeks until he sent a note via the copy girl, asking for a date. She agreed, saying that she had "nothing better to do." They continued dating, until Windham moved to New York to further his career. When he returned to Alabama he married Kathryn on February 10, 1946, in Thomasville's Methodist Church. Kathryn's brother Wood gave her away. Fourteen years passed before she was a newspaper reporter again.

The Windhams welcomed three children into their Selma home, and Kathryn became a full-time mother. Kathryn (Kitti) Tabb, Amasa Benjamin (Ben), Jr., and Helen Ann (Dilcy) presented Kathryn with new challenges. The Windhams lived in a wooded family community near Edgewood Elementary School where Kathryn was the first PTA president. Joining civic committees that promoted good causes, she baked cookies, raised funds, and taught Sunday School.

When she found time, she wrote with her typewriter on the dining room table or kitchen counter, submitting character sketches to *Inn Dixie*, a hotel chain's publication, the *Progressive Farmer* and *Birmingham News Magazine*. From 1950 to 1966, Kathryn penned a column entitled, "Around Our House," which appeared in weekly Alabama papers. Inspired by her children, Kathryn humorously profiled their activities, identifying them by age only, and offered household hints and recipes.

Her husband was chronically ill for several years and suffered a fatal heart attack in 1956. In 1960, when her youngest daughter was in first grade, Kathryn asked the *Selma Times-Journal* to hire her. She worked part-time in order to be with her children when they came home from school. She filled numerous positions, from reporter to city editor, and covered a variety of assignments. In 1961 she interviewed Selma flood victims for both the Red Cross and the newspaper.

In the early 1960s, Kathryn was an eyewitness to the Civil Rights movement. Aware of the first meetings, protests, and marches, she covered the federal court and interviewed Civil Rights leaders such as Stokely Carmichael. Kathryn knew many of the protestors who waited daily outside the Dallas County courthouse, attempting to register to vote. Watching Sheriff Jim Clark and his deputies, she used her camera and pen to capture images of emotional struggles and demonstrations in downtown Selma during this confusing era. She became a crucial information source for reporters from northern and foreign periodicals.

Kathryn, aware of the dangerously volatile climate, personally intervened in an effort to warn non-Selma white protesters to stay away from the city. Despite her pleas, the Concerned White Citizens of Alabama marched in support of blacks. They were cursed and harassed, and she feared for their lives. This was the only time, however, that Kathryn was truly afraid. Mostly she was angry and frustrated that she could not accomplish more.

Kathryn belonged to the United Methodist Church in Selma and was upset that its congregation approved of monitoring its doors to prevent integration of worship services. She was aware that one black man attempting to attend church had been hurt by a guard, but when she demanded that her minister condemn such hateful behavior, he refused to listen. She continued to attend the services, however, and regrets that she was there in church when the protestors crossed the Edmund Pettus Bridge on Bloody Sunday 1965. She somberly watched replays of the carnage on television.

Although she had been unable to mitigate conditions for protestors, Kathryn did aid in the integration of public schools. As a Democratic member of the Selma City School Board from 1960 to 1972, she expressed concern about the high rate of absences at the black elementary and high schools. In addition to outlining the reasons why children needed to be educated, Kathryn stressed that this truancy reduced state funding to Selma.

When a federal order was issued to integrate schools, Governor George Wallace asked Kathryn to meet with him and other school officials about the desegregation issue. He then requested a separate meeting with her and the Selma City School Board chairman. According to Kathryn, Wallace warned her of possible dangers that she might encounter if she approved the integration of Selma schools. She disregarded his threats, and continued to support integration.

Angry Selma citizens staged meetings, protesting against the school board. When Selma Mayor Joe Smitherman labeled Kathryn a "cornfield intellectual," she was thrilled, not angry, because that was the first time anyone had called her an intellectual. In response, she sent Smitherman a dried corn arrangement. Kathryn's support of integration resulted in hate mail and obscene phone calls. Former friends snubbed her, and her windshield was shot out. Sticking to her convictions, she wrote about the first day of integrated schools for the Selma newspaper. She continues to embrace civic commitments, including serving the city of Camden's Area Agency on Aging and acting as a community service planner.

When Kathryn's children were grown and in college, she focused on a new writing career, publishing her first cookbook in 1964. When the Selma newspaper was sold in 1973 to an "out-of-town chain," Kathryn realized that not only was she unprepared to use the newfangled computers in the press room, but also that the new owners were probably not thrilled with her part-time employment arrangement. After twelve years of reporting for the Selma paper, she was on her own.

Kathryn's writing efforts produced two more regional cookbooks offering only "real Deep South recipes." Kathryn spiced her books with legends and tales too, including the story of Brer Rabbit and other southern favorites. Her recipes included such regional fare as dandelion wine, Pine Mountain pralines, divinity, spoon bread, custards, Gulf coast shrimp gumbo, roast venison from the piney woods, and quail and grits from the Black Belt.

Her recipe books were well received, but Kathryn's next project earned her real acclaim throughout the South. On an October day in 1966, Kathryn was home alone when she heard footsteps and a door slam. Thinking that her son had come home from college, she called to him, but received no answer. Puzzled, she went to his room and saw that it was empty. Kathryn was not scared, but wondered what she had heard.

Her children and guests began to hear similar sounds in Kathryn's home, too. They found furniture mysteriously moved. Chairs rocked, lamps shook, chest of drawers blocked doors, and cakes balanced on the edge of the dining room table. The Windhams became convinced of an unusual presence when their cat, Hornblower, became upset, arched his back with fur fuzzed, and stared into the shadows. Naming their house ghost Jeffrey, the family, for the most part, enjoyed his friendly antics. They blamed him for lost items, malfunctioning lights and electrical equipment, and anything that went awry. Hornblower, however, was annoyed, afraid, and confused.

Kathryn credits Jeffrey for her interest in ghost stories. "I think his sole purpose was to involve me in collecting and preserving the true tales of the supernatural around the state." Inspired to discover Alabama's authentic ghost stories, Kathryn utilized her reporting skills. She contacted Huntingdon's folklore authority, Margaret Gillis Figh, with whom she collaborated. Emphasizing that ghost stories are an important facet of folklore, Kathryn believes that ghost stories help teach local history by making it exciting.

Kathryn and Figh traveled around Alabama, listening to hundreds of ghost stories, strange tales, and legends and visited ghostly haunts. Kathryn notes that almost every town and crossroad claims some type of supernatural activity, with some stories being well known and others having limited circulation. She and Figh selected stories that seemed to have historical veracity.

Kathryn investigated each story, staying in the area for several days to authenticate historical backgrounds. She consulted local libraries and archives to verify dates, places, and names related to every ghost story and considered variations of each tale. She photographed ghostly habitats to preserve pictures of decaying mansions and buildings. She became a familiar sight to many Alabamians, with her camera slung over her shoulder and her notepad and pen in hand. Kathryn visited many ghost story sites but admits that she never saw a ghost.

She and Figh selected thirteen stories from the hundreds that they collected. Their book, *13 Alabama Ghosts and Jeffrey,* was published by Strode Publishers in 1969. For the most part the stories are nostalgic and not horrifying. Kathryn emphasizes that she reported the stories accurately and sincerely. In her tales, Alabama ghosts include an architect, a Mobile sea captain, dancing Grancer Harrison, the red lady of Huntingdon College, and phantom steamboats. Many of the tales have Civil War themes and occur at Alabama's most prominent homes, including Selma's Sturdivant Hall and Gaineswood in Demopolis. Public buildings host haunts too, and Kathryn tells about the face in the Pickens County Courthouse window. She tells her readers that "The sites of all the stories can be visited—but I make no promise that the ghosts can be seen!"

When asked if she believes in ghosts, Kathryn diplomatically admits that strange things do happen, including Jeffrey in her home. "I cannot explain it and I don't even try to. We just enjoy it. It really doesn't matter to me if people believe in ghosts or not. I still think the stories of ghosts are important. They have been told since man's origins. I suppose that since man began to talk he has been fascinated with the supernatural. You don't have to believe in ghosts to enjoy ghost stories. They stretch the imagination and make us ask how they could happen."

She tries to be objective and not cynical. The people who have told her about personal contacts with ghosts are sincere about their experiences, truly believing that they happened. No matter what "those stories should be preserved as a part of our heritage."

She especially encourages historical groups to collect local ghosts stories before all the legends and their storytellers have died. She explains that ghost stories are disappearing because the custom of people relaxing by telling stories is being replaced by television.

After she finished her Alabama ghost book, Kathryn turned her attention to educational books. Hoping to inspire Alabama schoolchildren to learn about their state's history, she wrote a chapter on the Cahaba River for *Rivers of Alabama* and co-authored, *Exploring Alabama*, and *Our Alabama: Fourth Grade Social Studies Teacher's Guide*. She wrote these textbooks in a popular manner to make the history of an "amazing state" come alive. Kathryn sketched out tales of Alabama's earliest residents, who lived in Russell Cave, to modern Alabamians who have put men on the moon. She emphasizes that this book should not only educate, but be fun to read and help students understand how people lived in different eras. In the teacher's guide, Kathryn listed vocabulary words and activities, including collecting stories. Her ghost stories were adapted by public television to familiarize Alabama schoolchildren with state history and geography.

Kathryn claims that while she busily compiled these textbooks, Jeffrey prodded her to return to ghosts stories. She resumed her travels and produced several books about ghosts in neighboring states. In *Jeffrey Introduces 13 More Southern Ghosts* (1971), Kathryn describes ghosts waiting for long-lost loves, phantom music, and disappearing people. *Thirteen Georgia Ghosts and Jeffrey* (1973) features a ghost collie, revolutionary patriots, and chanting friars. Georgia ghosts also frequent the notorious Andersonville prison and Columbus's Springer Opera House.

Benevolent ghosts protected children, tucking in blankets, in *13 Mississippi Ghosts and Jeffrey* (1974), which hosted Civil War spirits, the eerie Black Cat, and ghostly lanterns and train lights that alerted passersby of danger. *Thirteen Tennessee Ghosts and Jeffrey* (1977) featured witches, snake charmers, a missing monk, rocking chairs, and stains that refused to vanish.

Returning to Alabama haunts, Kathryn told how Theophilus Jowers fell into a Birmingham furnace in 1887 to become the *Ghost in the Sloss Furnaces* (1978). She often visits the furnaces on Halloween to carve pumpkins and spin ghostly yarns. Kathryn's favorite ghost stories are in *Jeffrey's Latest: 13 More Alabama Ghosts* (1982). In "The Locket," Harvey Hammer died when he was only twenty months old, but he returned from the dead so that his mother could have a photograph taken of him. "Paint the Gallows Red" tells how a young woman sees the image of an executed murderer in her house, identifies his photograph, and tries to determine if he's innocent. Kathryn calls these stories amazing, stating that she has seen the photographs and is sure that they actually happened, although she is not sure *how* they occurred.

In addition to writing ghost stories, Kathryn, fascinated by Alabama history, prepared *Alabama: One Big Front Porch* (1975), which is filled with folklore, myths, and superstitions about bottle trees, hoop snakes, and gourd birdhouses. She reveals the origins of Auburn's battle cry, "War Eagle," and tells readers where to find Joe Namath's cleat-print on the University of Alabama campus. She explains how Vulcan came to Birmingham, what happened to the first meteorite that hit a human being, and presents other characters sketches of people and history that delight and inform readers.

Writing about topics close to her heart and home, Kathryn published *A Sampling of*

Selma Stories (1991), filled with Civil War tales and humorous anecdotes. One story about tells how Selma's plan to host an out-of-state tourist went awry when the city later discovered its honored guest was an escaped felon who had a stolen car and bounced checks all over town. Kathryn signed copies of this book, "With a touch of laughter."

She also wrote *Southern Cooking to Remember* (1978) and *Count Those Buzzards, Stamp Those Grey Mules!: Superstitions Remembered from a Southern Childhood* (1979). Illustrating the latter book, Kathryn explains that having been raised in a family steeped in superstitions, she wanted to record the games, folklore, songs, and social customs that she loved as a child. She tells the history of Selma's orphanage, the United Methodist Children's Home, from a bell's perspective in *The Autobiography of a Bell* (1991).

Kathryn has published two autobiographies in *A Serigamy of Stories* (1988) which chronicles her childhood through college years. She writes about her family and the eccentric but good people who resided in her hometown. She explains to confused readers that the word "serigamy" was specifically created by her family to mean "A whole lot, a heap of, a right smart, a goodly number" of things. She describes her journalistic experiences in *Odd Egg Editor* (1990).

When the Alabama Federation of Women's Clubs asked her to be their luncheon speaker at the University of Alabama in the early 1970s, Kathryn accepted. She chose to speak about Julia Tutwiler because of Tutwiler's historical work in Tuscaloosa. Kathryn found minimal library material about Tutwiler and commented that a book should be written about her but never considered that she would be the author. After she finished her talk, Kathryn believed that her work on Tutwiler was completed, but "Miss Julia would not let me forget her." Everywhere Kathryn went, Tutwiler "haunted" her.

Kathryn turned to the Alabama Department of Archives and History and Livingston University's and the University of Alabama's archives to read Tutwiler's letters. She listened to the recollections of townspeople and former Tutwiler students in nursing homes. Scouring old newspapers and family scrapbooks for tidbits, Kathryn filled notebooks and boxes full of information about Tutwiler.

Originally intending to write a book about Tutwiler, Kathryn remarks that her subject had a "spirit of her own." While she was writing, Kathryn lamented, "I don't know what I'm going to do with her. I've tried to put her in a book, but she doesn't want to be in a book—she wants to be alive." Abandoning her book idea, Kathryn produced a one-woman play, "My Name is Julia." Dressed in a long black skirt and jacket, emblazoned with a Women's Christian Temperance Union (WCTU) ribbon, Kathryn became Julia Tutwiler. She has presented her monologue about Tutwiler's efforts to secure women's education and jail reform to a variety of audiences, ranging from the Los Angeles' Museum of Contemporary Art to the 150th Julia Tutwiler birthday celebration at Birmingham's Linn-Henley Research Library. Alabama Public Television has aired the remarkable performance several times.

Wearing her trademark Jeffrey t-shirt, necklace, glasses, and straw hat, Kathryn's friendly face has greeted thousands of children and adults across the state. Telling her tales at libraries and public places, Kathryn has also been a featured storyteller at the National Storytelling Festival. She helped establish the annual Alabama Tale Tellin' Festival at Selma.

Kathryn was a charter member of the National Association for the Preservation and

Perpetuation of Storytelling, serving on its board of directors for several years. She has also been a member of the board of advisors of the Southern Women's Archives and the Alabama State Historical Commission. Considered one of Selma's most prominent citizens, Kathryn has generously given back to her community. She has also donated her papers to Auburn University's archives for scholars to use who obtain her permission.

Kathryn has won numerous awards for her writing. In 1975 the Alabama Library Association named *Alabama: One Big Front Porch* as the best non-fiction book in the state. Kathryn received journalism prizes from the Associated Press and Alabama Press Association for both her photography and reporting. Huntingdon presented her an honorary doctorate in 1979, and six years later, Kathryn earned the "Living for America" award.

Through the airwaves, she gained national renown as a southern humorist. Her radio commentaries began in 1985 at Tuscaloosa's public radio station WUAL. She became a National Public Radio commentator on "All Things Considered" the next year. Kathryn's commentaries most often are about ghosts and growing up in Alabama. *The Mother Earth News* printed her humorous story, "Tombstone in the Kitchen," about how her aunt used the smooth side of a tombstone to roll and chop dough and vegetables in the kitchen; the engraved side proved useful for decorating pastries.

Kathryn frequently travels to speaking engagements, reminiscing about her life, reading stories, and signing autographs (she signs ghost books "Hauntingly yours," followed by her name and Jeffrey's spiky signature). She likes to tell how she arrived at one speech only to discover that the room was filled with University of Alabama banners. Kathryn informed her hosts that Jeffrey was an Auburn fan and would be upset. They snickered until a large banner suddenly fell to the floor; then they became very attentive.

Kathryn's home on Royal Street in Selma is filled with collections of Alabama and Civil War relics, dirt dauber nests, door knobs, and insulators that she acquired during her writing adventures. She treasures items that her children unearthed on archeological expeditions with her and delights in visits with her grandchildren. She works on her pine writing desk, with metal legs engraved with Roman gods' faces, that she inherited from her father's bank.

Kathryn still collects ghost stories (and blames Jeffrey for misplacing papers on her desk), but she says that she probably will not publish them. The University of Alabama Press reprints her ghost story books in paperback, assuring that they will be available for future generations. Focusing on her writing and photography, Kathryn continues to records images of the changing South. She matter-of-factly comments that although she still feels young, as she ages she needs to be practical in order to be productive with the time that she has left.

When asked if she will return as a ghost after her death, "I've got a long list of people I'm going to come back to haunt. I think it would be fun." For the present she devotes her life to chronicling Alabama's rich folk culture because, as she inscribed in a copy of *Exploring Alabama*, she wants to preserve her home state's legacies "For everybody who loves Alabama."

written by Elizabeth D. Schafer

ZELMA FINCHER WYATT
1904 -

There Are No Excuses For Being Ignorant.
Anyone Can Be Well Educated If He Will Read.

On being informed that she'd been selected as one of Alabama's "women who made a difference," Zelma Wyatt's face flooded with astonishment. "Why, what have I done that made any kind of difference? All I did was raise five children."

When Zelma Fincher Wyatt was born on October 5, 1904, in Buchanan, Georgia, that's all a woman was expected to do. Women did not vote; neither did they usually go to college nor work outside the home; nevertheless, in her home everyone was expected to be educated. Zelma's mother, the tiny 90-pound Emma Jane Ayres Fincher, had borne seven children to Reuben Benjamin Fincher. She raised them to be responsible and productive adults. She taught all her children that they could be anything they wanted, but they must have an education. "There are no excuses for being ignorant," she told them. "Anybody can be well educated if he will read." The emphasis was not on being *able* to read, but on being *willing* to read.

Thus, when she was very young, the pattern was set for Zelma's education. She can't remember not being able to read. To the best of her recollection, no one ever taught her to read. "It was just something I picked up from Grandfather's books in the shed room," she explains. The importance of education was not a concept original to Zelma's mother. It had been deeply ingrained in her by her father, Alfred Ayres, who thought all people should be educated; and in furtherance of that goal he had purchased several well-bound sets of books by good authors—Dickens, Thackeray, Hawthorne, and so on. Born before the Civil War, Grandfather Ayres clearly remembered how Sherman's march through Georgia was preceded by the terrifying rumor that, like Herod of old, the Union general ordered his troops to kill all little boys. The family's home was not in Sherman's path, fortunately, and Alfred's fears were groundless. He lived to see his legacy—his belief in education—passed on like a twining strand of DNA to his grandchildren, almost as if Zelma had genetically inherited her keen appetite for learning.

After Grandmother Ayres' death, Grandfather "broke up housekeeping," and all his books were stored in a lean-to, the shed room, attached to his daughter's house. There Zelma learned to read, developing knowledge and understanding far beyond her years. Though sometimes she produced unusual pronunciations that amazed adults, like the astonished Sunday School teacher who heard "in the beginning, God *cretiated* Heaven and Earth."

When Zelma was five years old, the Fincher family moved to Heflin, Alabama, where Reuben bought a barber shop. There Zelma went to school, starting in the second grade because she already knew how to read. Ten years later, with Zelma in high school, they moved to Anniston, Alabama. Because the high school in Anniston did not have its own building and the curriculum was very poor, Zelma rode a street car to Oxford, about four miles away, to finish her last two years of high school.

After graduation she went to the Baptist Hospital in Selma for nurse's training. While in the midst of her schedule she met a young man just returned from completing a dairy management course at Michigan State University. He was managing an ice cream plant in Dublin, Georgia. With Dublin clearly too far away to permit a propitious courtship for the young couple, Zelma left nursing school after a year and a half to marry William Garner Wyatt on December 26, 1924.

With the onset of the Great Depression, the plant in Dublin failed and William Wyatt lost his job but soon found another which necessitated a move with two small children back to Alabama to take charge of a dairy plant in Sylacauga. The salary was ridiculously low and times were hard. It took skillful household management on Zelma's part to keep the family clothed and fed. Occasionally one of her children will still tease her saying, "We remember how you bought a steak for Daddy and gave us kids the gravy." But even that sort of economy was inadequate.

Although Zelma grew up in a time and place where women did not work outside the home, she solved the problem by setting up a flower shop in her own house which enabled her to make a contribution to the family finances and still be at home to watch her children. It was hard work. She remembers "thirty-six hour days" before Christmas or Easter and other times when a big wedding coincided with an equally large funeral. She also remembers many happy times. She remembers a husband whose quick sense of humor could remove the tension from almost any situation. Most of all she remembers being surrounded by love and, she observes, "you can never find love unless you are capable of giving it."

By the end of World War II times were easier. The Wyatts moved to Tuscaloosa where William managed a larger dairy plant. The children, five in number now, were all in school and because 1948 was the first year for Tuscaloosa to have a 12-year school system, high school was not a problem as it had been for Zelma. With her youngsters better able to care for themselves, Zelma had time to branch out along her own paths though still keeping the welfare of her family in mind.

She was determined that all her children should go to college. Well aware of the cost of five college educations—even with scholarships—Zelma continued to be anxious about the family budget. Having always faced problems honestly, resourcefully, and without compromise, she took a job selling World Book Encyclopedias door to door. When the need for greater mobility became obvious, she learned to drive a car even though she was more than 50 years old. She was good at selling the encyclopedias because she was selling something she sincerely believed in—knowledge and education.

About this same time Zelma's friend and neighbor, Emily Jo Strong, an avid activist in the cause of family planning and also a University of Alabama professor in the College of Home Economics, introduced her to the League of Women Voters. The League had several action programs including support of the local public library and establishment of a juvenile detention home for Tuscaloosa. It was the work to purge voting rolls of non-existing voters and to register new voters, however, that captured Zelma's greatest interest. She became Voter Services Chair of the League when Alberta Murphy, an attorney and law school professor, was president.

"We had registration booths set up all over town—grocery stores, drug stores, school houses, any place where people congregated; and we were quite successful, too. We registered a lot of people and felt really happy about our accomplishments," Zelma recalls.

"Well, just imagine, then, how I felt when the telephone rang one night, quite late, and a man's voice announced that he was from the Justice Department in Washington, DC. Oh, my! Oh, my! What *had* I done wrong to get involved with the Justice Department? He informed me that I was to make a deposition at the Federal Court House the next day; 'would I come willingly or will you have to be subpoenaed?' No, no, I didn't want any subpoena! I told him I'd just come."

Zelma would probably have felt much more at ease about the situation if she had known at the time that the representatives from the Department of Justice had come at the request of "The Deacons," a tightly organized and rigorously selected group of black activists whose purpose was to neutralize Klan efforts and ascertain the safety of all civil rights workers. Those men needed to produce authoritative evidence that registration of black voters was legal and being carried out in a legitimate and orderly fashion.

"Now," she continues, "let me set the scene. There I was in Federal Court with the judge's bench and the jury box high up in the front. It was very awe-inspiring. Then I noticed a tall, handsome, white-haired man—the perfect picture of a Southern gentleman—and two short, dark-haired young men coming toward me. The young men introduced themselves as being from Selma. The Southern gentleman said, 'Hell, they're not from Selma. They're those damn lawyers from Washington.' Frowning at me, he added, 'But what are *you* doing here?' I told him I was supposed to be there. I had to make a deposition. He looked quite surprised and then I understood that he had been expecting Alberta. There he was, prepared to confront an elegant, sophisticated lady lawyer, and instead he encountered a chubby, frumpy, little old housewife without a bit of makeup. I'd been so scared I'd forgotten all about cosmetics. Yes, I admit I was scared—scared to death—until he made me mad. I try to be nice all the time, but when folks don't do right—well, my husband used to say I reminded him of a hot Coca-Cola when you take the top off.

"You see, that man carried me off to one side and started asking me all kinds of things even before the deposition began. I wouldn't *think* of saying the words he used when he asked me if I didn't believe that white folks had more sense than other people. I told him I had never made a study of the subject. Then he asked me how I would feel if one of my children were to marry someone of another race and I said I hoped my children could make their own decisions.

"The deposition itself was not frightening. Those polite young lawyers asked me where we were registering, whether we registered white voters, and did we station only at black grocery stores. Then they asked me why we had booths at Tuscaloosa High School [now Central High East] and not at Druid High [Central West]. I had to confess that the Voters Service chair had fallen down on the job and forgotten about the other school. When he asked me if I had any prejudice toward registering black people to vote, I pointed out how important the vote is for *everyone*."

Zelma has always believed very strongly in the right to vote and the importance of exercising that right. She also supports the League of Women Voters premise that the voting public should be an informed public. Accordingly, with that purpose in mind, the Voters Service Committee diligently prepared questionnaires addressed to all candidates involved in the local elections. The questions, together with each candidate's answer, were to be published in *The Tuscaloosa News* before the election. To prevent any "lost in the mail" excuses, all questionnaires were sent by registered mail and replies were to be returned in the same manner. At first the response was very poor. The candidates, all male at that time, let it be known that they had no intention of sending in something for "those damn women to publish." Their attitude changed, however, when the newspaper started printing "no reply" after the names of those not responding.

As Zelma explains it, "When the 'no reply' policy started those men were dead serious about getting their answers to me. They didn't even trust registered mail. They came to my house and hand delivered their letters. I really felt like somebody then—all those men coming to my house. Of course, they were only politicians.

"The worst time I had with those questionnaires, though, came from a woman—the wife of one of the candidates. The committee had agreed that, after sending the questions by registered mail, it was unnecessary to telephone the candidates in addition. Anyway, I made an exception when one man did not return his statement. His wife said it must have been overlooked and promised that she would mail the letter immediately, but I still didn't get it. When the newspaper printed a 'no reply' after the man's name, she called me, very nastily demanding that I have the paper print a retraction. I told her I couldn't do that because there was nothing to retract. I hadn't received his letter. She was terribly insulting. When she finally admitted she had not addressed the envelope as instructed but sent it simply to the Tuscaloosa League Voters Service chair, I told her I had two daughters and a son who were teachers and if they had students who couldn't follow directions any better than *that*, those students failed.

"Well, when she called me again about the retraction, I told her my children had been here at home when she said those rude and ugly things to their mother. I asked her if she thought they would forget that when they went behind the curtain on election day. Nobody *has* to be stepped on. You have to lie down to be stepped on.

"There were four votes in my house that year; and you know, that man lost the election by *exactly four votes*! Now, doesn't that show the importance of every vote?"

Zelma handled not only her personal problems expeditiously; whenever she saw a problem, of whatever scope, she took the responsibility for doing what she could to resolve the difficulty. Her work for integration at the voting booth and the schools was not token effort performed through a formal organization. Zelma carried her convictions with her every day and acted accordingly. One Sunday evening Zelma and William went to church as was usual for them, and a nice-looking, well-dressed black man entered and sat in the pew directly behind them. The ushering Deacon approached with a perturbed look on his face and informed the visitor that the church was not integrated and therefore he was requested to leave.

"I don't know what happened," Zelma said describing the incident. "Something inside me just snapped and I flapped open my hymn book and handed it to the man. I told him that I had been a member of the church for many years, that my husband there beside me was a Deacon, and that we wanted him to stay and worship with us."

The usher retreated without another word and after the service Zelma and William walked their guest to his car. "We didn't know what some of those other Deacons might do," she said.

Frequently people approach Zelma with a question: "Mrs. Wyatt, how can a woman your age and brought up the way you were behave like you do? You act like a liberal."

Completely undisturbed by the question, Zelma has a ready answer. "I couldn't behave any other way," she replies. "I had a mother who was years ahead of her time. I remember her concerns that the black children had no school to go to—no where to learn—and how hard she worked to collect old books and find a place for those children to get some sort of education. My mother was a wonderful role model."

And so it is. Role models beget role models, and example is more important than words. With a heritage like that, Zelma Wyatt could do no less than be a wonderful role model herself. In a marriage founded in love and a strong faith in God, William and Zelma reared and nurtured a family in an atmosphere of security and self-respect. They were a wealthy family in everything except money, and that they didn't miss at all because it was never mentioned.

She saw to it that Grandfather Ayres' legacy—his firm belief in the value of education—was passed on to the third and fourth generations with every promise of its continuing to the fifth and sixth. In fulfillment of her longtime goal, Zelma's five children all have college degrees (two doctorates); all her 11 grandchildren are college educated (two are Phi Beta Kappa); and her four great grandchildren are destined to follow in the same direction very shortly. Even their puppy, Dodger, is expected to read his first words any day now.

How can Zelma Wyatt ask what she did to make a difference? Does anyone dare say all Zelma did was raise five children?

Parts of this story have previously appeared in *The Tuscaloosa News Senior Edition*

written by Joyce Mahan

THE WRITERS

Hazel Hendricker Bruchey

Hazel Bruchey is the office manager at the School of Music on the University of Alabama campus in Tuscaloosa, Alabama. Writing is both a part of her public relations work and an enjoyable hobby. She has a degree in education. Hazel has served as Environmental Portfolio chair on the Board of the Tuscaloosa League of Women Voters (LWV). She is active in the Sierra Club and Covenant Presbyterian Church. She has two adult daughters.

Suzanne Henson

Suzanne Henson works as a features reporter for *The Tuscaloosa News*. She also works with the Kentuck Museum in Northport, Alabama, and previously worked as a research assistant for *Alabama Heritage* magazine. Suzanne earned a bachelors's degree in Journalism from the University of Alabama. She calls Tuscaloosa her home.

Adeline F. Kahn

Adeline F. Kahn is editor of the Birmingham Botanical Gardens' newsletter and is a master gardener. She has been a member of the Birmingham League of women Voters for many years. Adeline was executive director of Common Cause from 1975 to 1978 and has served as an officer in many civic and community groups. She served as the senior case worker for Congressman Ben Erdreich. Adeline studied law at the Cumberland School of Law and has a B.A. from Vassar College. She has been married to Stanley S. Kahn, M.D. for forty-five years. They live in Birmingham, Alabama. Their daughter and two sons live on the West Coast.

Joyce Mahan

Joyce Mahan was born in Wisconsin. Her undergraduate degree is from Wisconsin State College and she has done graduate work at The University of Wisconsin in Madison and The University of Alabama in Tuscaloosa. She did research in genetics (before Watson and Crick discovered DNA) on a grant from the U. S. Department of Agriculture at the University of Wisconsin. Joyce taught English and biology in American overseas schools in Brazil for nine years. She taught freshman and sophomore English at the University of Alabama for five years

Joyce is an active member and past president of the League of Women Voters of Tuscaloosa. She is a member of the Advisory Board and contributor for *The Senior Edition* published by *The Tuscaloosa News*. She is married to Philip J. C. Mahan, former law professor at New York University and The University of Alabama. Tuscaloosa is their home. Between them they have five adult children.

Anne Permaloff, Ph.D., Ph.B.

Dr. Anne Permaloff is Professor of Political Science and Public Administration at Auburn University at Montgomery, Alabama. She has a Ph.D. in political science from the University of Minnesota, and a M.A. and Ph.B. from Wayne State University in Detroit, Michigan. She grew up outside Detroit in Royal Oaks, Michigan. She currently serves on the Board of the League of Women Voters of Alabama and is Secretary and Voter Editor for the Montgomery League. Together with her husband Carl Grafton, she is the co-author of two books on Alabama politics: *Big Mules and Branchheads: James E. Folsom and Political Power in Alabama* and *Political Power in Alabama: The More Things Changed...* They live near Montgomery.

Sarah Cabot Pierce

Sarah Cabot Pierce's biography appears in this book.

LaVerne Davis Ramsey

LaVerne Ramsey is a certified Financial Planner with Prudential Securities in Birmingham, Alabama. She grew up in Montgomery and graduated from Sidney Lanier High School. LaVerne has a B.A. degree from Huntingdon College with emphasis on English and History. She also studied art at the Art Students' League of New York, UAB, and the University of Montevallo.

A member of the League of Women Voters of Greater Birmingham, she served as secretary of the state League Board from 1993-95. She is an avid photographer whose picture of billionaire stock investor Warren Buffett has appeared in several of his biographies. LaVerne has an intense interest in Alabama's political history as well as current political trends. She is married to William T. Ramsey, a retired Financial Advisor, and lives in Indian Springs Village where she edited the town newsletter from 1991-92.

Elizabeth D. Schafer, Ph.D.

Dr. Elizabeth D. Schafer was born in Opelika, Alabama and grew up in Auburn where she graduated as valedictorian from Lee-Scott Academy and with honors from Auburn University. Her graduate work in the history of science and technology, studying with her major professor, Dr. James R. Hansen, a renowned aerospace historian and Pulitzer Prize nominee, culminated in her being the first woman to receive a Ph.D. in the history of technology at Auburn University. She has contributed articles to numerous encyclopedias and magazines.

Elizabeth has been a finalist in the *Writer's Digest* writing competition and received the Colonial Dames Award for the most outstanding paper on colonial history in 1988. Her mother Carolyn H. Schafer, an active member of the Auburn League of Women Voters and former president of the Auburn League and other civic organizations, has inspired her to preserve women's history. Elizabeth is currently a freelance writer who divides her time between Loachapoka, Alabama, and Burlington, Iowa, where she writes historical and biographical works; travel and feature articles; and fiction for both children and adults.

Cheryl Joanne Sloan

Joanne Sloan was born and raised in Texas. She has a B.A. in English & History from East Texas State University, Commerce, Texas; a M.ED. in Secondary Education and English from the University of Arkansas, Fayetteville, Arkansas. She has taught high school English in 4 states. Joanne is a freelance writer; the publisher of Vision Press, a press that specializes in communication textbooks; an instructor in University of Alabama College of Continuing Studies Independent Study Division (feature writing course); and the coordinator of the annual Southern Christian Writers Conference in Birmingham, Alabama.

Joanne has co-authored two books; written several book chapters; is a freelance writer of numerous magazine and newspaper articles (specializing in how-to's and biographical/historical articles). She is married to Dr. David W. Sloane, a University of Alabama Journalism Professor. They live in Northport, Alabama, and have a grown son and daughter. Joanne's great-grandparents were from Alabama (my grandfather moved to Texas when he was small), so she has an interest in Alabama history.

Miriam Abigail Toffel

Abigail Toffel is a Tuscaloosa native and a descendant of early American and Alabama settlers. She lived for fifteen years on the beach in Hawaii. She has two degrees from the University of Alabama, a B.A. from New college and a M.A. in Journalism. She has been a writer and editor for eighteen years. Work experiences include four years as head of public relations and copy writer with a national advertising agency; director of public Relations for Alabama Public Television; executive editor for a state magazine; writer and editor of eight books; freelance writer with clients like UAB and Bell South Services; and taught creative writing for UAB's Adult Studies and privately.

Abigail has served as president of the Tuscaloosa LWV and on the board of the Tuscaloosa, Birmingham, and State LWV Boards. She has served on the state board of the Foundation for Women's Health in Alabama (FWHA) and as president of the Birmingham chapter of FWHA. She was chairperson of Southern Danceworks' board, a fine arts dance company in Birmingham. She is divorced with two adult sons. Abigail is living with and caring for her disabled mother in Tuscaloosa, Alabama.

Kathy Yarbrough

Kathy Yarbrough is the former Director of Development at the Alabama Shakespeare Festival in Montgomery, Alabama.